THE
CHARACTER OF THE FOURTH GOSPEL.

AN ATTEMPT TO ASCERTAIN

THE CHARACTER OF

THE FOURTH GOSPEL;

ESPECIALLY IN ITS RELATION TO

THE FIRST THREE.

BY THE LATE REV.

JOHN JAMES TAYLER, B.A.,

MEMBER OF THE HISTORICO-THEOLOGICAL SOCIETY OF LEIPSIC, AND PRINCIPAL
OF MANCHESTER NEW COLLEGE, LONDON.

Φίλη καὶ προτιμοτάτη πάντων ἡ ἀλήθεια· ἐπαινεῖν τε χρῆ καὶ συναινεῖν ἀφθόνως, εἴ τι ὀρθῶς λέγοιτο, ἐξετάζειν δὲ καὶ διευθύνειν, εἴ τι μὴ φαίνοιτο ὑγιῶς ἀναγεγραμμένον.—Dionys. Alexandrin. ap. Euseb. H. E. vii. 24.

. . . . "acri
Judicio perpende et, si tibi vera videntur,
Dede manus, aut, si falsum est, accingere contra."
Lucret. II. 1041-3.

SECOND EDITION.

WIPF & STOCK · Eugene, Oregon

Wipf and Stock Publishers
199 W 8th Ave, Suite 3
Eugene, OR 97401

An Attempt to Ascertain the Character of the Fourth Gospel, 2nd Edition
Especially in its Relation to the First Three
By Tayler, John James
Softcover ISBN-13: 978-1-7252-9091-4
Hardcover ISBN-13: 978-1-7252-9093-8
eBook ISBN-13: 978-1-7252-9092-1
Publication date 11/2/2020
Previously published by Williams and Norgate, 1870

This edition is a scanned facsimile of the original edition published in 1870.

TO

THE REV. JOHN KENRICK, M.A., F.S.A.,

ETC.,

FOR MORE THAN THIRTY YEARS CLASSICAL AND HISTORICAL TUTOR IN

MANCHESTER NEW COLLEGE, YORK;

KNOWN TO THE LEARNED BY HIS ACUTE AND THOROUGH RESEARCHES

INTO THE HISTORY AND MYTHOLOGY OF THE ANCIENT WORLD:

NOT AS CLAIMING HIS ASSENT

TO CONCLUSIONS WHICH HE MAY NOT ACCEPT,

BUT AS A FEEBLE THOUGH SINCERE EXPRESSION OF THE LOVE OF SCHOLARLY

HONESTY IN THE PURSUIT OF TRUTH,

WHICH IT WAS THE CONSTANT AIM OF HIS INSTRUCTIONS TO INSPIRE,

THIS ATTEMPT

TO ELUCIDATE AN IMPORTANT CRITICAL QUESTION,

IS,

WITH EVERY SENTIMENT OF RESPECT AND GRATITUDE,

INSCRIBED

BY HIS FRIEND AND FORMER PUPIL,

THE AUTHOR.

PREFACE.

THE conclusion which I have undertaken to maintain in the ensuing pages has not been hastily adopted. It is a result of the gradual triumph of what has seemed to me preponderant evidence over an earlier belief. For years I clung tenaciously to the opinion, that the most spiritual of the gospels must be of apostolic origin. Twice I read through the "Probabilia" of Bretschneider, and the conviction still remained that, in the choice of difficulties which he has so forcibly stated, more truth would be lost by the admission than by the rejection of his theory. On investigating, however, more thoroughly the origin of the contents of our New Testament, I found how impossible it was, in every case but that of Paul, to establish satisfactory evidence of direct personal authorship: and I came at length to the full persuasion, that the one point of importance to ascertain respecting any particular book, was simply this;—that, whoever might have written it, it belonged to the first age, while the primitive inspiration was still clear and strong,—and that it could be regarded as a genuine expression of the faith and feeling which then prevailed. Not till I had decidedly embraced this view, was my mind open to admit the just inference from undeniable premises, and prepared to accept a legitimate result of honest criticism, without feeling that I had thereby relinquished what the distinctest voice of my inward being assured me must still be spiritual truth. I rested therefore in the general conclusion, that evidence of the immediate and powerful action of the Divine Spirit in the apostolic age, was a matter of infinitely greater moment than the question of the personality of any of its human agents.

The literature of this controversy respecting the Fourth Gospel has already become voluminous, especially in Germany. I do not profess to have made myself master of the whole of it; though it will be seen, that I am not unacquainted with what has been contributed by some of the most eminent scholars to its elucidation. In particular I have derived great assistance from the learned researches of Hilgenfeld on the Paschal question. But what I wished, without attempting to compare and combine the divergent theories of others, was to examine anew for myself the ancient testimonies on which they have founded them; in order to arrive, if possible, from personal investigation, at an independent conclusion. While engaged in this inquiry, I was unwilling to distract my attention by taking into view the bearing of contemporary researches in the same field; and this must plead my excuse for omitting to notice some works which have recently appeared, both in this country and on the continent, by men whose names entitle whatever they write to respectful consideration. If our conclusions should prove substantially identical, they will have more weight, as coming from independent witnesses. If they differ, they will help to correct and modify each other.

From the nature of the present investigation, I have to ask the reader's indulgence for a frequent citation of original authorities which may be felt wearisome, and even look pedantic. But the question is one which can only be settled by a direct appeal to the statements of ancient writers; and if those writers are quoted at all, they must be quoted in the language in which they wrote, as the applicability of a citation to the point at issue will often depend on the rendering of words, and the construction of phrases, which the supporter of a theory is always liable to the suspicion, and even open unconsciously to the temptation, of attempting to wrest from their proper meaning to his own purpose. Those who are best qualified to form a judgment on the case, will wish to have the whole evidence set before them at once. Mere references, however exact, would have subjected them to an unreasonable expenditure of time and trouble in hunting through different books not always at hand, to ascertain whether the authorities have been rightly used or not. I have confined the citations for the most part to the foot-notes. When, for special reasons, I have thought it necessary in a few instances to introduce them into the text, an English translation is always subjoined.

To some, perhaps, an apology may seem due for having appended to a purely critical disquisition, the practical and spiritual bearings of the question, which I have considered at some length, and traced to their probable consequences, in the concluding section of the Essay. It will be objected possibly, that I have mixed up in one inquiry, matters which are essentially distinct—the strictly critical and the properly religious. I think, however, that the artificial relation in which theology has been unhappily placed towards general science, has led to the drawing of too sharp and absolute a line of distinction between different spheres of mental activity. Our nature is a whole, all the elements of which should work together in harmony. I do not believe, that the most rigid demands of the intellect and the clearest intuitions of the moral and spiritual sense, when both are rightly understood, will ever be found at variance. I know from personal experience, that it was an apprehension of spiritual loss, which kept me for a long time from accepting the plain dictate of unbiassed scholarship. Not till I was aware of the gratuitous assumption on which that apprehension was based, did I become capable of admitting the full force of critical evidence. What I have found a relief to my own mind, I wished to suggest as possibly available for others also.

After all, there are excellent men who will regret, I am well aware, that I should have ever raised the question mooted in these pages. Constantly engaged in the noble work of practical Christianity, and grounding their benevolent ministry on the authority of the New Testament, such men look—not unnaturally, perhaps, from their point of view—on every attempt to invalidate the old traditional foundations of our Protestant theology, as an encroachment on the province of religion itself, as some weakening of the blessed power, which they conceive the popular system specially carries with it, of sustaining, warning, and comforting our weak, sinful, and suffering humanity. Words cannot express the reverence in which I hold the labours of such men as these. The chief value which I attach to critical studies arises from my belief, that they will ultimately procure a firmer standing point, a clearer vision, and a directer spiritual action for the preachers of the pure and everlasting Gospel of Christ. Men who are engaged in the practical administration of Christianity, draw out of its sacred books, by a sort of elective affinity, all those elements of a diviner life which belong to the essence of our spiritual being, which are imperishable and eternal,—and which qualify, at least, if they cannot wholly neutralize, the less pure and defensible adjuncts historically attached to them in the great tradition of the ages. With such men, the practical influence of Christianity is so overpoweringly strong, that it reduces all speculative difficulties to zero. Their disregard of these difficulties, which they do not pretend to deny,—arises from no want of sincerity, but from their entire absorption for the time in a higher interest. The scholar's position is of quite another kind; and it is difficult for men so very differently placed, fully to understand each other. The scholar, as a scholar, lives aloof from the practical interests of the world, and dwells in a clear and quiet atmosphere of thought, where his mind cannot fail to discern the mingled elements of truth and falsehood that enter into the composite mass of tradition and arbitrary interpretation, constituting the popular theology—its groundless assumptions, its illogical inferences, and its perverse apprehension of many statements of fact, which meant one thing to the simple age which first wrote them down, and mean quite another, with all the theories which have gathered round them, now. Yet he may feel as strongly as ever the deep beauty and intrinsic truth of the fundamental convictions and trusts which are imbedded in these old traditions, and which were infused into them at first, as they are still kept alive, by the Spirit of the Omnipresent God. What, then, is the scholar to do, when he has girded up his loins like a man to search for truth at all cost, and the demands of his intellectual and spiritual nature attack him with forces which he cannot at once bring into harmony; when he feels that there is truth on both sides of his being, which he cannot as yet make one? He can only go on trustingly and reverently, in the full belief that truth, wherever it leads him, is the voice of God; and that although the way for the moment may be perplexed and difficult, if that voice be honestly hearkened to, it will certainly conduct him to rest and refreshment at last. He can only say, in a far higher sense than blind old Samson, to the Invisible Power on which he leans—

> "A little onward lend thy guiding hand
> To these dark steps, a little further on;
> For yonder bank hath choice of sun or shade."

The true principle of Protestantism, carried to its legitimate extent, not only justifies but demands the fullest and most fearless investigation of the origin, authorship, and composition of the books which form our sacred Canon. Protestantism was avowedly a transference of authority from human councils to the direct utterances of the voice of God. But how are we to know what is the voice of God, except by exploring the sources through which it is declared to have come to us, and clearly understanding the conditions under which alone it can be credibly conveyed? One thing is certain, a true religion can never rest on false history. We must first test the historical foundations, before any system, however fair and well-proportioned, can be securely built on them. A Scripture utterance of divine truth cannot be interpreted like a legal instrument, merely by a literal acceptance of the words which it contains. We must go through the words to the Spirit which fills them from the Highest Mind, and which can only be interpreted by a kindred spirit within our own. The old Protestant confessions, broader than the theology which grew out of them, appeal to the witness of the Spirit in the last instance as the consummating evidence of divine authority. Luther, with a rough boldness of speech, which would have made our modern scripturalists stand aghast, maintained that the Spirit of Christ was the only decisive test of the apostolic origin: "Whatever does not teach Christ, cannot be apostolic, though it were taught by St. Peter and St. Paul; and again, whatever preaches Christ, will be apostolic, though it were preached by Judas, Ananias, Pilate and Herod." [1]

[1] Was Christum nicht lehrt, das ist noch nicht apostolisch, wenn es gleich S. Petrus oder Paulus lehrte; wiederum was Christum predigt, das wäre apostolisch, wenns gleich Judas, Hannas, Pilatus und Herodes thät?

If the essence of Christianity be the self-consecration of the individual soul to God in the spirit of Christ, then the Spirit, as the living power which effectuates that union, must be above every written record of its utterance and working. It wrought with marvellous strength in Christ and his apostles: and it works to this day in all who have any participation in their faith and love, and strive to prolong their mission to the world; and thus it makes the true people of God one from age to age and over all the earth. But the Scriptures are invaluable from the witness which they bear to its earliest effusion and freshest operation. It is this consideration which has enabled me to reconcile an undiminished reverence for the religious teaching of the Fourth Gospel, with the entertainment of views very different from those usually held, respecting its date and authorship. Should my conclusion find acceptance, I shall feel satisfaction in the thought of having made a small contribution to that advancing tide of liberal opinion which is irresistibly bearing onward men's minds to a more spiritual conception of Christianity, and to wider and nobler views of human duty and destination. If, on the other hand, it should appear that I have missed the truth, the copiousness, and, as I believe, the fidelity with which I have adduced the premises for my conclusions, will afford the reader means of my refutation.

CONTENTS.

SECTION I.
Statement of the Question 1

SECTION II.
The Fourth Gospel and the Apocalypse 9

SECTION III.
Historical Notices of the Apostle John 15

SECTION IV.
Comparison of foregoing notices with the Works ascribed to John 25

SECTION V.
Testimonies to the Apocalypse 28

SECTION VI.
Reaction against the Apocalypse 42

SECTION VII.
Testimonies to the Fourth Gospel 54

SECTION VIII.
Internal Indications of Age 88

SECTION IX.
The Paschal Controversy 99

SECTION X.
Chronology of the Paschal Question 124

SECTION XI.
Recapitulation and Result 143

SECTION XII.
The Religious Bearing of the Question 157

EDITOR'S NOTE.

NOTWITHSTANDING the thoroughness of the following treatise, the Author had designed, in a Second Edition, to strengthen his argument on some points, and on others to enlarge his exposition. In particular, he had intended to rewrite and expand the Supplementary Note on the chronology of the Paschal question; and, in the concluding Section, to answer objections advanced against his conclusion by some of his English and American Reviewers. It was almost the only purpose which his singularly complete life left unaccomplished. I had hoped to be able, with the aid of memoranda in his hand-writing, and the recollection of conversations which interpret them, to give some imperfect account of his latest thoughts on the subject of this book. But the materials which he has left are little more than slight *marginalia*; and I find it impossible to work them into any literary form without rendering him apparently responsible for judgments which can only be conjecturally his. With the exception, therefore, of a single footnote, giving Volkmar's correction of the Justin Martyr dates, this Second Edition is simply a revised reprint of the First.

J. M.

LONDON, *Feb.* 26, 1870.

THE
CHARACTER OF THE FOURTH GOSPEL.

SECTION I.

Statement of the Question.

"MAN KANN MIT RECHT BEHAUPTEN, ALLE DAS URCHRISTENTHUM BETREFFENDEN FRAGEN HABEN IHREN EIGENTLICHEN MITTELPUNKT IN DER EINEN FRAGE: WIE DER TIEF-EINGREIFENDE WIDERSPRUCH ZU LÖSEN IST, WELCHER IN DEN EVANGELIEN SELBST UNLÄUGBAR ZU TAGE LIEGT."—F. C. BAUR.

"HOW THE UNDENIABLE CONTRADICTIONS OF THE EVANGELISTS ARE TO BE SOLVED, IS THE ONE QUESTION WHEREIN CENTRES EVERY OTHER RELATING TO PRIMITIVE CHRISTIANITY."

ALTHOUGH the superstitious feeling with which the mere letter of Scripture is often regarded, hinders people from perceiving as readily as they otherwise would, the distinctive character of its several books, yet, I presume, no reader of ordinary attention can have failed to discover a marked difference between our Three First Gospels, or as they are now conveniently designated, from the common view which they take of Christ's ministry, the Synoptical Gospels—and the Fourth, which bears the name of John. This difference goes much deeper than mere diversity of style or individuality of conception—the mere omission, or insertion, or simple rearrangement of particular facts and particular sayings; for in these more superficial aspects, the Three First Gospels also differ very considerably from each other. The difference between the Fourth Gospel and the other three affects the whole conception of the person and teaching of Christ, and the fundamental distribution of the events of his public ministry. The

Synoptical Gospels, notwithstanding their frequent divergency on collateral points, agree generally in their representation of that ministry as a whole; often coincide to the very letter for entire sentences together, especially in their report of the words of Christ himself; and evidently contain at bottom the common Palestinian tradition respecting him. They describe him as undergoing with many of his countrymen the initiatory baptism of John,[1] and not commencing his own public ministry till that of the Baptist was concluded;[2] confining his labours, in the first instance, exclusively to Galilee and the surrounding districts; appealing with great effect to the Messianic expectations of his time, and gathering round him vast multitudes to listen to his teachings and witness his wonderful works, as he journeyed from town to town and from village to village to the extreme verge of northern Palestine; gradually unfolding to the more devoted and confidential of his disciples both the height of his claims and the destiny which awaited him, as the consciousness of his divine mission grew and deepened in his own mind; and only at the very close of his ministry, coming into direct collision with the sacerdotal and rabbinical party at Jerusalem which procured his execution by the Roman government.

If we except what is called the Sermon on the Mount, which contains apparently the substance of discourses delivered at various times on a hill-side near Capernaum, and that continuous series of parables occurring between the 9th and 19th chapters of Luke's Gospel, where we have probably the insertion of a similar collection,[3]—the teachings of Christ, as preserved in the Synoptical Gospels, are remarkable for their occasional character and aphoristic form, always called forth by some casual incident or encounter in the course of his missionary

[1] Matth. iii. 15; Mark i. 9; Luke iii. 21.
[2] Matth. iv. 12, 17; Mark i. 14. The same fact is indicated, though not so distinctly, by Luke. Compare iii. 20 with v. 33 and vii. 18.
[3] The limits of this series, Bishop Marsh, in his Essay on the Origin of the Three First Gospels (ch. xvii.) has fixed more definitely between ix. 51 and xviii. 14. He supposed it to contain the substance of a γνωμολογία or "collection of sayings," previously in existence. We find here some most beautiful parables peculiar to Luke.

STATEMENT OF THE QUESTION.

wanderings, and never expanding into any connected and lengthened argumentation. His first appeal was made, as he himself says (Matth. x. 6; xv. 24), "to the lost sheep of the house of Israel;" and although in the narrative of Luke, which was written under Pauline influence, we discern already the working of a broader and more cosmopolitan principle, yet generally we may say, that throughout the Synoptical Gospels the teachings of Christ assume the Law and the Prophets as their basis, and are intended to bring out the deep spiritual significance that was hidden in them.[1] The Three First Gospels divide the public ministry of Christ into two distinctly marked and broadly separated periods,—that which was passed in Galilee, and that which was passed in Jerusalem. The first of these periods is introduced by the descent of the Spirit on Jesus at his baptism by John; the second, by the transfiguration, which has all the appearance of being a renewal and a re-enforcement of the original consecration at baptism.[2] This distribution of events into two periods, with the initiations of the

[1] In Matthew (x. 5) Christ says expressly to the twelve: "Go not into the way of the Gentiles, and into any city of the Samaritans enter ye not." Luke, notwithstanding his mention of the refusal of some Samaritans to receive him into their village, "because his face was set to go to Jerusalem" (ix. 53), does not, however, represent him as limiting his instructions to the seventy by any such prohibition as Matthew puts into the commission of the twelve, and even tells us that, on his way to Jerusalem, "he passed through the midst of *Samaria* and Galilee" (xvii. 11). It is observable, moreover, that in the sections peculiar to Luke, the great lessons of human brotherhood and devout thankfulness are enforced by the example of a Samaritan (x. 33; xvii. 16). Yet Luke says, as distinctly as Matthew himself: "It is easier for heaven and earth to pass, than one tittle of the law to fail" (xvi. 17). Nowhere in Luke do we meet with such strong and apparently such exclusive language as occurs in John: ἐγώ εἰμι ἡ θύρα τῶν προβάτων· πάντες ὅσοι ἦλθον πρὸ ἐμοῦ, κλέπται εἰσὶν καὶ λῃσταί. (x. 7, 8).

[2] The words on the two occasions are nearly identical in all three Evangelists: Matth. iii. 17, and xvii. 5; Mark i. 11, and ix. 7; Luke iii. 22, and ix. 35. The transfiguration marks the turning point of the synoptical narrative, and divides it into two sections which differ perceptibly in character and significance from each other. Only Simon Peter and the two sons of Zebedee are admitted to the transfiguration, as best qualified of all the twelve to enter into the higher meaning and inevitable conditions of the Messianic office, which Jesus was now beginning more undisguisedly to assume. About this period of his ministry, we find him for the first time speaking quite openly of his death and resurrection. Compare Matth xvi. 21; xvii. 12, 22, 23; Mark ix. 9-12; x. 33, 34; Luke ix. 31, 44, 45.

baptism and the transfiguration severally prefixed to each, marks with the strongest characters the common type of the synoptical conception of the public ministry of Christ.

In all these respects the Fourth Gospel stands out in decided contrast and contradiction to the Three First. It omits all mention of the baptism of Jesus by John. It represents John as saying at once, on seeing the Spirit descend on Jesus, "Behold the Lamb of God, which taketh away the sin of the world"[1] (i. 29, comp. 31-34); and Andrew, after his first interview with Jesus, declaring to his brother Peter, "we have found the Messias" (i. 41); a declaration shortly afterwards repeated more at full by Philip to Nathaniel, "We have found him, of whom Moses in the law and the prophets did write, Jesus of Nazareth, the son of Joseph" (i. 45). Instead of postponing the commencement of Christ's ministry till John was cast into prison, the Fourth Evangelist describes it as subsisting for some time side by side with that of John,—the two preachers baptizing together in the same neighbourhood (John iii. 22, 23). Instead of cautiously advancing his claims, and only towards the close of his ministry distinctly announcing himself as the Christ— Jesus, in the Fourth Gospel, from the very first reveals his high character and office by an unreserved disclosure of the Divine Word that was incarnate in him, and engaged in open discussion respecting his claims to authority with the Jews at Jerusalem and elsewhere[2] (John i. ii. iii.). In no instance is the difference between the synoptical and the Johannine narrative more strikingly exemplified, than in the position which they respectively assign to the expulsion of the money-changers from the Temple. The Fourth Gospel puts it at the opening of Christ's ministry, on the occasion of the first Passover,—with a view, no doubt, to establish his prophetic authority from the first in the face of the Jews, and to give him at once the vantage-ground which

---

[1] This is irreconcileable with the later inquiry of the Baptist, recorded by Matth. xi. 3, and Luke vii. 19,—" Art thou he that should come, or do we look for another?"

[2] Compare Matthew xvi. 20.

STATEMENT OF THE QUESTION. 5

he is described as occupying in his subsequent controversy with them through the sequel of the history. The only wonder is, how at such a time, after such an act, he should have escaped alive out of the hands of his enemies; especially when we remember what befel him for not stronger language or more violent proceedings during his last visit to Jerusalem. The Synoptists,[1] with certainly far more semblance of probability, place this transaction at the end of his public life, after his triumphal entry into Jerusalem, when he had already acquired a wide-spread prophetic fame, and numbers believed in him, and he had an enthusiastic multitude at his back to support his claims. In the Three First Gospels we have the picture, exceedingly vivid and natural, of a great moral and religious reformer, cautiously making his way through the prejudices and misconceptions of his contemporaries, gradually obtaining their confidence and changing the direction of their hopes, and only reaching the full climax of his personal influence in the period immediately preceding his death. In the Fourth, on the contrary, the unclouded glory of the Son of God shines out complete from the first, and is sustained undiminished till the words "It is finished" announce its withdrawal from earth—saved through the whole intervening period from the extinction which seems every moment to threaten it, by the mysterious protection indicated in the significant phrase peculiar to this gospel, "My hour is not yet come." Interwrought inextricably with the texture of the synoptical narrative we meet with records of healing and restorative agency, which forms a large part of the daily work of the prophet of Nazareth; and amidst which the casting out of demons and unclean spirits holds a conspicuous place. Instead of this, the Fourth Gospel presents us with a selection of just seven miracles,[2] intended apparently to furnish

[1] The Germans use the word *Synoptiker*. But *synoptic* (συνοπτικός) more properly denotes the work than the author. There is sufficient authority for the Greek verb ὀπτίζω (see Liddell and Scott's Lexicon) to justify the adoption of so convenient a derivative as *Synoptist*, to express the collective writers of the Three First Gospels.

[2] (1) ii. 6-11 ; (2) iv. 46-54 ; (3) v. 5-9 ; (4) vi. 11-14 ; (5) vi. 19-21 ; (6) ix. 1-12 ; (7) xi. 1-46.

a specimen of the various modes and occasions of Christ's miraculous working, and closing with the greatest instance of all—the raising of Lazarus from the dead. Among these miracles not one case occurs of the cure of a demoniac, though cures of this description might almost be described as the characteristic feature of the miraculous element of the Synoptists. For the pithy sayings and popular parables of the Three First Gospels, the Fourth substitutes long argumentative discourses, reiterating incessantly (as if the writer was labouring with the weight of thoughts which he could not at once adequately express), in words but slightly varied, the same absorbing idea; at times apparently encountering forms of error and anticipating objections which, if the synoptic narration be true, could hardly yet have come into existence. We have not here the varied, interwoven miscellany of history and doctrine, of miracle and parable, which the Three First Gospels so graphically present, but one smooth, continuous flow of exhortation and disputation poured through the length and breadth of the book, with a few most exquisite narratives interspersed, standing out like islets of rare beauty in the broad expanse of some quiet lake. Instead of confining the earlier part of Christ's ministry, with the Synoptists, exclusively to Galilee, and bringing him up for only one Passover to Jerusalem, when he met his fate,—the Fourth Gospel represents him as dividing his time almost equally from the first between Galilee and Jerusalem, and attending two if not three Passovers in the Holy City.[1]

It must be obvious, I think, to every one who has carefully gone through the foregoing comparison, that the old theory which so long found favour in the Church, of John's having written his gospel to fill up and complete the earlier three, does not meet the actual conditions of the case.[2] John's is not so

---

[1] There is no uncertainty about two Passovers—those mentioned ii. 13, and xiii. 1. From comparing vi. 4 with vii. 2, we know that a Passover must have intervened, which vii. 1 renders it probable Jesus had attended.

[2] This theory was first broached by Eusebius (H. E. iii. 24), who says, "that John was induced to write, having previously confined himself ἀγράφῳ κηρύγματι, by observing that the Three First Evangelists—the correctness of whose actual narrative he

much another, as in one sense a different gospel.[1] It is impossible to harmonize the two forms of the narrative. One excludes the other. If the Three First Gospels represent Christ's public ministry truly, the Fourth cannot be accepted as simple, reliable history. If we assume the truth of the Fourth, we must reject on some fundamental points the evidence of the Three First. The question is, which of these two narratives are we to take as our guide, and accept as authentic for the main facts of the life of Jesus? Must we control the statements of the Synoptists by those of John, or those of John by the Synoptists? The decision of this question will be followed by consequences of some moment. It will affect our whole conception of the person and doctrine of Christ; modify to some extent our view of the religion originally taught by himself; and must doubtless contribute to the settlement of some contro-

confirmed—had omitted all notice of Christ's public ministry previous to the imprisonment of the Baptist, and had thus made it last but one year. It was this omission which he specially proposed to supply; and the simple recognition of this fact Eusebius thought sufficient to bring the Four Gospels into perfect harmony: οἷς καὶ ἐπιστήσαντι οὐκέτι ἂν δόξαι διαφωνεῖν ἀλλήλοις τὰ εὐαγγέλια, τῷ τὸ μὲν κατὰ Ἰωάννην τὰ πρῶτα τῶν τοῦ Χριστοῦ πράξεων περιέχειν, τὰ δὲ λοιπὰ τὴν ἐπὶ τέλει τοῦ χρόνου αὐτῷ γεγενημένην ἱστορίαν. (13.) How superficial and inadequate this solution of the difficulty is, the foregoing comparison will show. Jerome (de Vir. Ill. i. 9) has copied this explanation of Eusebius, with still looser application to the facts of the case. Clement of Alexandria (cited by Eusebius, H.E. vi. 14) has suggested another theory, viz., "That whereas the three earlier gospels contained the *corporeal* side of the history (τὰ σωματικά), John, at the earnest request of his friends, and under the influence of the Spirit, produced a *spiritual* gospel." (7.) This theory, rightly understood, is nearer the truth than that of Eusebius. When all the four gospels got a place in the canon, and the difference between the Fourth and the Three First was still undeniable, it was thought necessary to devise some mode of reconciling them, which should leave the historical authority of each untouched. The assumption of this necessity prevented, as it still prevents, the discovery of the true relation between them.

[1] I do not think this language too strong for the particular fact which it is intended to express; but I must not be understood as meaning to deny the *ultimate* ascription of *all* the gospels, the Fourth not less than the Three First, to a common spiritual source in Christ himself. Indeed, apart from the pre-supposition of some great spiritual power which had come into the world, quickening into intenser life the kindred elements of humanity, and diffusing among men a new religious awakening far beyond the limits of its own living presence on earth, the origin of a work like the Fourth Gospel would be to me a still more inexplicable enigma than even the simpler narrative of the Synoptists.

versies which have long hopelessly divided Christendom. The question, therefore, to the investigation of which the following pages are devoted, is not one of mere speculative and critical interest without obvious result, but carries with it a grave and practical import. To the early existence of the substance, at least, of two of our synoptical gospels—those of Matthew and Mark—we have direct and very early, if not contemporary, testimony;[1] and Luke's preface bears witness to the care which he took in sifting and tracing to their source, the various traditions which he found current respecting the life of Jesus. All three agree in the main outlines of their narrative; their style is marked with a strong character of simplicity and naturalness; and their very differences attest the presence of some great underlying historical reality, which different traditions had variously caught up, and transmitted through divers media of conception and realization to those who first put the history into writing. Against such obvious claims to general trust on the part of the Synoptical Gospels, we ought to possess the most unanswerable evidence of direct apostolic origin, to supersede them as historical authorities by a book—in which all the traces of primitive tradition, even the characteristic words of the great Teacher himself, seem dissolved and washed away in the sweeping tide of the writer's own thought—where doctrine, not history, has evidently been the animating impulse.

[1] In the fragments of Papias preserved by Eusebius (H.E. iii. 39). See also Routh's Reliquiæ Sacræ, Tom. i. p. 7 seq. Papias declared, he had conversed with those who had conversed with the apostles.

SECTION II.

On the possibility of the Fourth Gospel and the Apocalypse having the same author.

IN the New Testament are two books, each of which has been ascribed by tradition, and a certain amount of early testimony, to the apostle John—the Fourth Gospel and the Apocalypse. Can both of these have been the production of the same mind? The settlement of that preliminary question has a direct bearing on the determination of the authenticity of either. It has been urged by those who affirm the identity of authorship, that the difference of style and manner and underlying tone of thought, which is perceptible on the most cursory reading, between the Apocalypse and the Fourth Gospel, is simply the difference between a young and an old mind—between the sensuous fire and brillancy of a yet unsubdued imagination, and the serener light of a spirit mellowed by years and experience.[1] This explanation seems plausible, till we look more narrowly into the nature and grounds of the difference between the two writers. For it is a difference not resolvable into any conceivable amount of progressive development out of a common mental root, but a difference so marked and so characteristic as to imply a radical distinctness in origin. The writer of the Apocalypse has a mind essentially objective. He realizes his conceptions through vision. He transports himself

---

[1] Longinus explained on this ground the difference between the Iliad and the Odyssey, without doubting for a moment, that both were the production of Homer. The Iliad was the fruit of his mature genius (ἐν ἀκμῇ πνεύματος γραφομένη), the Odyssey of his age—γῆρας δ'ὅμως (he adds with graceful rhetoric) Ὁμήρου. (De Sublim. ix.) Modern criticism has not, however, ratified his judgment.

into an imaginary world, and speaks as if it were constantly present to his sense—introducing its ever-shifting scenes by "I saw," "I looked," "I heard," "I stood." His colouring is warm and gorgeous, and his lights and shadows are broadly contrasted. His whole book is pervaded with the glow, and breathes the vehement and fierce spirit, of the old Hebrew prophecy, painting vividly to the mental eye, but never appealing directly to the spiritual perception of the soul. When we turn to the Fourth Gospel, we find ourselves at once in another atmosphere of thought, full of deep yearnings after the unseen and eternal, ever soaring into a region which the imagery of things visible cannot reach; even in its descriptions marked by a certain contemplative quietness, as if it looked at things without from the retired depths of the soul within. It exhibits but a slight tinge of Hebraic objectiveness, and throughout seems striving to express its sense of spiritual realities in the more abstract phraseology which the wide diffusion of Hellenic culture had rendered current in the world at the commencement of the Christian era. It has been said, indeed, that both writers are distinguished by a remarkable power of objective presentation. In a certain sense this is true. But in how different a way is it shown? Compare, for instance, the awful description of the effect of opening the sixth seal, and that ghastly procession of the horses which precedes it, in the Apocalypse (vi. 12-17 and 1-8), where every word vibrates, as it were, with the throbbing pulse of an excited imagination,—and that marvellously graphic story of the man born blind, or the exquisite pathos with which the raising of Lazarus is narrated, in the Fourth Gospel (ix. and xi.), where all is so clear and yet so calm and still, as if the writer had looked the fading traditions of the past into distinctness, as enthusiasts for art have been said by dint of gazing to call back into their original vividness the decaying colours and crumbling outlines of the Last Supper of Da Vinci on the wall of the refectory at Milan. We at once recognise in the authors of the Apocalypse and the Gospel a genius essentially distinct.[1] The language of the two writers is as different as their characteristic modes of conception and thought. The style of the Apocalypse is perfectly barbarous—Hebrew done into Greek, with a constant violation of the most ordinary laws of construction.[2] The Greek of the Fourth Gospel, without being classical, is still fluent, perspicuous, and grammatical. Some diversity of style, it is true, might be expected in the two works, owing to the different subjects of which they treat, even supposing them to have come from the same hand. But there are certain little peculiarities of expression and con-

[1] This power of objective presentation, by which a scene is brought up distinctly before the reader's mind, has been assumed too readily as an evidence of autopsy. Unless supported by other testimony, it proves nothing but the peculiar genius of the writer—his way of realizing to himself the events which he has to record. How extremely vivid, how true, how real, are many of the descriptions in the book of Genesis, in Homer, and in Herodotus! We seem to see with our own eyes what they narrate. The men and women actually live and speak before us. Yet we know, that nothing but tradition, which lives through its very vividness, could have furnished the material of these stories. The oldest traditions in the world are the most picturesque. Tradition naturally produces vivid and picturesque narration. It is easy to perceive why it must be so. When men have a strong interest to throw their thoughts backward, and try to reproduce the vanished past, imagination is the faculty by which they arrest, and combine, and shape into definite form, and animate with a kind of secondary reality, the vague and floating rumours which dimly envelope their minds. The critical sifting of evidence is a process as yet unknown and inconceivable. The more distinct the picture which they can make out of their materials, the stronger is their assurance that it represents the truth. They accept it as a divine inspiration. For memory and imagination have hardly as yet acquired a distinct exercise. All early tradition is poetry. Mnemosyne was the mother of the Muses. When Homer is about to lay some unusual stress on his memory, as in the recital of the forces which came to the war of Troy, he invokes the Muses.

"Ἔσπετε νῦν μοι, Μοῦσαι Ὀλύμπια δώματ' ἔχουσαι·
Ὑμεῖς γὰρ θεαί ἐστε, πάρεστέ τε, ἴστε τε πάντα,
Ἡμεῖς δὲ κλέος οἷον ἀκούομεν, οὐδέ τι ἴδμεν. Β. 484-6. Compare also Α. 218.

The power under given circumstances still operates in the heart of modern civilization. Sir Walter Scott has thus described in his own felicitous manner the marvellously reproductive faculty of Old Mortality. " One would have almost supposed he must have been their contemporary, and have actually beheld the passages which he related, so much had he identified his feelings and opinions with theirs, and so much had his narrations the circumstantiality of an eye-witness." Ch. I. "Vetustas res scribenti nescio quo pacto antiquus fit animus, et quædam religio tenet." Liv. Hist. xliii. 13 (15).

[2] Dionysius of Alexandria (Enseb. H. E. vii. 25) describes it as ἰδιώμασι μὲν βαρβαρικοῖς χρώμενον, καί που καὶ σολοικίζοντα.

struction, clinging to the inmost texture of an author's style, and resulting from the very make and working of his own mind, which imprint themselves on everything that he writes, and the presence or absence of which supplies an unfailing criterion of authenticity. Such peculiarities in the Fourth Gospel are, among others, its constant use of ἵνα with the conjunctive for the ordinary construction with the infinitive—its fondness for οὖν as a connecting link in narration, and its employment of οὗτος and ἐκεῖνος with a singular union of demonstrative and relative force. These peculiarities are wholly wanting in the Apocalypse.[1] Some have insisted on the wide interval that probably separated the appearance of the two works, as affording time sufficient for a gradual change of views and the acquirement of a more complete mastery of the Greek language. The most probable date for the composition of the Apocalypse must be placed somewhere between 60 and 70 A.D. —the reign of Galba, and the destruction of Jerusalem.[2] Now, supposing John to have been not more than 18 or 20 when he joined the ministry of Jesus, he must have been close upon 50, at the very least, when the Apocalypse was written—a time of life when men's views and habits of thought and expression are for the most part permanently fixed. If he wrote his Gospel, as is usually maintained, in extreme old age, at the very close of the century, this would leave an interval of little more than thirty years between the composition of the two works. I do not hesitate to say, that so complete a transformation of the whole genius of a writer between mature life and old age, as is implied in the supposition that John could be the author at once of the Apocalypse and the Gospel, is without a precedent in

---

[1] De Wette has given a full recital of the peculiarities of expression which distinguish the Fourth Gospel and the Apocalypse from each other. (Einleit. ins N.T. § 105, c. b. § 189, b. c. d).

[2] Ewald (Comm. in Apocal. § 7), De Wette (Einl. N.T., § 187), Lücke (Einl. § 57), Bleek (Beitr. p. 81) agree substantially in this date, which carries internal probability along with it. Newton put it as far back as the reign of Nero. Irenæus carried it forward to the end of the reign of Domitian.

the history of the human mind, and seems to me to involve a psychological impossibility.

The case may be illustrated to the English reader from our own literature. Two of our greatest poets passed through remarkable mental changes. Milton's earliest and latest poems are separated by the chasm of the civil wars; and the stern Puritanism of the Samson Agonistes, with the severity of its Hellenic form, is strikingly distinguished from the joyous, romantic spirit and the cavalier-like appreciation of everything graceful and gay, which pervade the Comus and the Arcades, many of his early sonnets, and those exquisite pendents, L'Allegro and Il Penseroso. Dryden underwent mutations more extraordinary still. He began life as a Puritan, and passing through the intermediate stage of Anglicanism, ended his days in the bosom of the Catholic Church. The Hind and Panther, in which he justified this last change, breathes, as may be supposed, a very different spirit from the lines in which he bewailed the death of Cromwell. Yet, if we compare the poems written at the opposite ends of the lives of these great men—notwithstanding the revolution of thought and feeling which came over them in the interval—every mind that has any sense of mental characteristics, will at once perceive that it is dealing at bottom with the same individual genius;—that it is a case of growth and development, not of original difference;—and will feel it to be utterly impossible that, even had they passed through changes of opinion more radical still, Milton could ever have written the Hind and Panther or the Veni Creator, and Dryden, the Paradise Lost or Samson Agonistes. No living writer has exhibited a more remarkable change of style in the course of his literary career than Mr. Carlyle; yet, if we compare his Life of Schiller with his French Revolution or his History of Frederic the Great —notwithstanding the great disparity of form—every reader of ordinary discernment will recognize the same fundamental characteristics of his peculiar genius in his earlier and his later works. Apply this standard to the two books now under consideration; and the conclusion will be irresistible, that if the Apostle John be the author of the Apocalypse, he cannot have written the Gospel: if he wrote the Gospel, he cannot be the author of the Apocalypse.—We have next, then, to inquire what is the tenour of early testimony on this point. Does it speak most decidedly in favour of the authenticity of the Gospel or of the Apocalypse? Before adducing this testimony, it will be well to consider, in the first place, what is the impression conveyed to us, by the New Testament and the oldest ecclesiastical traditions, of the spirit and character of the Apostle John, and to compare it with the contents of the two books which bear his name. We shall thus be furnished with an additional criterion of the probability of his being the author of the one or the other.

SECTION III.

Notices of the Apostle John in the New Testament and the oldest ecclesiastical traditions.

IN citing the collective evidence of the New Testament on the character of the Apostle John, we must, of course, exclude, in the first instance, such as might be furnished by the two books which are the subject of comparison; since our purpose is to decide on the claims of each to a specific authorship, by testimony which is external to them both. This is the more necessary, as the popular conception of the Apostle, which has been invested with a kind of halo by religious poetry and art, and which influences the mind almost unconsciously in the question of authorship, is mainly derived from the Fourth Gospel itself. We gather from the synoptic narrative, that John was the younger of the two sons of Zebedee, a Galilæan fisherman of some substance on the Lake of Gennesaret—of whom we hear little, and who probably died soon after the conversion of his family. With their mother Salome, the two sons, James and John, appear to have shared enthusiastically in the Messianic hopes which were then rife and stirring throughout Palestine. It was probably the ardour of their religious temperament which attracted the notice of Jesus, drew him into close intimacy with them, and induced him to bestow on them the significant title of Sons of Thunder.[1] Their nobler qualities were not, however, unmingled with the carnal and selfish aspirings of the popular Messianic faith, and with some fierceness of Jewish intolerance; and these tendencies were encouraged by their mother, who, on one

---
[1] We learn this fact from Mark alone (iii. 17). He had it probably direct from Peter.

occasion, preferred a particular request to our Lord that her sons might fill the two most conspicuous places in his future kingdom. (Matth. xx. 21 ; Mark x. 35.)[1] It was the same two brothers who, on the refusal of some Samaritans to admit Jesus and his followers into their village, were for invoking fire from heaven, in the spirit of Elijah, to consume them, and received the significant rebuke, that their master's mission was not to destroy, but to save. (Luke ix. 54-56.) Of John it is specially remarked by two of the evangelists (Mark ix. 38, 39; Luke ix. 49, 50), that about the same time, when he saw one casting out devils in Christ's name, he forbade him because he was not of their company; and how he was again reproved by Christ for his exclusiveness. It should be observed that these instances of intolerance occur when the brethren were no longer recent converts, towards the close of Christ's ministry on his last journey to Jerusalem.[2] Notwithstanding their infirmities, which were, perhaps, inseparable from their mental constitution, Jesus shewed his appreciation of their higher nature by admitting the sons of Zebedee, with Simon Peter, into closer familiarity with his inmost thoughts than the rest of the twelve. They were with him during the transfiguration (Matth. xvii. 1 ; Mark ix. 2 ; Luke ix. 28). They, with Andrew and Peter, asked him privately, as he sate on the Mount of Olives, fronting the Temple, when and how the destruction of the city should be (Mark xiii. 3). John is sent with Peter to prepare the Passover (Luke xxii. 8). The same three are again present during the agony on Gethsemane (Matth. xxvi. 37 ; Mark xiv. 33). There is no further notice of the sons of Zebedee in the Synoptical Gospels; but their mother, Salome, is mentioned among the women who waited on Jesus to the last—watching him as he expired on the cross, and after his burial bringing sweet spices to the sepulchre. (Matth.

---

[1] Luke has omitted all notice of this request, and of the indignation which it excited in the minds of the ten.

[2] Lücke has called attention to this fact. (Comment. Evang. Johan. § 2).

xxvii. 56 ; Mark xv. 40, xvi. 1 ; Luke xxiii. 56, xxiv. 1.) Her deep love and trust were unshaken by the great and terrible catastrophe which had blighted her earlier expectations. Doubtless, she had hoped with the two disciples who walked to Emmaus, " that it had been he who should have redeemed Israel." (Luke xxiv. 21.) When we get into the apostolic age, after the death of Jesus, we find John actively engaged with Peter in building up the primitive church in Jerusalem. The two names are constantly associated through the earlier chapters of the book of Acts. How essentially Jewish in spirit their ministry was, we learn from the question proposed to the risen Jesus, with which they opened it: "Lord, wilt thou at this time restore again the kingdom to Israel?" (Acts i. 6) and from the course of action by which it was followed. When a persecution broke out against the more liberal movement originated by Stephen, and those who shared in it were scattered abroad, it is remarkable that the apostles were left undisturbed in Jerusalem, as though it did not affect them.[1] Again, after Samaria had been converted by Philip, one of Stephen's followers,[2] it is significant, that Peter and John, induced probably by a sort of conservative precaution, go over the same ground, with the view, as it would seem, of correcting or neutralizing any mischievous effects that might have resulted from Philip's preaching.[3] For it deserves notice, that, at this period, numbers of the Pharisees, changing the tactics which they had pursued in the life-time

[1] The exception in the case of the apostles is expressed in the most decided manner: πάντες διεσπάρησαν—πλὴν τῶν ἀποστόλων (Acts viii. 1). The author, writing from a later point of view, and with the evident purpose, as his whole book shows, of reconciling the Petrine and Pauline tendencies of the primitive church, is betrayed into apparent inconsistency. He says a great persecution attacked τὴν ἐκκλησίαν τὴν ἐν Ἱεροσολύμοις (using the word ἐκκλησία in its broader ultimate sense), and yet represents the acknowledged heads of that church as untouched by it.

[2] Acts vi. 5; Comp. xxi. 8.

[3] Acts viii. 5-13 (preaching of Philip with the baptism of Simon) ; ibid. 14-25 (preaching of Peter and John, with refusal of the Holy Spirit to Simon, for offering money); Acts viii. 26-40 (preaching of Philip along the coast of the Mediterra1ean) ; ix. 32-43 (preaching of Peter through the same district).

of Christ, appear to have prudently sided with the new religion, which was already making way with the multitude, and to have now tried to influence its counsels and imbue it with their own narrow spirit.[1] There is not a trace in the history of John's having ever taken any part or shown any sympathy with the liberal movements either of Stephen or of Paul. On the contrary, all subsisting evidence from the book of Acts goes to show, that John was closely connected with the Jewish party, who formed, it should be recollected, the original nucleus of believers at Jerusalem. Of his brother James, so constantly associated with him in the gospel narrative, we hear nothing, except that he was put to death by Herod—very possibly in consequence of some opposition raised by his Messianic zeal to the Hellenizing tendencies of the king (xii. 2).[2]

When Paul went up the second time to Jerusalem, to confer with the apostles about the treatment of heathen converts, he found John there (as he tells us himself, Gal. ii. 9)—associated with Peter, whose irresolution and fearfulness about the vexed question of eating with Gentiles he so sharply reproves—and with James the Less, the recognised head of the Jewish party and their first bishop,—enjoying with them the distinction of being considered " a pillar" of the church, and not occupying, be it observed, a neutral position, but thrust into conspicuous prominence as one of the acknowledged chiefs of the then Jewish Church, whose mission was exclusively to the circum-

---

[1] See especially Acts xv. 5, Comp. vi. 7, and the part taken by Gamaliel in the Sanhedrim, v. 34-39. The Sadducees were now the great open opponents of Christianity.

[2] It has been objected (National Review, No. ix. Art. v. p. 112) that the subordinate position which John occupies in relation to Peter throughout the earlier chapters of Acts, is inconsistent with the supposition of his being a leading member of the Jewish party at Jerusalem, and the author of the Apocalypse, which so vividly reflects its spirit. But the fact is easily explained, if we keep in mind the evident principle of the construction of the book of Acts—that of balancing and harmonizing the rival claims of Peter and Paul—which made it impossible to put any one on the same level with Peter in the first part of the history. It is sufficient for our purpose to remark, that everywhere in Acts, John is closely associated with the Jewish party.

cision.¹ So far, then, as the New Testament throws any light on the character and history of the Apostle John, it exhibits him as a Jewish Christian. This conclusion is remarkably confirmed by a passage in Irenæus, referring to this very conference with Paul at Jerusalem—which may be thus translated: "the apostles themselves, by raising the question whether disciples ought still to be circumcised or not, clearly showed that they still worshipped the God of their fathers"—and, therefore, by implication still observed the old law.² The book of Acts (iv. 13), in speaking of Peter and John, describes them as "unlettered and unlearned men"³—that is, as persons who had not, like Paul, been trained in the higher rabbinical discipline, and who might thereby have acquired some tincture of Hellenic culture, but who merely possessed such rudiments of Hebrew education as could be furnished by an ordinary Galilæan school attached to the synagogue. John's name never once occurs in the latter half of Acts. On Paul's last visit to Jerusalem, at the end of his third missionary journey, not later than 60 A.D. —both he and Peter would seem to have been away; as only James the Less is mentioned (xxi. 18). Had they been in the

---

¹ There is a latent irony in Paul's language,—οἱ δοκοῦντες στῦλοι—as though he did not recognise them as such himself, from their failure to perceive the breadth of the foundations of the true gospel.

² The passage exists only in the Latin version. "Ipsi autem (*i.e.* the apostles at Jerusalem, including John) ex eo quod quærerent: an oporteret circumcidi adhuc discipulos necne, manifeste ostenderunt, non habuisse se alterius Dei contemplationem" (Iren. adv. Hær. III. xii. 14). To apprehend the complete force of this passage, we must notice its place in the argument of Irenæus. He is replying to the Gnostics, who contended that the God of the Old Testament was not the God of the Christians. To refute them, he appeals to the practice of the apostles themselves, who, after their conversion, still observed the usages of the Jewish law. That this in his meaning, is clear from what he adds in the next section : " Hi circa Jacobum apostoli gentibus quidem libere agere permittebant, concedentes nos Spiritui Dei : ipsi vero eundem scientes Deum, *perseverabant in pristinis observationibus.*" The sense of the whole passage is well given by Stieren: "Ipsi legis præceptis satisfacere anxie studebant, quum iis persuasum esset, Deum legis et evangelii esse unum eundemque." Lücke expresses himself more strongly than I have ventured to do: " So lange Johannes in Jerusalem war, meint Irenæus, habe er mit den übrigen Aposteln das mosaische Gesetz noch streng beobachtet" (Comment. § 2, p. 16, 2te Aufl.).

² ἀγράμματοι καὶ ἰδιῶται.

city, it is hardly conceivable, how persons of such eminence should not have taken part in the proceedings on so important an occasion, and how, if they had been present, it should not have been noticed. When John finally quitted Jerusalem, and to what place he immediately transferred his residence, there are no data extant for determining. Dr. Lardner (Works, vi. p. 170) and De Wette (Einl. N. T. § 108 a. b.) agree in thinking it not unlikely, that the apostle removed into Asia on the breaking out of the war in Judea. This in itself would appear not improbable; but we have just seen that he could not have been in Jerusalem as late as 60 A.D.—and connected as he was with the Jewish party, he could hardly have settled at Ephesus, till the influence of Paul's ministry there had ceased. On the other hand, the imprisonment of that apostle for two years at Cæsarea (Acts xxiv. 27), and his subsequent removal to Rome, may have separated him so completely from the Asiatic churches, as to leave room for the planting of another church on the ground originally broken up by him. Some have doubted whether John ever resided at Ephesus at all. But the tradition of antiquity seems to be too clear, constant and uniform to admit of such entire scepticism. Polycrates, bishop of Ephesus, in the latter half of the second century, in a letter to Victor of Rome on the paschal controversy, says distinctly that John described particularly as ὁ ἐπὶ τὸ στῆθος τοῦ Κυρίου ἀναπεσών— was buried at Ephesus;[1] and Eusebius tells us, that in his day the apostle's tomb still existed in that city.[2] It is singular, no doubt, that neither Polycarp, nor the letters which bear the name of Ignatius, should anywhere allude to the fact; but we must set off, against their silence, the express testimony of Irenæus, who had been instructed by Polycarp in his youth, and who speaks of John's living and working at Ephesus as an universally acknowledged fact.[3] In another place he states

---

[1] Eusebius, H. E. iii. 31, v. 24.   [2] Eusebius, iii. 39.
[3] Adv. Hær. II. xxii. 5; III. i. 1. He appeals to uninterrupted tradition from the time of those who had conversed with the apostles.

that the church which had been founded by Paul in Ephesus, was a true witness of the apostolic tradition under the ministry of John till the age of Trajan.[1] That there was a strong Jewish party in Ephesus, is plain from Paul's being obliged to abandon the synagogue, and discourse in the lecture-room of the sophist Tyrannus (Acts xix. 9). According to all appearances, after Paul's final separation from the Asiatic churches, some Judaic reaction had taken place.[2] An apostle from the mother-church of Jerusalem, who had leaned on the bosom of the Lord himself, would be eagerly welcomed in that great centre of religious life; and the churches of that district, as we learn from later history, long adhered to the Jewish usages of the first generation of Christian believers.

Associated with this period of the apostle's life at Ephesus some interesting traditions have been preserved by ecclesiastical writers. Irenæus tells a story—on the authority of Polycarp, whose youth joined on to the old age of John —that on the apostle's finding himself one day in the same bath at Ephesus with the notorious heretic Cerinthus, he rushed out, lest the walls should fall in and overwhelm him in a common destruction with this enemy of the truth. If this story represent a fact, it furnishes evidence of the same spirit of which we have already had an example in the New Testament (Luke ix. 54-56, 49, 50; Mark ix. 38, 39).[3] A far

---

[1] Ἡ ἐν Ἐφέσῳ ἐκκλησία ὑπὸ Παύλου μὲν τεθεμελιωμένη, Ἰωάννου δὲ παραμείναντος αὐτοῖς μέχρι τῶν Τραϊανοῦ χρόνων, μάρτυς ἀληθής ἐστι τῆς τῶν ἀποστόλων παραδόσεως (Adv. Hær. III. iii. 4). Eusebius has cited this passage (H. E. iii. 23). Its object is to authenticate the Christian tradition by tracing it through John to Paul. It implies, therefore, that John was the successor of Paul.

[2] We know from himself, what pains it cost him to resist such reaction in the churches of Galatia. The Christ party (1 Cor. i. 12) possibly furnish another example of similar reaction at Corinth. See F. C. Baur, Das Christenthum der drei ersten Jahrhunderte, ii. (Die Judaistischen Gegner).

[3] Adv. Hær. III. iii. 4. Irenæus does not say, that he had the story direct from Polycarp, but at second-hand through others: εἰσὶν οἱ ἀκηκοότες αὐτοῦ. Partly on this account, and partly perhaps from some tenderness for the memory of the apostle, Dr. Lardner treats the whole narrative as doubtful (Credib. P. II. chap. vi.) Lücke, on the other hand (Einl. Comm. § 2, p. 19) thinks it bears strong internal marks of

more pleasing tale is that of the apostle mounting his horse in his old age, and, with characteristic ardour and intrepidity, riding into the very centre of a stronghold of robbers, to rescue a young man in whom he took a deep interest, but who, having fallen into evil courses, had become the captain of the band; and how he succeeded in restoring him at last to the church which he had forsaken.[1] Jerome narrates, that in extreme old age, when no longer able to make a lengthened and connected discourse, the apostle used to be carried in the arms of his disciples into the midst of the church, when he would repeat day after day the simple words, " Little children, love one another;" and that, on being asked why he said this continually, he replied, " This is the sum and substance of the Lord's teaching." The story rests on the authority of Jerome alone, some three centuries after the age of John;[2] but it contains nothing in itself incredible. Polycrates of Ephesus, in the letter already cited—enumerating a number of Asiatic bishops who adhered with himself to the old Jewish usage of observing the 14th of Nisan[3]—puts John second in this list, immediately following Philip of Hierapolis, one of the twelve apostles (τὸν τῶν δώδεκα ἀποστόλων), and has this remarkable passage respecting him : " John also, who leaned on the bosom of the

probability, and compares it with 2 John 10. Eusebius (H. E. iii. 28) quotes the story from Irenæus. Epiphanius (Adv. Hær. xxx. 24) has repeated it with much amplification—substituting the name of Ebion for that of Cerinthus. This fact is significant, as suggesting the possibility that the story from its origin may have had some connexion with a rumour of Jewish Christianity; though, to save the apostle himself from the suspicion of any such tendency, the orthodox father makes the mythic founder of Ebionitism the special object of his abhorrence. This whole section in Epiphanius deserves to be read, as showing the complete change of character and object which a story often underwent in the course of ecclesiastical tradition.

[1] This story is first told in the little treatise usually printed along with the books of Clement of Alexandria : " Quis dives salvetur ?" Thence it has been copied by Eusebius (H. E. iii. 23). Lardner and Lücke both think, it probably contains substantial truth. Herder has pleasingly worked it up among his " Legends," under the title of " The Rescued Youth." (Zur Litt. u. Kunst. Werke, VI. 31).

[2] Comm. in Galat. c. 6. He cites it, without any introduction, as a tradition current in his time.

[3] " Cum cæteris episcopis Asiæ, qui juxta quandam veterem consuetudinem *cum Judæis* decimaquarta luna Pascha celebrabant." Hieron. de Vir. Illustr. c. xlv.

Lord, who was a priest wearing the *petalon*, both martyr and teacher." The *petalon* (πέταλον) was a gold plate in front of the high priest's turban or tiara, inscribed with the words, "Holy to Jehovah." Various interpretations have been given of this passage: some, with Lücke, supposing it simply to express the eminent episcopacy of John in Ephesus and its neighbourhood; other understanding it, in a figurative sense, of John's deep penetration into the inner mind of Christ; others, lastly, with Baur and the critics of the Tübingen school, of John's upholding the Jewish form of Christianity, and being, in the hierarchical sense of the Old Testament, a representative of the high priesthood of Christ on earth. The context, with some other considerations referred to in the note, appear to me to render this altogether the most probable interpretation.[1] The

[1] Ἔτι δὲ καὶ Ἰωάννης——ὃς ἐγενήθη ἱερεὺς τὸ πέταλον πεφορεκώς, καὶ μάρτυς καὶ διδάσκαλος. (ap. Euseb. H. E. v. 24.) Many commentators, not knowing what to make of these words in their literal sense, have been disposed to understand them figuratively, as, for instance, Routh (Reliquiæ Sacræ, ii. p. 28).—Le Moyne (Var. Sacr. ii. 25), cited by Heinichen (Euseb. H. E. v. 24), has strongly pressed the difficulties of the literal interpretation, and yet candidly admits that the writer may be speaking "de Joanne sacerdote et lamina instructo, dum adhuc viveret inter Judæos."—Epiphanius, in speaking of James the Less, the so-called brother of the Lord, the first bishop of the Jewish church at Jerusalem, of whose Ebionitish asceticism and piety, and final martyrdom, Hegesippus, himself a Jewish Christian and employing Hebrew materials (Euseb. H. E. iv. 22), has given so strange an account in his Records of the Apostolic Age (comp. Josephus's account of the death of James, Antiquit. XX. ix. 1.), —has twice ascribed to this undoubted head of a Jewish Christian Church, the very same peculiarity which we have already seen given by Polycrates to John (xxix. 4 Panarion). Τὸ πέταλον ἐπὶ τῆς κεφαλῆς ἐξῆν αὐτῷ φορεῖν and (ibid. lxxviii. 14) πέταλον ἐπὶ τῆς κεφαλῆς ἐφόρεσε. There is much, no doubt, that is legendary and fabulous in the narratives of Hegesippus and Epiphanius; but both meant to describe a Jewish Christian, and they knew the characteristics that would mark one.—Valesius quotes a passage from a MS. treatise on the passion of the Evangelist Mark, where the same expression is used of him, and with the same intent, *i.e.* to indicate, as I understand the words, the Jewish type of his Christianity: *pontificalis apicis petalum in populo gestasse Judæorum.* That such expression, however strong, did not imply the exercise of any sacerdotal function, properly so called, is evident from a passage in Irenæus. He is arguing, against the heretics, for an unbroken continuity of religious privileges from the Old dispensation to the New—the apostles in the spiritual kingdom occupying the same position with the former priests under the outward law. *Sacerdotes sunt omnes Domini apostoli, qui neque agros neque domos hereditant hic,*

same conclusion might be drawn from the appeal of the Quartodeciman party in the Asiatic churches, to the authority of the apostle John traditionally preserved among them, in favour of their own usage; but as this is a question still open to controversy, which I shall have to examine more at length in an ensuing section, I will not enter on it now.

On the whole, we gather from the united testimony of the New Testament and ecclesiastical tradition, that the apostle John, so far as we can trace his history through the dimness of the past, belonged to the Jewish section of the primitive Christian Church. There is much evidence that points directly to that conclusion, and none that bears against it. The few distinct glimpses that we get, are just of such a character as we should naturally expect to find in the first generation of Palestinian converts to Christianity—full of Messianic eagerness and zeal, and warmly attached to the person of Jesus; marked by strong prejudices and bitter national antipathies, but generous, impulsive and confiding, susceptible of the deepest and tenderest love where the object seemed worthy of it;—a simple, honest, unlettered Jew, with the better life of Christianity gradually kindling within him, but incapable of breaking loose entirely from the bonds of early prepossession, and of throwing himself with unreserved freedom into the broad catholicity of the spirit of Paul.

sed semper altari et Deo serviunt. (Adv. Hær. IV. viii. 3.) Irenæus designates the head of a Jewish communion, though it had nothing sacerdotal in its constitution, by a sacerdotal title. He calls Jairus, who was merely the ruler of a synagogue (Mark v. 22) *summus sacerdos* (adv. Hær. V. xiii. 1).—On the whole, in spite of the doubts of Dr. Lardner and others (Credib. P. II. Ch. cxiv., Hist. Apost. and Evang. Ch. ix. 4), I incline to think, that the most obvious meaning of this obscure expression, is John's presidency over an association of Jewish Christian churches. The early Protestant divines were averse to admit any suppositions that dispelled their ideal of an apostolic age, as conceived from the modern point of view. I may further remark, that the result of the most recent criticism seems to show, that the sacerdotal element came into the Catholic Church out of the Jewish Christianity. See, among others, Ritschl, "Die Entstehung der altkatholischen Kirche."

SECTION IV.

Comparison of the foregoing notices with the works ascribed to John.

IF I have drawn a fair inference, from the scattered notices which have been preserved to us, of the personal character of the apostle John—of the two works that bear his name, which must strike a thoughtful reader as most in harmony with it? Let us briefly recall the salient features of each. The Apocalypse is intensely Jewish both in its spirit and in its form. In its conception of the fulfilment of the Messianic hope—the final conflict of heathenism with the people of God, the complete destruction of the former, and the gathering of the latter into a glorious kingdom under a triumphant Messiah—in its retention of the old prophetic diction and imagery—in the importance which it attaches to the atoning efficacy of the blood of the Lamb that was slain (vii. 14, v. 12)—in its doctrine of a first and second resurrection, with the splendid vision of the New Jerusalem—it represents the popular belief of the early Jewish Christians more truly and vividly than any other book of the New Testament, not excepting the gospel of Matthew, in which, as we now possess it in its later Greek form, the original Jewish element is already tinged and qualified by some infusion of a Catholic spirit. The Apocalypse is strongly impregnated with the idea of Chiliasm; and Chiliasm, we know, was the general belief of the primitive Church, and more or less pervaded all sections of it, till Catholicism—which was a mixed result of reaction against Gnosticism and of a compromise with the Pauline tendency—subdued and excluded, in the course of the second and third centuries, the old Judaic form of Christianity, and recognised it only as a lingering heresy among the Ebionites and Nazarenes.[1] When the churches of Smyrna and Philadelphia are warned in the opening chapters of this book (ii. 9, iii. 9) " against the synagogue of Satan, which say they are Jews and are not,"—it is difficult not to believe that the allusion must be to the same liberal party, headed successively by Stephen and Paul, who were charged, as we find it stated in Acts (vi. 14) with a design " to change the customs which Moses had delivered to the Jews." The Greek of the Apocalypse is just such as we should expect from a man who had never learned it grammatically, but had picked it up from mere intercourse with those who spoke it. It is precisely the diction of one who is described in Acts as " unlettered and unlearned," but who had been thrown in his maturer years into the society of Greeks.

In all these respects the Fourth Gospel exhibits a character the very opposite to that of the Apocalypse. From beginning to end, though indicating acquaintance with Jewish history and Jewish modes of thought, its spirit is anti-Jewish. The habitual opponents of Christ are constantly distinguished as " the Jews." It has all the spiritual breadth of the mind of Paul, and is chiefly distinguished from it by a more quiet and contemplative tone, and a pervading consciousness of assured superiority, as though it came from one who had passed beyond the stage of controversy, and felt his faith to be resting on unassailable foundations. It betrays in more than one passage strong interest for the conversion of the Greeks (vii. 35, 36, xii. 20-23); and of the Chiliasm, which enters so largely into

[1] In the first age both Papias and the heretic Cerinthus were strongly attached to Chiliasm. Many eminent fathers of the second century, Justin Martyr, Irenæus, and Tertullian, undoubtingly upheld it ; and it was an object of enthusiastic belief with the Montanists. The first decided opposition to it came out of the philosophical school of Alexandria, headed by Origen. Yet down to the opening of the fourth century, we find no less a man than Lactantius, the tutor of the sons of the first Constantine, distinctly asserting it, and arraying it in all the colours of his rhetorical eloquence. (Divin. Instit. vii. 19-26, Epitom. lxxi. ii.) It only became a heresy by degrees. See Münscher's " Dogmengeschichte " (II. i. § 25, 26).

the descriptions of the Apocalypse, and formed so conspicuous a belief of the early Jewish Church, we do not find a trace in this gospel. Its Greek, though neither pure nor elegant, is that of a person who had been long in the habit of speaking and writing it, and with whom it had become a ready instrument of thought.

Without some direct outward testimony, there is nothing, it is true, in the interior form and character of the Apocalypse to link its authorship of necessity with the apostle John. The writer's description of himself as δοῦλος χριστοῦ, is undecisive. But there is certainly nothing to render it incredible, that John might have been the author of the book; for its spirit agrees with what we know of his own. On the other hand, it is difficult to conceive how the John, who is exhibited to us by the New Testament and ecclesiastical history, could possibly have written the Fourth Gospel, without so complete a transformation of his deeply marked character, and so entire a reversal of the powerful influences of his early life, as we can find no adequate means of accounting for within the widest limits of his later career. But this is a question mainly of external testimony, to which we must now direct our attention.

SECTION V.

Direct Testimony to the Authorship of the Apocalypse.

THE first witness to be adduced is Papias, whose fragments, preserved in Eusebius, throw so valuable a light on the apostolic sources of our two first gospels, and whose martyrdom has been placed on apparently good grounds in 164 A.D.[1] His testimony, therefore, goes back to the first half of the second century. As Papias informs us what pains he took to make himself acquainted, from eye and ear witnesses, still surviving, with the circumstances of the primitive church,[2] it is not in itself improbable that he should have known one of the earliest works which it produced, and that we should have his witness to the existence in the first age of our two oldest gospels and of the Apocalypse. But this testimony is not without its difficulties. In the first place, it is not direct, and comes to us through two authors of a comparatively late date—Andreas and Arethas, who were bishops of Cæsarea in Cappadocia towards the end of the fifth century.[3] These writers cite Papias with other ancient fathers, of whom they place him at the head—Irenæus, Methodius, and Hippolytus—as asserting the θεόπνευστον and ἀξιόπιστον of the Apocalypse. But they do not state from what

[1] See Rettig (Theologische Studien und Kritiken, for 1831, p. 769) who cites the Chronicon Paschale as his authority, and notices the coincidence of this date with that of the accession of his successor in Hierapolis, furnished from an independent source.

[2] Οὐ γὰρ τὰ ἐκ τῶν βιβλίων τοσοῦτόν με ὠφελεῖν ὑπελάμβανον, ὅσον τὰ παρὰ ζώσης φωνῆς καὶ μενούσης. ap. Euseb. H. E. iii. 39.

[3] Rettig (ubi supr.) has determined the limits of their literary activity by a very exhaustive process of reasoning, as falling somewhere between 470 A.D. and the opening years of the sixth century.

book of Papias they produce this testimony, nor furnish any evidence of his opinion respecting authorship. When Papias wrote, *inspiration* and *credibility* did not necessarily imply an apostolic source. They simply intimated that, in the judgment of the writer, the work was imbued with an apostolic spirit, and felt to be conducive to faith and edification. But remoteness and indirectness of allusion is not the only circumstance which detracts from the value of this testimony. Eusebius, who was familiar with the writings of Papias, and has quoted from them at some length, never once alludes to anything that he had written on the Apocalypse. This is the more remarkable, as he was much interested in the subject, and would have been glad, it might be thought, of some early testimony to fix his opinions respecting it; as he vacillated, we know, in his views of the authorship of the Apocalypse, and was half inclined to ascribe it to the presbyter John.[1] In consequence of too much having been made of this slight and indirect testimony of Papias, and the groundless assumption that he must have written a commentary on the Apocalypse, which has perished,—there has been perhaps a not unnatural tendency on the other side to depreciate it below its actual worth. It is not at all improbable, that Papias may have alluded to and cited the Apocalypse in the only work which we know him to have written, his "Expositions of the Oracles of the Lord" (λογίων κυριακῶν ἐξηγήσεις); nor does there seem any reason to reject the cautious inference of Rettig, that possibly Papias ascribed the book to a John, perhaps even John the Divine, without our being thereby justified in assuming that Papias claimed the apostle as its author.[2] To Papias we may,

---

[1] H. E. iii. 39, p. 283. Tom. i. ed. Heinichen.

[2] The whole question of the value of this testimony of Papias, contained in the writings of the two Cappadocian bishops, especially in its bearing on the authenticity of the Apocalypse, has been discussed with great thoroughness and impartiality by Rettig, in the article already referred to in the "Theologische Studien und Kritiken." I think, however, he attaches too much weight to the silence of Eusebius. It is quite evident, that the historian thoroughly disliked the chiliastic notions of Papias, and did not know what to make of their seeming to be sanctioned by a book so old and of

perhaps, add the still earlier testimony of Clement of Rome, who, in a passage of his first epistle to the Corinthians, appears to me distinctly to allude to, if he does not actually cite, the Apocalypse.[1]

Our next testimony is more direct and explicit. It is that of Justin Martyr, whose period of literary activity occurs between 139 and 160 A.D., and the time of whose death is assigned by Semisch, following the Chronicon Paschale, to the year 166.[2] He was a contemporary, therefore, of Papias. Justin was born a heathen at Flavia Neapolis, the ancient Sychem, in Samaria, and was converted to Christianity, it has been supposed, at Ephesus, where the scene of his celebrated dialogue with the Jew Trypho is laid. It is certain that he passed the latter years of his life in Rome, where he suffered martyrdom. From the places with which the few notices of his personal history are associated, it is evident that he must have been familiar with the traditions which were then current among the Christians, and at Ephesus with those more particularly which related to the apostle John. To him also we are indebted for the account

such high traditional authority as the Apocalypse. He was one of that class of philosophical Christians (in his time rapidly increasing under the influence of a court), who, like the Alexandrine Jews under the Ptolemies, had grown ashamed of the homely and popular faith of their forefathers. I can hardly doubt, that he would have taken, if he could, from the Apocalypse the credit of an apostolic source: and had he found any clear indication in Papias, that it had been written by the presbyter John, or any other John than the apostle, it is difficult to believe, that he would not have mentioned it. If any inference can be drawn from the silence of Eusebius, it seems to me as much in favour of Papias's attesting the apostolic origin of the book, as against it. The passages from Andreas and Arethas about Papias are cited by Kirchhofer (Quellensammlung zur Gesch. d. N. T. Canons xxxiii. Papias). See his note on them, p. 300.

[1] The passage runs thus (I. ad Cor. xxxiv.), and has a close verbal agreement with Apocal. xxii. 12: προλέγει ἡμῖν· (a form of scriptural citation) ἰδοὺ ὁ κύριος, καὶ ὁ μισθὸς αὐτοῦ πρὸ προσώπου αὐτοῦ, ἀποδοῦναι ἑκάστῳ κατὰ τὸ ἔργον αὐτοῦ. There may in both writers be a remoter reference to the LXX. Isaiah xl. 10, and lxii. 11. But it is remarkable, that Clement and the Apocalypse much more nearly resemble each other, especially in the concluding words of the sentence, than either of them Isaiah. I cannot but think the passage furnishes a proof that the Apocalypse was known and read in the time of Clement. The death of Clement is usually placed about 100 A.D. If my inference be correct, this is the oldest witness to the existence of the Apocalypse as a part of Scripture.

[2] Otto (de Justin. Martyr. Scriptis et Doctrina, p. 6), following the same authority, puts it at 165 A.D.

—still circulating in Samaria when he was young—of the kind of rural industry in which the early years of Jesus had been engaged.[1] Although, therefore, the testimony of Justin represents, after all, only a tradition, it was, it must be remembered, a fresh and living tradition. In the Dialogue with Trypho (c. 81) we find the following passage. Justin is arguing with the Jew in support of the evidence which his own Scriptures furnished—especially the prophets, Ezekiel and Isaiah—on behalf of the doctrine of the resurrection of the body, and of the reign of a thousand years on earth with Christ—and against those false Christians, as he regarded them, who denied that doctrine, and contended for the immediate transition of the soul at death into the heavenly world.[2] He then, as it were, clenches his argument by adducing the direct evidence of a Christian himself in these words : " Among us, too, a certain man named John, *one of the apostles of Christ*, in a revelation made to him, prophesied that the believers in our Christ should fulfil a thousand years in Jerusalem—and that after that, there would be the general and final resurrection and judgment of all men together." This language is so express, that Rettig, under the influence of pre-conceived theory, was disposed to reject the words, εἷς τῶν ἀποστόλων τοῦ Χριστοῦ, as a later interpolation. Lücke, who agrees with Rettig respecting the authorship of the Apocalypse, has shown that such criticism is indefensible; and Eusebius, whose tendencies run all in the same direction, admits that Justin distinctly affirms John the apostle to have written the Apocalypse.[3] This explicit testimony deserves the more notice, as it is the only passage in the works of Justin, where any book of the New Testament is cited with the name of its author.

[1] τὰ τεκτονικὰ ἔργα—ἄροτρα καὶ ζυγά. Dial. c. Tryph. c. 88.
[2] ἅμα τῷ ἀποθνήσκειν τὰς ψυχὰς ἀναλαμβάνεσθαι εἰς τὸν οὐρανόν. It should be noticed here, that Chiliasm in the age of Justin was orthodoxy ; and that the view of the Future Life entertained in later centuries by Channing and others, was then considered not merely heresy, but an absolute denial of Christianity : μὴ ὑπολάβητε αὐτοὺς Χριστιανούς. (c. 80.)
[3] H. E. iv. 18. σαφῶς τοῦ ἀποστόλου αὐτὴν εἶναι λέγων.

Melito, bishop of Sardis (one of the seven churches spoken to by the Spirit in the Apocalypse), the author of an Apology for Christianity, addressed to Marcus Antoninus, of which a fragment has been preserved by Eusebius (H. E. iv. 26), wrote, we are told, a work on the Apocalypse of John.[1] This, of itself, does not prove much for our immediate object. But there are some collateral circumstances connected with the name of Melito, which render the allusion to him not wholly unimportant. He belonged to the same cycle of Asiatic churches with Papias and Irenæus, in which we know that chiliastic views widely prevailed. He appears to have studied the Old Testament for the same purpose as Justin in his Dialogue with Trypho—viz., to discover proofs and illustrations of Christianity; and, with this view, he made a selection from it in six books for the use of a friend (ἐκλογὰς ἔκ τε τοῦ νόμου καὶ τῶν προφητῶν περὶ τοῦ Σωτῆρος καὶ πάσης τῆς πίστεως ἡμῶν. Euseb. ibid.)— actually travelling into the East for fuller information, and to familiarize himself with the scene of the old prophetic action and preaching. Polycrates, who flourished a little later at Ephesus, speaks of him as leading a singularly ascetic and holy life (τὸν εὐνοῦχον, τὸν ἐν ἁγίῳ πνεύματι πάντα πολιτευσάμενον. Euseb. H. E. v. 24). Putting all these indications together, we may perhaps not unreasonably conclude, that Melito adhered to the primitive type of the Christian faith, and was anti-Pauline in his tendencies; that he was a Chiliast, like most of his contemporaries in that part of Asia, and possibly, as we seem to gather from the description of his asceticism, inclined to the Ebionitism, of which James the Just, the first bishop of Jerusalem, is the standing ecclesiastical type. He represents, therefore, the class of minds among which the Apocalypse would be sure to find a welcome reception; which cherished its peculiar doctrine, and accepted it with reverence as an authoritative expression of apostolic truth. So far as it goes, his witness may be allowed

---

[1] It is mentioned in a list of several other works ascribed to him (Euseb. H. E. iv. 26).

TESTIMONIES TO THE APOCALYPSE.

to contribute its atom of probability to the directer evidence of the apostolic authorship of the Apocalypse. At all events, it throws no weight into the opposite scale.[1]

We learn from Eusebius (H. E. iv. 24) that Theophilus of Antioch (author of the treatise "To Autolycus") in a work (now lost) in reply to the heresy of Hermogenes, had cited witnesses from the Apocalypse of John.[2] This Hermogenes appears to have been an anti-Montanist; if so, he was opposed to the doctrines contained in the Apocalypse. Theophilus must, therefore, have cited the book against him, as a New Testament authority already widely acknowledged; and this justifies us in assuming that it was at that time received and respected, not only by Theophilus himself, but in the church of Antioch generally. Such is the inference of Lücke, no partial witness (Einl. Offenb. Johan. § 37. 2.), who further thinks it probable that Theophilus, with Justin Martyr, regarded the apostle John as its author.

In the last instance, we saw the Apocalypse alleged probably against an anti-Montanist. In the next, we find it used by an anti-Montanist himself. Apollonius, who flourished in the reign of Commodus and Septimius Severus, wrote a very strong treatise against the Phrygian or Montanist heresy, in which we are told by Eusebius (H. E. v. 18) that "he made use of witnesses from the Apocalypse of John." As, in immediate connexion with this statement, we are told that he gives an account of John's having raised, by divine power, a person from the dead in Ephesus, the probability is that Apollonius must have meant by John, the apostle. Had he intended any other John, Eusebius would certainly have noticed it.

The fifth book of Eusebius's Ecclesiastical History (1-3) contains the celebrated letter of the Christians of Vienne and Lyons to their brethren in Asia and Phrygia (whence they had

---

[1] The subsisting fragments of Melito have been collected by Routh, Reliquiæ Sacræ, Tom. I. p. 113-153.

[2] Theophilus flourished in the reign of Marcus Aurelius, 161 A.D.—180 A.D.

originally emigrated to the banks of the Rhone), giving an account of the dreadful persecution which they had undergone in the reign of Marcus Aurelius, about 177 A.D. Now, in this letter not only are characteristic phrases literally quoted from the Apocalypse—*e.g.*, ἀκολουθῶν τῷ ἀρνίῳ ὅπου ἂν ὑπάγῃ (xiv. 4)—but Christ himself is called πιστὸς καὶ ἀληθινὴς μάρτυς, πρωτότοκος τῶν νεκρῶν (i. 5, iii. 14), and sentences are given as if from memory, where the sense is retained, though the expression is slightly varied—*e.g.*, ὁ ἄνομος ἀνομησάτω ἔτι, καὶ ὁ δίκαιος δικαιωθήτω ἔτι (xxii. 11). What is still more remarkable, this last passage is cited as a fulfilled Scripture (ἵνα ἡ γραφὴ πληρωθῇ)—showing, beyond a doubt, that the Apocalypse was received at that time as authoritative Scripture, and put on the same level with the Law and the Prophets—as well among the Gaulish Christians as among their co-religionists in Asia, and attesting, therefore, the widely diffused recognition of the book in the latter half of the second century. This renders it in the highest degree probable, that both the Gaulish and the Asiatic Christians regarded it as a work of the apostle John; and the probability rises almost to a moral certainty, when we bear in mind that this, as we shall presently see, was the decided conviction of Irenæus himself, who, if not the author of the letter, stood in the most intimate relation to the two communities between which it passed.

The author of a MS., entitled "A Refutation of all Heresies," discovered in Greece some years ago, and now deposited in the Imperial Library at Paris, which was first published under the name of Origen, but which its last editors, Duncker and Schneidewin, in accordance with the judgment of the late Baron Bunsen, have unhesitatingly ascribed to Hippolytus—bears the following distinct testimony to the authorship of the Apocalypse by John, at the opening of the third century.[1] Speaking of

---

[1] We gather its date from its allusion to Zephyrinus and Callistus (as the author's contemporaries) who became bishops of Rome respectively in 201 A.D. and 218 A.D. (Lib. ix. 7.)

the Nicolaitans, who are referred to with abhorrence in the Apocalypse (ii. 6), he adds : " the disciples of this school, doing despite to the Holy Spirit, John, in the Apocalypse, has charged with fornication and eating meats offered to idols" (vii. 36). It is noticeable, that this is one of the few passages in this treatise where the writer of any book of the New Testament is mentioned by name. Mark's gospel is alluded to (vii. 30), and Paul is cited several times (v. 7, 8; vii. 30, 31 ; viii. 20), and, in some places, is called " the apostle," in others, " the blessed." Whether Matthew be referred to is doubtful, as he is described as the author of an apocryphal work used by the Basilidians : and the recent editors read not Matthew, but Matthias (vii. 20). The gospels of Luke and John are not once quoted with the names of their authors. That, in the foregoing passage, John the apostle is intended as the author of the Apocalypse, can hardly be questioned.[1] In the year 1551, there was dug up at Rome, a statue of Hippolytus sitting in a chair, on one side of which is inscribed a list of his works ; and from this, though now imperfect, we learn that he wrote on the Gospel and Apocalypse of John.[2] In his treatise on " Christ and Anti-Christ," he cites John, who was in Patmos, as the author of the Apocalypse, and addresses him as an " apostle and disciple of the Lord."[3]

[1] The passage as now corrected runs thus: " οὗ (Nicolai scil.) τοὺς μαθητὰς ἐνυβρίζοντας τὸ ἅγιον πνεῦμα διὰ τῆς ἀποκαλύψεως Ἰωάννης ἤλεγχε πορνεύοντας καὶ εἰδωλόθυτα ἐσθίοντας. Had the original readings of the Paris MS. been retained —ἐνυβρίζον τὸ—and Ἰωάννου—the assertion of apostolic authorship would have been still more explicit, as the spirit would then have been represented as rebuking the Nicolaitans through the revelation of John. But both the first and the later editors have concurred in the change of reading. Ἐνυβρίζον is so harsh an expression, that it could hardly have been used with reverence of the Holy Spirit, even if the occurrence of the word in Hebrews (x. 29) did not sufficiently show in what sense it must be employed here, and fully justify the conversion of ον into οντας and νου into νης. A passage in Irenæus (Adv. Hær. I. xxvi. 3) with similar reference to the Nicolaitans, which Hippolytus must have had in his eye, when he wrote the words in question, leaves no room for doubt, what John is intended. For Irenæus certainly believed that John the apostle was the author of the Apocalypse.

[2] ὑπὲρ τοῦ κατὰ Ἰωάννην εὐαγγελίου καὶ ἀποκαλύψεως. Jerome (Catal. 61) says only " de Apocalypsi."

[3] Kirchhofer (Quellensammlung etc. p. 310) gives the original passage from the

In Irenæus and Tertullian, in whom first we discern the traces of a recognized and authoritative scripture, the references to John as the author of the Apocalypse are so numerous and so unquestionable, that it is unnecessary to consume much time in adducing them. In Irenæus, John is usually described as "the disciple of the Lord;" but in the same way he speaks of the author of the first epistle (III. xvi..8), which he unquestionably regarded as apostolic. If there could be any doubt, it is removed by his statement, on citing the Apocalypse (i. 17, 18), that the John alluded to, as overpowered by the vision, was he that leaned on the bosom of the Word at supper (IV. xx. 11). There is weight, too, in the remark of Lücke (p. 571 and note), that, by the mode of citation frequently employed — "John beheld in the Apocalypse"—the identity of the seer and the writer is clearly indicated.

Tertullian abounds in citations from the Apocalypse, as well as from the other books in the New Testament, now forming, as he expressed it, a part of the great *instrumentum literaturæ* (Apologet. c. xviii.) or body of written documents on which, furnished alike by the Old and New Testament, he grounded his proofs of the divine origin and authority of the Christian religion. All these writings he considered to possess, immediately or mediately, an apostolic character. What was his opinion of the authorship of the Apocalypse, the following passages from his writings place beyond a doubt. In his treatise, "de Pudicitia" (c. xix.), comparing the apparently conflicting opinions of Paul (1 Cor. v. 9-13) and John (Apocal. ii. 18-22) about the re-admission to church communion of a fornicator, he calls both of them "apostles," and speaks of their equally enjoying the Holy Spirit (æqualitatem spiritus sancti).

works of Hippolytus. Ebedjesu, a Syrian bishop at the end of the 14th century, in his catalogue of the different books of Scripture, mentions that Hippolytus wrote in defence of the Apocalypse as a book of the apostle and evangelist John. Dr. Lardner, Credibility of Gospel History (Works, iv. p. 442 and ii. p. 412).

Still more explicit is his language, (adversus Marcionem, xii. 14) —" Apostolus Joannes in Apocalypsi ensem describit ex ore Dei prodeuntem etc." Apocal. i. 16). It is not, indeed, to be supposed that the opinion of Irenæus and Tertullian on this point were the result of any critical investigation. They merely represent the strong, unquestioned tradition of their own time. If Tertullian's notorious leaning and final accession to the Montanist heresy, which specially appealed to the Apocalypse in support of its peculiar views, may be thought in some degree to affect the independence of his judgment; yet, on the other hand, the very appeal of the Montanists may be taken as evidence of the wide diffusion of the tradition in that part of Asia where they originated: while Irenæus's close connexion with Ephesus, and his knowledge of the belief which existed there, must be allowed to give peculiar value to his testimony as coming from the fountain-head of the tradition.

The witnesses hitherto cited have been taken entirely from the Asiatic and the Western Churches. It will be interesting to notice what opinion prevailed in the more learned school of Alexandria. Clement of Alexandria (Strom. VI. xiii. § 106) quotes the Apocalypse of John, referring distinctly to iv. 4 and xi. 16. That he means John, the apostle, is evident from the treatise, " Quis dives salvetur " (§ 42), where he speaks of his exile in Patmos (Apocal. i. 9). In his " Pædagogus" (II. xii. 19) he quotes Apocalypse xxi. as an utterance of the *apostolical* voice (τῆς ἀποστολικῆς φωνῆς).

His successor in the Catechetical School, the celebrated Origen, is not less explicit. Eusebius (H. E. vi. 25) quotes a passage from the 5th book of his " Exposition of the Gospel of John," in which he says, that the same John, he who leaned on the bosom of Jesus, wrote also the Apocalypse; and his testimony is the more remarkable, as he speaks doubtfully in the same passage of the second and third epistles. In his Commentary on the book of Joshua, he asserts that John was the author of the Gospel, the Epistles, and the Apocalypse; where he must, of course, mean the apostle.[1] Citing the Apocalypse (xiv. 6, 7), he calls it the work of John, the son of Zebedee, (Comment. in Evangel. Joann. Tom. I. 14). In his Commentary on Matthew (Tom. xvi., quoted by Kirchhofer, p. 309) he leaves no doubt as to the personality of the author of the Apocalypse, who was exiled to Patmos, by describing him as a son of Zebedee, and a brother of the James who was put to death by Herod (Acts xii. 2). In his Commentary on John (edit. Huet. p. 51 ; Kirchhofer, p. 310), he calls the author of the Apocalypse an apostle and evangelist (ἐν τῇ ἀποκαλύψει ὁ ἀπόστολος καὶ εὐαγγελίστης). I believe there is not a passage in the writings of Origen, in which he expresses a doubt of the apostolic origin of the Apocalypse. He is said to have meditated a commentary on the book.[2] Yet he was decidedly opposed to Chiliasm and Montanism, which found a strong support in the Apocalypse. Without, therefore, supposing that either Clement or Origen had critically investigated the authenticity of the Apocalypse, their unhesitating acceptance of it may be taken as an evidence of the steadiness and constancy of the original tradition, the truth of which they had met with no objection of sufficient weight to induce them to doubt.

Before I close this list of witnesses, I must notice two facts, which seem for the first time to indicate the awakening of doubt. In the first half of the last century, Muratori discovered in the Ambrosian library at Milan—brought apparently at an earlier period from the ancient convent of Bobbio founded by Columban—a MS. which contained, in Latin, a mutilated list of the books of the New Testament, and of some apocryphal works often associated with them in the first age of the Church. This fragment is referred by the general consent of scholars to the

---

[1] As this Commentary exists only in the Latin version of Rufinus, who often took liberties, as he himself confesses, with the original Greek, it is only right to observe, that with respect to this particular version, Rufinus says, " simpliciter expressimus, ut invenimus." See Kirchhofer, Quellensammlung, etc. p. 26.

[2] See Lücke (Einl. § 39, 4), who refers to his Commentary on Matthew. Oper. Tom. iv. p. 307. edit. Lommatzsch, and Huet. Origen. III. ii. 4.

latter part of the second century, or, at the latest, to the beginning of the third. It makes mention of our book in the following terms: "There is an Apocalypse also of John; and one of Peter we simply receive, which some of our people do not like to have read in church."[1] The passage is somewhat obscure, and it has been variously interpreted. I do not think we can safely infer from it more than this;—that, at the time of the construction of this canon, an Apocalypse was in existence which bore the name of John; and that there was then also in circulation along with it, another ascribed to Peter, which was not universally received in the Church.

A more remarkable circumstance is the omission of the Apocalypse in the oldest Syriac version of the New Testament, called the Peschito. When this version was made, it is impossible to decide with any approach to precision. The great antiquity claimed for it by J. D. Michaelis, who carried it up to the first century, has been shown by his translator and com-

[1] The Latin of the whole fragment is exceedingly corrupt. I have translated the passage as it stands. With the preceding article (which I give for the sake of a clearer view of the context) it runs thus : " Epistola sane Judæ et superscripti (tæ) Joannis duas (duæ) in catholica habentur. Ut (et) Sapientia ab amicis Salomonis in honorem ipsius scripta. Apocalypsis etiam Johannis, et Petri, tantum recipimus, quam quidam ex nostris legi in ecclesia nolunt." Credner (Zur Geschichte des Kanons, p. 76) changes 'apocalypsis' into 'apocalypses,' and suppressing the points after 'Johannis' and 'Petri,' refers the words 'tantum recipimus' to both the apocalypses, putting them apparently on the same level: but then that leaves the difficulty of the singular 'quam,' which we should expect in this case to be 'quas.' Hug (Introduction to New Testament, Sect. xix. Wait's Transl.) thinks the difficulty may be partly got over by regarding the Latin as a barbarous version by some incompetent person of a Greek original ; and to show the probability of this, he renders back some passages into Greek. He puts a full stop at 'Johannis,' and connects the sentence with the preceding article, which speaks of the epistle of Jude and two Catholic epistles of John. By assuming 'tantum' to be a mistranslation for $\mu \acute{o}\nu\eta\nu$, he thinks he recovers an allusion to the first epistle of Peter; and supposing 'quam' to represent the Greek for 'alteram,' he finds in the concluding words a denial of ecclesiastical authority to the second. His explanation seems to me far-fetched and unsatisfactory. But he is perhaps right in affirming that the words 'Apocalypsis etiam Johannis' belong in their general connexion to the preceding paragraph of the fragment. Put a fuller stop at 'Johannis;' supply 'Apocalypsin' after 'Petri;' and the passage yields a tolerable sense without any alteration. This fragment is usually described as "Fragmentum de Canone acephalum," and was first published in the 3rd vol. of Muratori's Antiquit. Ital. Med. Ævi. Milan : 1740.

mentator, Bishop Marsh, to be contradicted by all existing evidence.[1] Nevertheless, it must be very old; for it represents a text which harmonizes with the most ancient Greek MSS. and the oldest Latin versions, and which modern criticism has rendered it probable was anterior to the fourth century. After the middle of the second century, Bardesanes and his son, Harmonius, made a commencement of Syriac literature; and as this was altogether of ecclesiastical origin, and dated from the introduction of Christianity, it can hardly be supposed that the translation of the New Testament would be deferred long after the time when Syriac began to be employed as a written language. This brings us to the end of the second or the opening of the third century, the period when we first discover traces of a recognised scriptural canon throughout the Church. To this date the majority of recent scholars assign the Peschito. In this version, the second epistle of Peter, the second and third of John, the epistle of Jude, and the Apocalypse, are wanting. That Theophilus of Antioch (in Syria) should have known and cited the Apocalypse before that time, notwithstanding its absence from the Peschito, is not, perhaps, so extraordinary, as he belonged to western Syria, where Greek civilization predominated, and the Greek language was universally spoken. But that Ephraem Syrus, towards the end of the fourth century —the earliest writer by whom we find the Peschito used— should constantly quote the Apocalypse with the name of its author, is certainly not a little surprising, as he belonged to a district beyond the Euphrates, where Syriac was the popular dialect; and we know from the distinct witness of contemporaries, that he did not understand Greek.[2] Eichhorn and

---

[1] Michaelis, Introduction to New Testament, Part I. Ch. vii. and Marsh's note on sect. 6, p. 554.

[2] Hug, Introduction, Sect. lxv. vol. I. p. 349, note c. Ephraem was obliged to employ an interpreter in his intercourse with Basil of Cæsarea. The late Cardinal Wiseman states, that the earliest indication of the existence of the Peschito occurs in the writings of Ephraem, though he supposes the version to be much older than his time. " Quamvis de Peschito testem nullum habeamus Ephraemo anteriorem, tamen antiquiorem longe ipso fuisse mihi certo constat." Horæ Syriacæ, II. § v. p. 139.

TESTIMONIES TO THE APOCALYPSE. 41

Hug explain the fact, by supposing that the Apocalypse did originally form a part of the Peschito, but was gradually excluded from the later copies in consequence of the growing dislike to the book which pervaded the Eastern Church; and that our oldest MSS. do not go back to the time when this aversion first began to operate.[1] Lücke does not go so far as this; but, assuming that the Apocalypse was originally wanting in the Peschito, he accounts for its exclusion, not on historical or dogmatic grounds, but from the circumstance that, in the MSS. which came into the hands of the Syriac translator, whether derived from Antioch or Alexandria, it was not yet incorporated with the other books of the New Testament.[2]

With the exception of the two last instances, which we may be allowed, perhaps, to leave in a neutral position, all the witnesses that we have so far produced, down to the middle of the third century, speak distinctly in favour of the apostolic origin of the Apocalypse, without the occurrence of any positive testimony on the other side. In summing up their united weight, the verdict of Kirchhofer can scarcely be considered as too strongly expressed: "Hardly one book of the New Testament has such a list of historical witnesses marked by name on its behalf."[3] Soon after the middle of the third century, however, we discern the rise of an altered feeling in regard to the Apocalypse, which left a considerable impression on the future judgment of the Church. Of the nature and origin of that feeling, I must now give some account.

[1] Hug, Sect. lxv.-lxviii. Eichhorn, Einleit. N. T. § 56, § 195.
[2] Lücke, Einl. § 39. 7.
[3] " Kaum ein Buch des N. T. hat eine solche namhafte Reihe von historischen Testimonien für sich." (Quellensammlung etc. p. 296.)

SECTION VI.

On the reaction of feeling against the Apocalypse.

TOWARDS the end of the second, and still more in the course of the third and fourth centuries, we discover unmistakeable traces of the change of character that inevitably overtakes every form of religious belief, which, originating in intense enthusiasm and demanding at first an almost entire renunciation of the world, has, nevertheless, acquired a permanent footing in society, and is compelled to adjust itself to the state of things that actually exists. No man who reads with unbiassed mind the different books of the New Testament, not excepting the Fourth Gospel itself,[1] can possibly deny that the great idea which, amidst many differences, is profoundly imprinted on them all, is the expectation of an approaching judgment-day and the end of the world. The gospel in its first, fresh outburst was a solemn utterance of this expectation, and a protest against the selfishness and carnality of an extremely corrupt civilization, gathering strength and taking shape from the Messianic hope which had been developed by Hebrew prophecy, and which the diffusion of Jewish synagogues and Alexandrine literature through the Græco-Roman world, had rendered not unfamiliar to many inquisitive minds among the heathen. Its effect was vehement reaction against the strongest tendencies of the age—its lavish expenditure on self-indulgence, and its heartless voluptuousness —its worship of power and worldly success, and its contempt for the masses—its passion for war, and the mimic slaughters of the amphitheatre. In the awful shadow of impending doom all these sensuous splendours grew pale and dim. The future over-

[1] See xiv. 3.

powered the present. The believer walked by "faith, not by sight," and lost every other hope and fear in the one absorbing solicitude to "make his calling and election sure" at the great crisis which would separate for ever the evil and the good. As described in the opening chapters of the book of Acts, the earliest Christian Church was based on a principle of religious communism; for a true disciple was expected to "sell all that he had and give it to the poor;" and the Master himself had said, it was "easier for a camel to go through the eye of a needle, than for a rich man to enter the kingdom of heaven." Primitive Christianity was, therefore, an absolute abandonment of the world—a forswearing of its pleasures, its literature, its favourite occupations, made additionally offensive to a devout and holy mind by their inextricable involution with the impure associations of heathenism. But such seclusion from living interests demanded an unnatural strain on the mind, which must ultimately give way, especially when the expectation which had sustained it was found not to be literally fulfilled. The great day came not. It was continually put off further and further into an uncertain future. Already, in the time of the author of the second epistle of Peter,[1] we read of "scoffers" who asked, "Where is the promise of his coming? for, since the fathers fell asleep, all things continue as they were from the beginning of the creation."

The little treatise on the "salvability of rich men," which is found among the works of Clement of Alexandria, and which, if not his, belonged to the same period, the beginning of the third century, and is worthy of his pen, for its refined style and philosophic elevation of sentiment—throws an interesting light on the transition of opinion which was then taking place in the minds of thoughtful Christians with respect to the possession of worldly goods. It takes as a sort of text the strong saying about the "camel" and "the eye of a needle,"[2] and argues that this and similar passages must be understood

[1] iii. 3, 4.   [2] Matth. xix. 24; Mark x. 25; Luke xviii. 25.

mystically or spiritually, and not in a coarse and carnal sense; that men may be rich in desire, though poor in actual possession; and poor in spirit, though abounding in worldly wealth; and that riches—things indifferent in themselves—merely diversified the course of earthly discipline, and might be sanctified by wise and beneficent use.[1] This doctrine was not in accordance with the letter of the original teaching, though it was a legitimate inference from its underlying spirit. By the first Christians any denial of their faith before rulers and magistrates was regarded as the height of disloyalty to Christ and God; and all who had borne witness to the truth with their blood were believed to have acquired a title to immediate admission into the beatific presence. But, with the spread of philosophical principles in the Church, and the reaction of the world on the primitive fervour, men hesitated to sacrifice life and social position for a profession; and, in times of persecution, often stooped to unworthy expedients to secure immunity. One of the controversies which most sharply divided the Church, especially in the West, during the third century, related to the treatment of those who had thus "*lapsed.*" The stricter party were for excluding them for ever from church communion. The laxer would have reduced them again to the condition of the unconverted, and re-admitted them after a due course of intervening penance.[2] Even war became less odious

[1] "Ὥστε τοὺς πλουσίους μυστικῶς ἀκουστέον, τοὺς δυσκόλως εἰσελευσομένους εἰς τὴν βασιλείαν μὴ σκαίως, μηδὲ ἀγροίκως, μηδὲ σαρκικῶς. Οὐ γὰρ οὕτως λέλεκται, οὐδὲ ἐπὶ τοῖς ἐκτὸς ἡ σωτηρία, οὔτε εἰ πολλὰ, οὔτε εἰ ὀλίγα ταῦτα — ἀλλ' ἐπὶ τῇ τῆς ψυχῆς ἀρετῇ, πίστει, καὶ ἐλπίδι, καὶ ἀγάπῃ, etc. etc. ὧν ἆθλον ἡ σωτηρία. c. 18. Again, wealth is an instrument of good to those who know how to use it : ὕλη τις καὶ ὄργανα πρὸς χρῆσιν ἀγαθὴν τοῖς εἰδόσι τὸ ὄργανον. c. 14. Why should God have permitted wealth to spring out of the earth, if it only procured death : τί δὲ ὅλως πλοῦτον ἐχρῆν ἐκ γῆς ἀνατεῖλαί ποτε, εἰ χορηγὸς καὶ πρόξενός ἐστι θανάτου. c. 26. This treatise, though pleading for the right use and enjoyment of the present world, is pervaded by a deeply spiritual tone, breathing the spirit of love which fills the Fourth Gospel. We enter into the nature of God, the more we love him, ὅσον ἀγαπᾷ τις θεόν, τοσούτῳ καὶ πλέον ἐνδοτέρω τοῦ θεοῦ παραδύεται. c. 27.

[2] This was the subject of the Novatian controversy, which raged under different relations at Carthage and Rome.

in the eyes of Christians, and councils shut out from communion those who refused to fulfil its obligations.[1] Among the more educated Christians the study of heathen literature and philosophy was resumed with ardour; and many of the apologists, with the great Greek fathers of the fourth century, were accomplished classical scholars.[2]

It was precisely at the juncture when this change of sentiment was beginning to be felt throughout the Church, and the wide diffusion of philosophical culture was irresistibly modifying the broad popular conceptions and bold imagery of the primitive Jewish Christianity, that we hear uttered for the first time strong doubts of the apostolic authorship of the Apocalypse. Coming out of the very heart of the first circle of believers, and representing in the most fervid language the enthusiastic faith which possessed them, the Apocalypse of all the books of the New Testament was the best fitted by its pervading idea of Chiliasm, to keep alive in the mind of the multitude, all those beliefs and expectations which were most at variance with the form and order of the existing civilization, and which it was the desire of the philosophical professors of Christianity to soften down and explain away into a merely figurative expression of general and abstract truth. This relaxation of primeval strictness and fervour was followed by a two-fold effect. The cultivated and intellectual justified it, and tried to show that it was a necessity; while those of a more enthusiastic temperament regarded it as a sure indication of the decline of the good old faith, which they made feverish efforts to restore

[1] This occurred in Gaul. " Un concile retrancha de la communion des fideles ceux qui se croyaient le droit de jeter leurs armes." Gaston Boissier: " Le Christianisme dans la Gaule." Revue des Deux Mondes, Juin, 1866.

[2] It became not unusual to adopt the form and diction of Greek poetry for the purpose of popular instruction. The histories of the Old Testament were versified in the language of Homer: and there is still extant a drama on Christ's passion, made up almost entirely of lines from Euripides, which has been used by modern scholars as a source of textual criticism. The plays from which it was a cento, are said to be the Hippolytus, Medea, Bacchæ, Rhesus, Troades, and Orestes. See Valckenaer, prefat. in Eurip. Hippolytum, p. xi.

and uphold. The Montanist movement in Phrygia, which, though it may have been fomented by the traditional influences of the locality, assumed importance about this period, was in its essence a reactionary and spasmodic endeavour to bring back the strong, undoubting faith of the first age; and it carried away in its contagion all the excitable spirits of the time, among them the fiery genius of Tertullian: just as in the last century the preaching of the Wesleys was a counteraction to the rationalistic coldness that was creeping over the Church and the old Dissenters, or as, at a still later period, what took the name of Primitive Methodism was an attempt to restore in its original power the spirit of early Wesleyanism. The Revivals of more recent times are another example of the same enthusiastic spirit.[1] Now the Apocalypse was the favourite book of the Montanists. It encouraged their hopes and nourished their zeal; for they had re-animated a faith in the approaching end of the world, and believed that the New Jerusalem would descend from heaven on Pepuza, the centre of their religious community in Phrygia. "After me," said Maximilla, one of their prophetesses, " comes the end of all things."[2]

It is not surprising that the first and most decided resistance to these revivals should proceed from the learned school of Alexandria. The controversy was begun by Dionysius, bishop of that city, from 247 to 265 A.D. Eusebius has given a full account of it in his Ecclesiastical History (vii. 24, 25), from which I have here abbreviated the most important particulars. Dionysius was of heathen extraction, but had been a pupil of Origen, and was

---

[1] The "Shepherd of Hermas," which probably belongs to the end of the second century, is the expression of a parallel endeavour after revival in a mitigated form within the limits of the Catholic Church. See a series of articles by Lipsius, "Der Hirte des Hermas und der Montanismus in Rom," in Hilgenfeld's " Zeitschrift für wissenschaftliche Theologie," 1865 and 1866. Hermas is quite apocalyptic in its tone, and constantly reminds the reader of the allegory of Bunyan, which had its origin in a similar desire to uphold the primitive fervour of Puritanism, at a time when Latitudinarianism was spreading in the upper regions of the Church.

[2] Μετ' ἐμὲ συντέλεια. Epiphan. Panar. xlviii. We are reminded of Metternich's celebrated phrase: " après moi le déluge."

for some time president of the Catechetical School of Alexandria. The office had been filled by some of the most eminent Alexandrine divines, including his celebrated master. From this position he was at length raised to the patriarchate. Origen, as we have seen, acknowledged the Apocalypse as a work of the apostle John, getting over the difficulties which the literal acceptance of its doctrines might have occasioned him, by his favourite system of allegorical interpretation. But the mass of simple believers could not be satisfied with these philosophical refinements, and protested against them. It was in encountering their scruples that Dionysius was led to apply his superior critical faculty to a discovery of the signs of distinct authorship in two works bearing the same name. He is the earliest critical theologian in the history of the Church.

There had been a former Egyptian bishop, of the name of Nepos, who taught that the promises of Scripture would be fulfilled in the Jewish sense (Ἰουδαϊκώτερον), and that for believers there would be a thousand years of bodily enjoyment on earth (χιλιάδα τρυφῆς σωματικῆς). So at least the doctrine of Nepos was represented by those who were unfriendly to it. At all events he was a Chiliast. He justified his own views from the Apocalypse of John, and set them forth in a treatise which he entitled, "A Refutation of Allegorizers."[1] As this book was considered by many at that time as an unanswerable plea for Chiliasm, Dionysius felt himself called upon to reply to it, which he did in two treatises on "The Fulfilment of the Promises,"[2] in the first of which he stated his own opinion, and in the second subjected the Apocalypse to a critical examination.[3]

[1] Ἔλεγχος ἀλληγοριστῶν.   [2] Περὶ ἐπαγγελιῶν.
[3] As these treatises were understood to be a general reply to the Chiliasts, of whom Irenæus (with in fact all the early fathers and apologists) was one, Jerome (Comm. Esaiam, lib. xviii. præfat.) according to Valesius (Euseb. H.E. vii. 24, 25, n. 1) represented Dionysius as writing against Irenæus. What was Jerome's opinion of the difference between the more recent and the older interpreters of the Apocalypse, appears very clearly from the following passage: " Apocalypsin Johannis si juxta litteras accipimus, judaizandum est; si spiritualiter, ut scripta est, *multorum veterum videbimur opinionibus contraire.*" Cat. Ill. Vir. Cited by Heinichen. Euseb. H. E. vii. ibid.

Dionysius held the memory of Nepos himself in great respect, for his faith and energy and familiarity with Scripture, and his large contribution to the psalmody of the church "by which," he says, "many were still refreshed;" and he was entitled to the more reverence, as he was now dead and gone. But truth, he contended, should prevail over all other considerations, and we must oppose those whom we most honour, when we think they are wrong. Had Nepos been still alive, a personal colloquy might have sufficed. But as the treatise which he had published was very popular, and believed to unfold some great and hidden mystery (μέγα τι καὶ κεκρυμμένον μυστήριον), and as it tended to lower the tone of religious sentiment among the multitude, by holding up to them the future kingdom of God in a mean and earthly light, like the present state of things (οἷα τὰ νῦν)—it ought not, Dionysius thought, to be left unanswered. These small indications of personal feeling are not uninstructive, as showing that the Chiliasts, though gradually sliding down into the position of heretics, were still very highly respected, probably with a dim, half-conscious belief that in their fervour and simplicity they represented the most ancient type of the Christian life. They seem also to bring clearly into view the considerations which led the more cultivated class of believers to dislike and resist Chiliastic opinions.

The controversy, as narrated by Dionysius himself, commenced and terminated in the following way.—Happening to be in the Arsinoite Nome, where the doctrine of Nepos had long been ascendant, and had drawn entire churches into schism and apostasy,[1] Dionysius assembled the presbyters and teachers from the neighbouring villages, and with their full concurrence entered into a public discussion of the question. The book of Nepos was produced, as an impregnable defence of Chiliasm.[2] For three days Dionysius sate with them from morning to

---

[1] Ὡς καὶ σχίσματα καὶ ἀποστασίας ὅλων ἐκκλησιῶν γεγονέναι. The question is, after all, whether the innovation was on the side of Nepos or of Dionysius.

[2] Ὡς τι ὅπλον καὶ τεῖχος ἀκαταμάχητον.

night, discussing the book, section by section, and correcting its errors.[1] Dionysius says he was delighted with the patience and sobriety, the candour and openness to conviction, of the Arsinoite brethren. At last Korakion, who had been the chief representative and supporter of Chiliasm in the district, confessed that he had been confuted, and declared that he would abandon the doctrine, and never teach it or allude to it again. The brethren present rejoiced at the issue of the conference and the mutual adjustment of opinion which it involved.[2]

Dionysius's criticism of the Apocalypse is of higher interest and importance.[3] Before his own time, some, he informs us, had rejected this book and denied it a place in the canon.[4] They declared, that it furnished proof in every chapter of an uncultivated and illogical mind (ἄγνωστόν τε καὶ ἀσυλλόγιστον); that it assumed a false title, and was not a work of John; that it was not even a revelation, being covered with a thick veil of ignorance; that it was not only not the work of an apostle, but not even of a saint or any member of the church; that it was the production of Cerinthus, who wished to give a name of authority to this fiction of his,—inasmuch as Cerinthus was a Chiliast, inculcating a very gross and carnal view of the happiness of Christ's earthly reign. Dionysius himself did not venture wholly to repudiate this book, as it was held in esteem by many brethren; but, assuming that it had a meaning beyond his comprehension, he left every man to take his own view of its hidden and marvellous sense. He would not measure it by his own

[1] Διευθύνειν ἐπειράθην τὰ γεγραμμένα.
[2] Ἐπὶ τῇ κοινολογίᾳ καὶ τῇ πρὸς πάντας συγκαταβάσει καὶ συνδιαθέσει. This is not the only instance in the history of Christianity, of the effect of one powerful mind, at once decided and conciliatory, in determining the religious profession of an entire community.
[3] The substance of it will be found in Eusebius (H. E. vii. 25).
[4] Ἠθέτησαν καὶ ἀνεσκεύασαν. This last word Rufinus interprets: (Heinichen in loc.) "a canone Scripturarum abjiciendum putarunt," *i.e.* " broke up and removed from its place in the σκεῦος=*instrumentum*,"—as used by Tertullian in the sense of an authentic document,—hence equivalent to *literæ sacræ*. Semler, Index Latin. Tertull. sub voce. The same verb occurs Acts xv. 24 : ἀνασκευάζοντες τὰς ψυχὰς ὑμῶν, " unsettling your minds."

reason, but handed it over to faith. He did not deny things which he had not seen; but as not having seen them, was only filled with more wonder.[1]—Dionysius admits, that this so-called prophecy was the work of a John, and of some holy and inspired man (θεοπνεύστου), but not of John the apostle, son of Zebedee and brother of James,—author of the gospel inscribed with the name of John, and of the catholic epistle. That these two last works cannot have come from the same hand as the Apocalypse, he argues from the marked difference which characterises each in regard to the pervading tone of feeling (ἤθους) and style (τῶν λόγων εἴδους) and the whole form of the composition (τῆς τοῦ βιβλίου διεξαγωγῆς λεγομένης). The author of the gospel never mentions his own name nor distinguishes himself from another; whereas, the reverse is the case with the author of the Apocalypse. The gospel and the epistle begin with the announcement of the incarnation; and our Lord (Matth. xvi. 17) calls Simon Peter blessed for having this higher spiritual revelation imparted to him. In the second and third epistles John is not named, but only the Presbyter. Who the John of the Apocalypse was, does not appear; but he nowhere, as many times (πολλαχοῦ) happens in the gospel, speaks of himself as the beloved disciple, nor as the brother of James, nor as an eye and ear-witness of the Lord; and it might have been thought, that under one or other of these titles he would have made himself known.[2] Many persons have borne the name of John, assuming it from their love and admiration for the apostle, and their wish to be equally beloved by the Lord with him; and for the same reason many believers have called their children after Peter or Paul. John Mark, who is mentioned in the Acts of the

---

[1] Οὐκ ἀποδοκιμάζω ταῦτα ἃ μὴ συνεώρακα, θαυμάζω δὲ μᾶλλον ὅτι μὴ καὶ εἶδον. It would appear from this that Dionysius regarded the whole as a vision, which he wished to leave where he found it, without coming to any decided opinion respecting it.

[2] Dionysius has made a slip here. The two last designations nowhere occur, either in the gospel or in the epistle. He has mixed up expressions in the opening verses of Luke and Jude, with a vague remembrance of the language in the first verse of the epistle.

Apostles, could not have written the Apocalypse, as he did not accompany Paul into Asia, but returned to Jerusalem.[1] It must have been some other John living in Asia. Now there appear to have been two Johns in Ephesus, as there is a tomb still existing in that city for each. The whole structure of thought and language in the Apocalypse is different from that in the gospel and epistle, which both begin in the same way and lay an equal stress on the manifestation of Christ in the flesh. This is the continuous theme of both gospel and epistle. Dionysius notices words and forms of expression which are peculiar to the gospel and epistle : such are ζωὴ, φῶς, ἀλήθεια, χάρις, κρίσις, and others.[2] In fine, the colour of the gospel and epistle is one and the same. The style of the Apocalypse is different in every respect, having no affinity with them whatever, not even a syllable in common.[3] Passing over the gospel, Dionysius remarks that the epistle never notices the Apocalypse, nor the Apocalypse the epistle. The language of the gospel and the epistle never offends against the laws of the Greek tongue, but is most exact in its choice of words and in the dependence and connexion of its construction, without a single barbarism or solœcism, or, generally, one vulgar or provincial expression— the Lord bestowing on it the double grace both of knowledge and of utterance.[4]—"I do not deny," adds Dionysius in conclusion, "that the author of the Apocalypse saw a revelation and had knowledge and prophesy conveyed to him. I cannot, however, overlook the fact, that his dialect and mode of expression are not pure Greek, but disfigured by barbarous idioms,

[1] It should be noticed that ετs is here quoted by its proper title, and that the words are exactly reported from xiii. 13.

[2] In this enumeration Dionysius has introduced some words, as υἱοθεσία, which do not belong to John, but occur in other books of the New Testament, though they are not found in the Apocalypse.

[3] Μηδὲ συλλαβὴν πρὸς αὐτὰ κοινὴν ἔχουσα.

[4] This is equivalent to saying, that the language of the gospel and epistle is pure, correct and perspicuous Greek. In the words ἑκάτερον τὸν λόγον —— τόν τε τῆς γνώσεως, τόν τε τῆς φράσεως, Valesius discovers a reference to the Philonian doctrine of the λόγος ἐνδιάθετος καὶ προφορικός.

sometimes falling even into solœcism. Of this it is unnecessary to produce examples; for it must not be supposed I have said this, to ridicule his style, but merely to point out how unlike it is to that of the gospel and epistle."

With some allowance for the rather exaggerated eulogy of the pure Greek of the Fourth Gospel and the first epistle, the foregoing criticism leaves on the mind a very favourable impression of the philosophical culture and refinement of the Alexandrine School in the third century of our era. It is acute and conclusive, and by all who can appreciate the force of the considerations on which it rests, must be admitted to establish unanswerably that the Fourth Gospel and the Apocalypse cannot have proceeded from the same hand. But it will be noticed that, throughout, the writer disproves the apostolic authorship of the Apocalypse by tacitly assuming that of the gospel. What authority he had for such an assumption, he nowhere states. The style and sentiments of the gospel corresponded more to his ideal of an apostle; and if, in this silence on his own part, we may form any conjecture as to the probable grounds of his conclusion, they would appear on this point to have been rather subjective than critical. We have seen, that his predecessors in the Catechetical School, Origen and Clement, acknowledged the Apocalypse, without hesitation, as a work of the apostle John. What can have occurred in that short interval to produce so entire a change of opinion, we are unable to surmise, except it be the fact, that Chiliastic doctrines were found increasingly offensive to the philosophical tendencies of the age, and that the allegorizing interpretation of Origen proved inadequate to neutralize their disturbing force. Within less than a century, from the time of Dionysius, we observe Eusebius of Cæsarea, the historian, betraying the same alienation, and sharing the same doubts.[1] But it is remarkable, that neither Dionysius nor Eusebius ventured beyond the expression of hesitation and doubt, resulting from a want of mental sym-

---

[1] Hist. Eccles. iii. 24, 25, 39.

pathy. They were still sufficiently restrained by the old traditional belief of the Church, to keep them from going the length of the Alogi (whose opinion was wholly subjective, and grew out of antipathy to the Montanists[1]), and repudiating the book unconditionally as heretical. Free search on such matters ceased altogether with the reign of Theodosius at the end of the fourth century. The limits of the Canon had by that time been authoritatively fixed; and the gospel and the Apocalypse, irrespective of any critical scruples, were both embraced as works of the apostle within them. Neither Greek nor Latin Church raised any more difficulty; and so the question slumbered till the Reformation, when Erasmus awakened it anew. Having disposed of the testimony for and against the Apocalypse, I must now proceed to that which bears on the gospel.

[1] They used to ask, according to Epiphanius, "What is the use of this book, with its talk about seven angels and seven trumpets?" Epiphanius, who represents the feeling of the Catholic Church in the latter part of the fourth century, replied, "That these things were to be understood spiritually, as revealing the hidden meaning of the Old Law." (Panarion, li. § 32.)

SECTION VII.

Testimony to the Apostolic origin of the Fourth Gospel.

WE are told by Eusebius that Papias, whose martyrdom occurred 164 A.D.,[1] " made use of witnesses from the first epistle of John."[2] Polycarp, who suffered martyrdom not earlier than 160 A.D., probably as late as 166 or 167, ctrtainly some time after the middle of the second century,[3] and who in his youth, according to tradition, had conversed with the apostles,[4] has a passage in his epistle to the Philippians (vii.) which bears a close resemblance, both in sentiment and in language, to 1 John iv. 3. It applies the epithet ἀντίχριστος, which is found only in the epistles of John, to every one who denies that Christ is come in the flesh. Whoever compares the two passages can have little doubt left on his mind, that the author of this epistle to the Philippians was acquainted with the first epistle of John. These are the earliest witnesses that we are able to cite; and as there is the highest probability that the Fourth Gospel and the first epistle were written by the same hand, they prove, so far as we can rely on them, that the author of the gospel must have been in existence when Papias and Polycarp cited the epistle. But the language of Eusebius furnishes no certain proof, that Papias knew the apostle John to be the author of the epistle. With regard to Polycarp, many learned men have expressed their

---

[1] See Section V. n. 1, p. 28.

[2] Κέχρηται μαρτυρίαις ἀπὸ τῆς Ἰωάννου προτέρας ἐπιστολῆς (H. E. iii. 39). In the same passage he is said to have made similar use of the first of Peter.

[3] The various dates of this event, with the authorities for them, are given by Hefele (Patres Apostolici, Prolegomena, V. p. 66).

[4] Eusebius, H. E. v. 20. Irenæus, adv. Hær. III. iii. 4. There is such a tendency in ecclesiastical tradition, as it proceeds downwards, to amplify itself, that we cannot perhaps safely infer more from these passages, than that the youth of Polycarp, according to the general belief, joined on to the apostolic age.

doubts of the genuineness, at least throughout, of the epistle to the Philippians.[1] But without pressing these doubts, and taking the two witnesses as they come to us, what they establish is this : that sometime in the first half of the second century, and before the death of the emperor Antoninus Pius, the first

[1] It is unfortunate for the early history of Christianity, that so many of the writings ascribed to the post-apostolic age, lie under the suspicion of spuriousness, or at all events of large interpolation. This suspicion became almost a morbid feeling in the minds of the early Protestant scholars. Hence the doubts of Daillé, of the Centuriators of Magdeburg and of Semler respecting the epistle of Polycarp, may be considered to have originated too much in mere subjective distrust. But these doubts are shared by critics of more conservative tendency, by Mosheim (De Rebus Christ. § liii. p. 161) and by Lücke (Comment. Br. Johan. c. i. p. 3), who says of the authenticity and integrity of this epistle, that "the former is not provable, and the latter not yet proved." Many years ago, in carefully reading through the remains of the so-called Apostolic Fathers—before I was under the bias of any pre-conceived opinion respecting the authorship of the writings which bear the name of the apostle John—I thus recorded the impression which the alleged epistle of Polycarp left on my mind. "Polycarp, it is said, had conversed much in his youth with John and other companions of Jesus, and heard from them accounts of our Lord's miracles and discourses ($\pi\epsilon\rho i \tau \tilde{\omega} \nu \delta \upsilon \nu \acute{a} \mu \epsilon \omega \nu \ a \grave{\upsilon} \tau o \tilde{\upsilon} \ \kappa a i \ \pi \epsilon \rho i \ \tau \tilde{\eta} \varsigma \ \delta \iota \delta a \sigma \kappa a \lambda \acute{\iota} a \varsigma$, Iren. ad Florin. ap. Euseb. H.E. v. 20.) It is remarkable, then, that we meet with so few indications of this traditionary information in his epistle. Not one living trait of Jesus Christ is recorded. His name occurs more as that of a *religious abstraction* than of a *historical personality*. Paul is introduced once or twice in a far more living way to the reader. The epistle itself is written without any apparent object. It is a loose string of moral precepts, a cento from the New Testament, chiefly the epistles, and especially of Peter and Paul—texts from various parts fused into one phrase, without the mention of any writer by name, except, twice only, Paul. On the whole, this epistle wants that impress of life and reality which is so conspicuous in the Pauline letters." On the other hand, the encyclic epistle of the Church of Smyrna, giving an account of the martyrdom of Polycarp, which has been inserted by Ruinart in his "Acta Martyrum Sincera," produced a very different feeling. I thus wrote of it at the time referred to. "With the exception of the conclusion, and a few insertions in the earlier chapters, this record—from its particularity, and its avoidance of the vague generalities that occur in the martyrdom of Ignatius—its specification of names and times and places, and even its special address to a city, of which we hear so little as Philomelium (a town in Phrygia, halfway between Antioch in Pisidia and Laodicea —possesses all the internal signs of genuineness and veracity. It is a vivid, interesting, and impressive narrative, and well deserves the encomium of Joseph Scaliger : " Nihil unquam in historiâ ecclesiasticâ vidi, a cujus lectione commotior recedam, ut non amplius meus esse videar?" (quoted by Hefele, Prolegom. vi.)—An important chronological datum is furnished by this piece. Polycarp says (ix.) that he was eighty-six years old when he suffered martyrdom ; so that he must have been a youth of at least twenty at the time usually assigned for the death of the apostle John.

epistle of John was read and quoted as a book of authority in the Christian Church; but how soon in that century, we have now no means of determining.

Such extreme uncertainty attaches to the origin and authorship of the so-called epistles of Ignatius, that no reliable use can be made of them in the present inquiry. They exist, it is well known, in three distinct forms, the mutual relations of which are still very obscure. Were they genuine, they would carry us back to the reign of Trajan, 98-117 A.D. But any one at all acquainted with the Ignatian controversy, would be inclined to infer from allusions in these epistles to the Fourth Gospel, rather the lateness of the epistles than the early origin of the gospel. In the three epistles to Polycarp, the Ephesians, and the Romans, which have recently been recovered in a very brief form from the Syriac, and which are considered by Dr. Cureton, the translator,[1] and the late Baron Bunsen, to exhibit the genuine nucleus of the posterior, amplified edition—there is no clear and certain reference to the Fourth Gospel.[2] The epistles of the former seem evidently to have been the model; in the same way as the author of the martyrdom of Ignatius has clearly had in his eye the account of Paul's last journey to Jerusalem contained in Acts xx. xxi. Peter and Paul are mentioned by name (Romans, c. 48), but John not once, not even in the epistle to the Ephesians. The style and sentiment of these three epistles found in the Syriac MS., which Cureton and Bunsen regarded as so great a discovery, seem to me very weak and puerile.

When the work "Against Heresies," now ascribed to Hip-

[1] Corpus Ignatianum, pp. 227-231.

[2] Allusions have been traced in the following passages; but they seem to me to carry no weight with them: Romans, c. 45, comp. 1 John iii. 18, ibid. c. 47, comp. John xv. 18, 19, ibid. c. 53, comp. John vi. 53-56. This last instance exhibits the greatest similitude in its reference to eating the flesh of Jesus as divine bread and drinking his blood as divine drink. But this would appear to have become a customary mode of speaking of the eucharist early in the second century. These three passages occur with some amplification in the two larger forms in Greek.

polytus, first appeared, the then Chevalier Bunsen thought it furnished conclusive evidence of the authenticity of John's gospel, as showing that Basilides, who flourished at Alexandria in the reign of Hadrian, 117-138 A.D., wrote a commentary on it. In answer to those who argued, that the references in Hippolytus did not apply to Basilides himself, but to his followers, and did not, therefore, establish so early a date, he insisted that the constant use in the citations of the singular verb "says" (φησί), was a clear indication that Basilides and nobody else could have been meant.[1] Should we admit this reasoning, it would prove, no doubt, that the Fourth Gospel existed between 117 and 138 A.D.; but we should still be left without any witness from Hippolytus as to its author. For it is a curious fact that, throughout his work, notwithstanding numerous and unquestionable references to the Fourth Gospel, the name of John is never mentioned but once, and then as the author of the Apocalypse (vii. 36). But if we turn to the passages, where the use of the singular verb seems to Bunsen to imply an allusion to Basilides alone, they do not, as I read them, bear out the conclusion which he draws. In vii. 20, Hippolytus mentions Basilides and Isidore, his son, and πᾶς ὁ τούτων χορός, and then cites them collectively through the whole of the following paragraph by the word φησί. Nor is this the only instance. In vi. 29, speaking of Valentinus, Heracleon, Ptolemy, καὶ πᾶσα ἡ τούτων σχολή, he quotes the opinion of the school, as before, by the singular verb φησί. It is surprising that so great a scholar as Baron Bunsen should have laid all this stress on so small a matter. "It says" (φησί) is the familiar mode of citing the doctrines of a particular school, whether represented by many writers or by one. Scripture, notwithstanding its multifarious contents and numerous authors, is constantly quoted by writers of the second century in this form.

The testimony of Justin Martyr is very important. In the pieces that are undoubtedly his—the two Apologies and the Dialogue with Trypho, which must be dated from the year 138

[1] Christianity and Mankind, I. p. 114.

A.D. and subsequently[1]—forms of thought and expression frequently occur which bear a considerable affinity to those we meet with in the Fourth Gospel. I must be allowed, therefore, to make a tolerably full citation of them. In the Dialogue (c. 17) Christ is called " the blameless and just Light sent by God to men." In the gospel, " light " is an epithet constantly applied to Chirst.[2] Ἀληθινός is a favourite adjective with John. It occurs twelve times in the gospel and first epistle. In the Dialogue (123) we have the expression, " true children of God."[3] But in John τέκνα is never conjoined with ἀληθινά. Consequently a reference to such passages as John i. 12 and 1 John iii. 1, 2, is not to the point. The Dialogue (c. 63) speaks of the " blood of Christ, sprung not from human seed, but from the will of God." This resembles John i. 13 ; but it is not a citation.[4] The following remarkable passage from the Dialogue (c. 105) it will be necessary to give at length in the Greek : μονογενὴς γὰρ ὅτι ἦν τῷ πατρὶ τῶν ὅλων οὗτος, ἰδίως ἐξ αὐτοῦ λόγος καὶ δύναμις γεγενημένος, καὶ ὕστερον ἄνθρωπος διὰ τῆς παρθένου γενόμενος, ὡς ἀπὸ τῶν ἀπομνημονευμάτων ἐμάθομεν. " He was an only-begotten son of the Father of the

---

[1] In the inscription of the first Apology to Antoninus Pius, Verissimus, afterwards Marcus Aurelius, is associated with him under the simple title of φιλόσοφος. Now, as Marcus was created Cæsar in 139, and it is not to be supposed, that this title, if already conferred, would have been omitted in the dedication, we must conclude that the Apology was written prior to that date. From an allusion in the Dialogue (c. 120) it appears that the first Apology was then in existence. The second Apology was probably written in the reign of Marcus Aurelius. As Antoninus Pius succeeded to the empire in 138 A.D., the first Apology cannot have been written at an earlier period. The limits of the time of its appearance are thus determined with great exactness. See Otto (de J. M. Scriptis et Doctrina, P. I. Sect. i.), also on Dial. c. Tryph. c. 120, n. 17. [Compare however, in the Tübingen Theolog. Jahrb. 1855, pp. 227. 412., Volkmar's revision of this chronology; assigning both Apologies (the second a postscript to the first) to about A.D. 150, and the Dialogue to about A.D. 155.]—*Ed.*

[2] Τοῦ μόνου ἀμώμου καὶ δικαίου φωτὸς τοῖς ἀνθρώποις πεμφθέντος παρὰ τοῦ Θεοῦ. Dial. c. Tr. c. 17. Comp. John i. 9, viii. 12, xii. 46, and many other passages.

[3] Θεοῦ τέκνα ἀληθινά.

[4] It may be convenient to place the two passages in juxta-position : Τοῦ αἵματος αὐτοῦ (scil. Christi) οὐκ ἐξ ἀνθρωπείου σπέρματος γεγενημένον, ἀλλ' ἐκ θελήματος Θεοῦ. Dial. c. 63.—οὐκ ἐξ αἱμάτων οὐδὲ ἐκ θελήματος σαρκὸς, οὐδὲ ἐκ θελήματος ἀνδρὸς ἀλλ' ἐκ θεοῦ ἐγεννήθησαν. John i. 13.

universe, sprung from Him by a special act as his word and power, and afterwards born a man through the Virgin, as we have learned from the apostolic records." Μονογενής is an epithet in this sense, as applied to the primal word—peculiar to John. It is so used four times in the gospel (i. 14, 18, iii. 16, 18), and once in the first epistle (iv. 9). But the conjunction of παρθένος with ἀπομνημονεύματα shows, that the reference must here be to the synoptic narrative; as no mention is made in the Fourth Gospel of the miraculous conception. Μονογενής, so applied, was a word already current in a certain Christian school. Exclusive of John, it is found only in Luke,—three times (vii. 12, viii. 42, ix. 38), and once in Hebrews (xi. 17); but in none of these passages is it used of Christ. There is a description of the baptism of Jesus in the Dialogue (c. 88) where John is represented as saying, "I am not the Christ."[1] These words are only found in the Fourth Gospel (i. 20); the remainder of the sentence coincides verbally with Matthew. Justin mentions in this account of the baptism —from what source he does not state—that when Jesus descended into the water, "fire was kindled in the Jordan."[2]

In the first Apology (c. 61) we find this passage: "Christ said, unless ye be born anew, ye cannot enter into the kingdom of heaven. Now that it is impossible for those once born to enter the wombs of them that bare them is obvious to all men." This is very like John iii. 3-5; the difficulty started by Nicodemus being distinctly alluded to, but only to show what must have been the real meaning of Christ's words.[3] On the other hand, it should be noticed, that for γεννηθῇ ἄνωθεν, Justin uses ἀναγεννηθῆτε, a verb which never occurs in John, nor even

---

[1] Οὐκ εἰμὶ ὁ Χριστός.   [2] Πῦρ ἀνήφθη ἐν τῷ Ἰορδάνῃ.
[3] I place the two passages side by side: Ὁ Χριστὸς εἶπεν,"Ἂν μὴ ἀναγεννηθῆτε οὐ μὴ εἰσέλθητε εἰς τὴν βασιλείαν τῶν οὐρανῶν. "Ὅτι δὲ καὶ ἀδύνατον εἰς τὰς μήτρας τῶν τεκουσῶν τοὺς ἅπαξ γεννωμένους ἐμβῆναι φανερὸν πᾶσίν ἐστι. Apol. I. (c. 61.) Ἰησοῦς—εἶπεν—Ἀμὴν, ἀμὴν λέγω σοι ἐὰν μή τις γεννηθῇ ἄνωθεν, οὐ δύναται ἰδεῖν τὴν βασιλείαν τοῦ θεοῦ. λέγει πρὸς αὐτὸν ὁ Νικόδημος, Πῶς δύναται ἄνθρωπος γεννηθῆναι γέρων ὤν; μὴ δύναται εἰς τὴν κοιλίαν τῆς μητρὸς αὐτοῦ δεύτερον εἰσελθεῖν καὶ γεννηθῆναι; etc. John iii. 3, 4.

in the Synoptists, being used twice in the New Testament—viz., in the participial form, in 1 Peter i. 3, 23.[1] Again, Justin says βασιλεία τῶν οὐρανῶν, which is the characteristic formula of Matthew—John (with Mark and Luke) everywhere using βασιλεία τοῦ θεοῦ. Apol. i. 60, and Dial. c. 94, refer to the brazen image set up in the wilderness by Moses, as a type of the cross of Christ; John iii. 14, 15, has a similar reference; but there is no other resemblance between the passages. The following passage on baptism and the eucharist (Apol. i. 66) is very remarkable, and must be transcribed in full: ἡ τροφὴ αὕτη καλεῖται παρ' ἡμῖν εὐχαριστία, ἧς οὐδενὶ ἄλλῳ μετασχεῖν ἐξόν ἐστιν ἢ τῷ πιστεύοντι ἀληθῆ εἶναι τὰ δεδιδαγμένα ὑφ' ἡμῶν, καὶ λουσαμένῳ τὸ ὑπὲρ ἀφέσεως ἁμαρτιῶν καὶ εἰς ἀναγέννησιν λουτρόν, καὶ οὕτως βιοῦντι ὡς ὁ Χριστὸς παρέδωκεν. Οὐ γὰρ ὡς κοινὸν ἄρτον οὐδὲ κοινὸν πόμα ταῦτα λαμβάνομεν· ἀλλ' ὃν τρόπον διὰ λόγου θεοῦ σαρκοποιηθεὶς Ἰησοῦς Χριστός ὁ σωτὴρ ἡμῶν καὶ σάρκα καὶ αἷμα ὑπὲρ σωτηρίας ἡμῶν ἔσχεν, οὕτως καὶ τὴν δι' εὐχῆς λόγου τοῦ παρ' αὐτοῦ εὐχαριστηθεῖσαν τροφήν, ἐξ ἧς αἷμα καὶ σάρκες κατὰ μεταβολὴν τρέφονται ἡμῶν, ἐκείνου τοῦ σαρκοποιηθέντος Ἰησοῦ καὶ σάρκα καὶ αἷμα ἐδιδάχθημεν εἶναι. "This nourishment is called with us eucharist, and no one is allowed to partake of it unless he believes that the things taught by us are true, and has undergone the ablu-

---

[1] The words ἀναγεννάω and ἀναγέννησις are used by the Fathers of spiritual regeneration. So the author of the treatise, "Quis dives salvetur," c. 23, Ἄκουε τοῦ σωτῆρος· Ἐγώ σε ἀνεγέννησα, κακῶς ὑπὸ κόσμου πρὸς θάνατον γεγεννημένον.— Ἀναγεννηθῆτε occurs also in the Clementine Homilies (xi. 26) in a passage which bears a close resemblance to John iii. 3, 5, mixed up strangely with language peculiar to Matthew, and with a distinct reference to what is called the baptismal formula (Matth. xxviii. 19). Under these circumstances, there has been much difference of opinion whether in such passages there could be any actual reference to John. That there is, has become additionally probable since the recovery of the wanting portion of the Homilies by Dressel. The curious phenomena exhibited by these and similar passages have led Volkmar to the conclusion, that Justin Martyr and the author of the Homilies must have used an uncanonical gospel which formed a kind of transition-document between the Synoptists and John. Ritschl more reasonably, as I think, suggests, that such passages were ultimately derived from the Fourth Gospel, but became known to these writers through oral communication. See Uhlhorn, "Die Homilien und Recognitionen des Clemens Romanus, etc." p. 125.

tion for the remission of sins and for regeneration, and lives as Christ has enjoined. For we do not take these things as common bread or common drink; but as Jesus Christ, our Saviour, incarnate through God's word, assumed flesh and blood for our salvation, so also this nourishment, blessed by the form of blessing prescribed by him, from which our blood and flesh are nourished by conversion—we have been taught is the flesh and blood of that incarnate Jesus." Justin in this passage is describing to the Jew Trypho the usages of the early Christian Church, and the explanation which he gives of the eucharist, closely resembles the doctrine contained in John vi. 47-58, where there is an evident allusion to the same rite, and the belief which had become prevalent, that eating and drinking the flesh and blood of Jesus Christ was indispensable to the attainment of "life eternal" (ζωὴ αἰώνιος). To those who were not prepared for this strong symbolism, it might well seem σκληρὸς λόγος ("a hard saying"). It is more harshly expressed in the Fourth Gospel than in Justin. From both we may infer, that participation in the eucharist was already regarded as the outward token of Christian communion, after the analogy of heathen sacrifices, where the persons offering partook of the victim that had been slain. Justin has evidently reference to the account of the Last Supper in the Synoptists; for, in the course of the chapter, he blends the words of Matthew (xxvi. 26-28) with those of Luke (xxii. 19), without any allusion to John. At the close of it he notices a certain affinity between the eucharist and the initiations of Mithras, where bread and a cup of water formed elements in the celebration; supposing, in accordance with the usual belief of the early Fathers, that evil demons had borrowed this usage from the Christian ceremony.

In the Dialogue, c. 69, allusion is made to Christ as a "misleader of the people" (λαοπλάνος). The same description of him occurs in John (vii. 12); but also in Matthew (xxvii. 63). Apol. I. 33 has these words: "that when it happens, it may not be disbelieved" ἵν' ὅταν γένηται, μὴ ἀπιστηθῇ), precisely corresponding to John (xiii. 19 and xiv. 29). In the first preaching of Christianity, things had a religious import given to them as being a fulfilment of ancient prophecy; and the objections of unbelievers to circumstances in the life and death of the founder of the religion, were met by the answer, that these, however strange and startling, had been all foretold and predestined. The remark had grown into a sort of established formula with the apologists of the time. In the following words of the Dialogue (c. 110) we are reminded of the beautiful imagery in John xv.: "As, if any one should prune the fruit-bearing parts of a vine, it sprouts out anew into a fresh growth of other flourishing and fruit-bearing branches, so is it also with us."[1] The vine is a favourite image with Hebrew writers; and it may have been suggested to Justin by the prophets and the psalms. It should be noticed, that the vine is not in this passage, as in John, Christ, but the people of Christ planted by him and God.

These are all the passages in the undoubted writings of Justin Martyr, which, to the best of my knowledge, can be supposed to contain any reference to the writings which bear the name of John. If there be reason to believe, on independent grounds, that the Fourth Gospel was generally received as an authoritative and apostolic work before the year 138 A.D., it would not be an unfair inference, that familiar acquaintance with the gospel had occasioned the general similarity of thought and expression which I have pointed out in several passages between the Martyr and the Evangelist. But the similarity in no one instance amounts to a quotation; and the conformity to the presumed original is much less close than what it is in innumerable passages to the gospels of Matthew and Luke, which are cited everywhere so copiously and so verbally, that it has been often remarked, a very complete history of the life and teachings of Jesus might be made up in the language

---

[1] Ὁποῖον ἐὰν ἀμπέλου τις ἐκτέμῃ τὰ καρποφορήσαντα μέρη, εἰς τὸ ἀναβλαστῆσαι ἑτέρους κλάδους καὶ εὐθαλεῖς καὶ καρποφόρους ἀναδίδωσι, τὸν αὐτὸν τρόπον καὶ ἐφ' ἡμῶν γίνεται.

of the Synoptists from the writings of Justin alone.[1] I do not here lay much stress on the entire omission of the name of John in all those passages which are supposed to refer to the Fourth Gospel; because this is a peculiarity common to John with Matthew and Luke: though it is certainly remarkable, that on the only occasion in Justin when the name of the apostle John is mentioned, it should be where he is expressly quoted as the author of the Apocalypse.

On a subject like the present, where the data for arriving at a conclusion are so few and imperfect, it would be presumption to dogmatize either on the positive or on the negative side; and therefore every suggestion must be offered provisionally, subject to future correction, as new facts are brought to light. The kind and degree of affinity between the Fourth Gospel and the writings of Justin would, however, seem to me fully explicable on the supposition, that both had drawn from a common source, and expressed the deepening conviction of their age. Already in the first half of the second century, the theological atmosphere was impregnated with the fermenting doctrine of the Logos; and, under its influence, modes of thought and forms of expression had got into extensive circulation, which were powerfully though silently modifying the old Palestinian tradition of the life and teaching of Jesus, and which must of necessity enter into every work that was written, while this change was taking place. It is noticeable, that although Justin had fully embraced the doctrine of the Logos, he still clung on many points to the original Jewish apprehension of the gospel, as, for instance, in his retension of Chiliasm; and that for his history, he in-

---

[1] The narrative followed is principally that of Matthew; in a somewhat less degree that of Luke; though the two texts are often blended together. In only one passage is reference made to a circumstance (the calling of the sons of Zebedee, Boanerges) which is mentioned by Mark alone. Dial. c. Tr., c. 106, and Mark iii. 17.—Curiously enough, the reading of all the MSS. in this passage of Justin would seem most naturally to ascribe this statement to certain "records of Peter," from whose teaching, according to the traditions of the Church, confirmed by Papias, Mark derived the materials of his gospel.

variably goes to the Synoptists. We do not meet in Justin with that complete amalgamation of the historical and the spiritual elements which is so conspicuous in the Fourth Gospel. I find it difficult to believe, that Justin could have been acquainted with the long and mystical discourses there put into the mouth of Jesus—at least, as accepted on the authority of an apostle. I cannot reconcile with such a supposition, the very particular description which he himself has given (I. Apol. 14) of the character of Christ's teaching.[1] In his address to the Antonines, he disclaims, on the part of the Christian apologists, all the arts of the rhetorician. They follow the simplicity of Christ. βραχεῖς δὲ καὶ σύντομοι παρ' αὐτοῦ λόγοι γεγόνασιν. οὐ γὰρ σοφιστὴς ὑπῆρχεν, ἀλλὰ δύναμις θεοῦ ὁ λόγος αὐτοῦ ἦν. "His words were brief and concise; for he was no sophist: but his word was a power of God." Nothing could more exactly describe the condensed wisdom, the short, aphoristic maxims, which characterize the teachings in the Synoptists; and nothing could be more wholly unlike the protracted argumentation which is so marked a feature in the gospel ascribed to John. The designation of Christ's words, as "a power of God," corresponds to what is said in Matthew vii. 29 and in Luke iv. 32.[2] The citations which Justin gives in the sequel of this passage, to justify and illustrate his statement, are all from the Synoptists—chiefly Matthew and Luke.

In the two treatises of Athenagoras—his ".Plea for the Christians," and that on "the Resurrection of the Dead,"—which belong to the latter part of the second century (for the former is inscribed to Marcus Aurelius and his son Commodus, as joint emperors, and is therefore assigned by the best critics to the year 177 A.D.),[3] there is not a trace of any quotation

---

[1] Weisse (Evangelienfrage. Zuzätze I. p. 127) has drawn special attention to this passage in Justin, with some very good remarks.

[2] Διδάσκων—ὡς ἐξουσίαν ἔχων (Matth. vii. 29), ἐν ἐξουσίᾳ ἦν ὁ λόγος αὐτοῦ (Luke iv. 32).

In this date Mosheim, Schroeckh, Neander, Gieseler, Credner, Semisch and Otto concur. See Otto's Prolegomena, p. 74.

from the Fourth Gospel. The citations, as in Justin Martyr, are from Matthew and Luke. Nevertheless, Athenagoras held decidedly the doctrine of the Logos; and some expressions which marked the common belief of those who held it, occur in his writings as in the Fourth Gospel. For instance, he speaks of the One God "who had made all things through the Word proceeding from Him" (πάντα διὰ τοῦ παρ' αὐτοῦ λόγου πεποιηκότα, Suppl. 4); and with still closer approximation to what we find in John —" by and through Him were all things made" (πρὸς αὐτοῦ καὶ δι' αὐτοῦ πάντα ἐγένετο, Suppl. 10); and again—"the Son being in the Father, and Father in the Son, by the unity and power of the Spirit" (ὄντος τοῦ υἱοῦ ἐν πατρὶ, καὶ πατρὸς ἐν υἱῷ, ἑνότητι καὶ δυνάμει πνεύματος, ibid.). This is the same doctrine which we have in John i. 3 and xvii. 21-23. Yet no one who reads the context, can feel any confidence that there is even a reference here to the Fourth Gospel. We already discern in Athenagoras the germ of the doctrine of the Trinity, as it was soon after developed by Tertullian. " It was part of the faith of Christians," he says, " to understand at once the union and the distinction of Father, Son, and Spirit" (τίς ἡ τῶν τοσούτων ἕνωσις καὶ διαίρεσις ἑνουμένων, τοῦ πνεύματος, τοῦ παιδός, τοῦ πατρός. Suppl. 12).

The first, and probably the original, portion of the beautiful Epistle to Diognetus, which there is reason to think was written about the time, or soon after the time, of Justin Martyr,[1] is deeply imbued with Johannine thought; but only in two passages have I been able to discover anything like a citation or a reference. " He sent his son in love, not to judge" (ἔπεμψεν ὡς ἀγαπῶν, οὐ κρίνων, c. 7). The sentiment is the same as in John iii. 17. Again: " Christians dwell in the world, but are not of the world" (Χριστιανοὶ ἐν κόσμῳ οἰκοῦσιν, οὐκ εἰσὶ δὲ ἐκ τοῦ κόσμου, c. 6): which closely agrees with John xvii. 16. " They are not of the world, as I am not of the world." But the author does

---

[1] See Otto, De Epist. ad Diognet. Jenæ, 1845, c. iii.

not indicate any particular source from which the sentiment in either case is taken.

We are now approaching the time, towards the end of the second century, when the citations from the Fourth Gospel, as a recognized portion of authoritative scripture, become distinct and unquestionable. Tatian, a pupil of Justin Martyr, in his " Address to the Greeks," written after the death of his master, and therefore subsequent to 165 A.D.,[1] has these words : " all things were made by him, and without him not a thing was made" (πάντα ὑπ' αὐτοῦ καὶ χωρὶς αὐτοῦ γέγονεν οὐδὲ ἕν). They are, it will be observed, almost literally those of John i. 3; but as they are here affirmed of the one only God, and not of the Word, and ὑπὸ, expressive of the primal, is substituted for διὰ the instrumental, cause, we might have felt uncertain of their origin, but for other passages in Tatian which leave no doubt of his acquaintance with the Fourth Gospel. The same remark might apply to πνεῦμα ὁ θεός, c. 4, which is identical with John iv. 24, and to Θεὸς ἦν ἐν ἀρχῇ, τὴν δὲ ἀρχὴν λόγου δύναμιν παρειλήφαμεν, c. 5 (compare John i. 1). But the following passage announces itself by the well-known formula as a citation from Scripture, even if the exact coincidence of the words did not prove that they came direct from John i. 5 : " And this is in truth what is said (τὸ εἰρημένον, a constant mode of Scriptural quotation), the darkness comprehendeth not the light."

In the work of Theophilus of Antioch, addressed to Autolycus, which must have been written in the reign of Commodus, and therefore subsequent to the year 180 A.D.[2]—we have *for the first time* a citation from the Fourth Gospel, with the name of its author—John. In explaining the doctrine of the Logos (ii. 22), Theophilus adds : " as the holy scriptures teach us and all the inspired—of whom John being one, says : In the be-

[1] Otto, Prolegom. vi.
[2] In his third book, c. 28, Theophilus brings down his chronological computation to the death of Marcus Aurelius, 180 A.D.

ginning was the Word," etc. (John i. 1). The Fourth Gospel is here classed among αἱ ἅγιαι γραφαί, and its author is described as πνευματόφορος; which, of course, gives him a place among canonical or authoritative writers: though even here it is to be noticed, that he is not called an apostle.[1] There are several other passages in this work which have their counterpart, sometimes to the very words, in the gospel. See, for instance, ii. 29, on the introduction of death into the world by Cain's murder of Abel, at the instigation of Satan (Comp. John viii. 44, and 1 John iii. 12)—i. 13, the grain of wheat which dissolves in the ground before it rises again (comp. John xii. 24, κόκκος σίτου occurs in both passages)—ii. 23, women forget the pangs of child-birth when they are past (so John xvi. 21)— i. 14, where we have almost the very words of John xx. 27. No one can doubt that Theophilus was acquainted with the Fourth Gospel, and considered it a part of holy Scripture; but there is only one passage in which he mentions its author by name.

Two works are mentioned in connexion with the names of Tatian and Theophilus, which are significant as showing, that about this time, in the latter part of the second century, four histories of the life and teaching of Jesus had begun to be accepted by the Church as authoritative, and that attempts were already being made to reconcile and explain their apparently discordant statements. These works appear to have corresponded in their object to our modern harmonies of the gospel narrative; and it should not be overlooked, that they bear the name of men in whose extant writings we meet for the first time with citations from the Fourth Gospel as recognised

---

[1] That by the holy scriptures, Theophilus understood writings which possessed the same authority with the books of the Old Testament, as being the work of inspired men, is evident from the following passage: (ad Autol. iii. 12) περὶ δικαιοσύνης— ἀκόλουθα εὑρίσκεται καὶ τὰ τῶν προφητῶν καὶ τῶν εὐαγγελίων ἔχειν, διὰ τὸ τοὺς πάντας πνευματοφόρους ἐνὶ πνεύματι θεοῦ λελαληκέναι. It is noticeable, that the gospels are here put on the same level as the prophets—a clear indication, that the idea of a New Testament canon was now in process at least of formation.

scripture, and with the name of the Author. Tatian's work is lost; but its title sufficiently explains its design: τὸ διὰ τεσσάρων (εὐαγγέλιον) "the gospel as exhibited by four." It was probably a compendious, harmonized view of Christ's ministry, with the omission of those passages in each of the four evangelists, that were irreconcilably at variance, and did not subserve the particular purpose of its author. It was put together, we may not unreasonably suppose, to meet the wants of the numerous class of believers who were bewildered by the conflicting accounts of the person and teaching of Christ, as represented in the Palestinian tradition given by Matthew and the other Synoptists, or as exhibited, under the strongly modifying influence of the doctrine of the Logos, in the more recent gospel which bore the name of John. The Diatessaron of Tatian was still used by some in the time of Eusebius (παρά τισιν εἰσέτι νῦν φέρεται, H. E. iv. 29), who seems to have known very little about it.[1] In some parts of the world it appears for a considerable time to have taken the place of the four gospels, as they exist in our present canon, being used not only by the followers of Tatian, but even by the Catholics, as a convenient and compendious book.[2] So, at least, we are informed by Theodoret, who says that when he took possession of his bishopric at Cyrus, in the first half of the fifth century, he found more than two hundred copies of the Diatessaron highly esteemed in the churches, all of which he collected and put away, and superseded by the four evangelists.[3] We have

[1] He describes it vaguely as συνάφειάν τινα καὶ συναγωγὴν οὐκ οἶδ' ὅπως τῶν εὐαγγελίων (iv. 29). In the same passage Eusebius tells us, that the party of which Tatian was regarded as the leader, used the law, the prophets, and the evangelists, interpreting them in a way of their own (ἰδίως); but that they spoke ill of the apostle Paul, and rejec ed his epistles, and did not even admit the Acts of the Apostles.

[2] οὐ μόνον οἱ τῆς ἐκείνου συμμορίας, ἀλλὰ καὶ οἱ τοῖς ἀποστολικοῖς ἑπόμενοι δόγμασι.

[3] πάσας συγαγαγὼν ἀπεθέμην, καὶ τὰ τῶν τεττάρων εὐαγγελιστῶν ἀντεισήγαγον εὐαγγέλια. Hæret. Fabul. Compend. I. 20. Theodoret says, that the Diatessaron cut off the genealogies, and the other passages which represented Jesus as sprung from the seed of David according to the flesh. It may be supposed, therefore, to have had a Docetic tendency.

other proofs that the Diatessaron gradually acquired a heretical character; in the same degree, no doubt, as the canonical gospels established their authority. Epiphanius, in his loose way, confounded it with the gospel according to the Hebrews.[1] It penetrated into Syria—of course in a Syriac version. Ephrem Syrus wrote commentaries on the gospels, following the order of the Diatessaron. If Abulfaragius (Bar Hebræus) really refers, in his "Short Commentaries on Scripture," to the genuine Diatessaron, we learn from him, that it commenced with the opening words of the Fourth Gospel—"In the beginning was the Word."[2] It fell at length, however, into disrepute; and, to supersede such heretical harmonies, Ammonius of Alexandria constructed his well-known canons for the comparison of the four canonical gospels, the nature and use of which have been described by Eusebius in his letter to Carpianus.[3]

Theophilus of Antioch is also said to have framed a harmony of the four evangelists, which, as it meets with the commendation of Jerome, must have escaped the imputation of heresy incurred by the work of Tatian. We may conclude, however, that it was written with the same conciliatory view; and this is rendered additionally probable by the allegorical mode of interpretation which it seems to have adopted.[4]

With Irenæus and Tertullian, who mark the transition from

[1] λέγεται δὲ τὸ διὰ τεσσάρων εὐαγγέλιον ὑπ' αὐτοῦ γεγενῆσθαι, ὅπερ καθ' Ἑβραίους τινὲς καλοῦσι. Panar. xlvi. 1.—There might, however, be some remote affinity between the two works.

[2] Assemani Bibliotheca Orientalis, Tom. I. p. 57, from the Syriac of Bar-Salibi, Jacobite bishop of Amida in Mesopotamia.

[3] This letter, with the canons of Ammonius, and Jerome's explanation of them to Pope Damasus, will be found at the end of the first volume of Lachmann's edition of the Greek Testament.

[4] Quatuor evangelistarum in unum opus dicta compingens, ingenii sui nobis monumenta reliquit. Hieron. Epistol. 151, ad Algasiam (quoted by Lücke, Comm. Evang. Johann. Einleitung, § 4). Jerome in the sequel gives a specimen of Theophilus's allegorical interpretation of the parable of the unjust steward. If the "Commentary on the Fourth Gospel," now extant in Latin under the name of Theophilus (which Otto has printed at the end of his recent edition of the Address to Autolycus) be to any extent based on the original work of Theophilus, it confirms the idea that his style of interpretation was throughout allegorical.

the second to the third century, the testimony to the apostolic origin and authority of the Fourth Gospel becomes so clear, express and full, and the verdict of the Catholic Church respecting it is so decisive, that it is quite unnecessary to pursue the line of witnesses any further. Nevertheless, it may be useful to dwell for a moment on the form in which these writers present this judgment to us, and on the influences under which it was apparently formed. Irenæus's work "Against Heretics" throws a most instructive light on the state of opinion in the Church at the close of the second century. In the course of that century it had been almost rent asunder by the fierce antagonism of opposing parties;—by the Jewish zealots on the one hand, who took their stand on the Old Law, and accepted as historical truth the concrete imagery of the prophets,—and by the extreme Paulinists on the other, who, under one or other of the many phases of Gnosticism, repudiated all connexion between the Old dispensation and the New, substituted a higher and unknown God for Jehovah, reduced the historical Jesus to a phantom, and transformed his ministry into a metaphysical theory of the universe. While these systems, which seemed actuated by wholly irreconcilable tendencies, were at the height of their conflict with each other, the doctrine of the Logos was gradually developing itself as an element of possible mediation between them. Itself a product of mingling Jewish and Hellenic influences, conceived in the prolific womb of Alexandrine thought, it took up, and moulded into a more scientific form, the new elements of moral and spiritual life that were being diffused through the world by the earnest missionaries of the Galilæan prophet and martyr. It furnished a terminology, by which the Jew could penetrate into the mind of heathenism, and by which the heathen could appropriate the great truths of Judaism. The converts from heathenism, who were the great apologists of the new faith in the second century, had, without an exception, embraced the doctrine of the Logos. It bridged over, in fact, the chasm which had hitherto separated the Jewish and Gentile worlds; and rendered possible that fusion of the elements of distinct spheres of thought, which laid the basis of a new idea in the development of humanity, and which yielded, as its earliest positive result, the tendencies that coalesced in a Catholic Church. Irenæus wrote at the crisis when this important amalgamation was consummating itself, and when it was beginning to be strongly felt, that something more fixed and definite than tradition was needed to sustain the issue. Tradition must now be supplemented by authoritative Scripture. Men had wandered away into vague speculation; they must be recalled to the concrete facts of history. One principal object of Irenæus's controversy with the heretics, was to restore the authority of the Old Testament as the necessary foundation of the New. His great aim was to show, that Jehovah and the God and Father of Jesus Christ are one and the same being, who made all things and revealed himself to the ages by his Son, the incarnate Word, and that he is ever acting by his providence on one plan, and with one view—the final salvation of them that believe. This, he argues, is the substance of all reliable tradition in all true Scripture. Scripture is the embodiment in a permanent form of apostolic tradition (τὸ τῆς ἀληθείας κήρυγμα, III. iii. 3), which is ever one and the same (ἡ δύναμις τῆς παραδόσεως μία καὶ ἡ αὐτή, I. x. 2), delivered in different languages, and carefully guarded by the Church, which is diffused through the whole world. Even were there no Scripture, the tradition of the oldest churches would suffice; for there are many barbarous nations who believe in Christ and yet have no written word to guide, but believe through the witness of the Spirit in their hearts.[1] This apostolic tradition

---

[1] The faith imparted to these barbarous nations is described (III. iv. 2) as a faith —" in one God, the maker of heaven and earth, and of all things that are therein, through Christ Jesus, the Son of God; who, on account of his exceeding love to the work of his hands, submitted to be born of a virgin, in himself uniting man with God, both suffering under Pontius Pilate, and rising again and received into glory, who will come in glory as the Saviour of them that are saved, and the judge of them that

is preserved by the succession of presbyters in the churches. Without attempting to trace this succession in all the churches, Irenæus deems it sufficient to insist on that of Rome (of which he enumerates the bishops from Linus, mentioned by Paul (2 Tim. iv. 21), to Eleutherus, twelfth from the apostles, who was his own contemporary) as the greatest and oldest, known to all men, founded by Peter and Paul—with which, on account of its commanding eminency and headship, all other churches that have faithfully kept the apostolic tradition, must of necessity agree.[1]

If I rightly interpret the reasoning of Irenæus, contained in the earlier chapters of his third book, it amounts to this: that apostolic truth is to be found in the tradition of successive presbyters, in the churches founded by apostles; that the test of genuineness in any book claiming to possess apostolic authority (an inference which is clearly implied, though not stated in so many words) must ultimately lie in its conformity with this apostolical tradition: and that, consequently, the admission of any work into the canon was not determined by the critical examination of its credentials in the sense of modern scholarship, but was a simple result of its acceptance by the general *consensus ecclesiæ*—expressed as that *consensus* was understood to be, most clearly and authoritatively, owing to the

are judged—sending into eternal fire those who pervert the truth and despise the Father and his Son." This passage, it should be observed, exists only in the Latin version.

[1] Maximæ et antiquissimæ et omnibus cognitæ, a gloriosissimis duobus apostolis, Petro et Paulo, Romæ fundatæ et constitutæ ecclesiæ, eam quam habet ab apostolis traditionem et annunciatam hominibus fidem, per successiones episcoporum pervenientem usque ad nos indicantes, confundimus omnes etc.—Ad hanc enim ecclesiam propter potentiorem principalitatem necesse est omnem convenire (Thiersch explains this word by *concordare cum ea*: in the modern Greek version it is rendered συμβαίνειν) ecclesiam, hoc est, eos qui sunt undique fideles, in qua semper ab his, qui sunt undique, conservata est ea quæ est ab apostolis traditio" (III. iii. 2). The old disputes of Catholics and Protestants on this celebrated passage, as represented by Massuetus and Grabe, are now out of date. Those who are still interested in them, will find what they want in the Apparatus to Stieren's edition of Irenæus. What is alone of importance, is to recognize the fact which these words indicate. I have endeavoured to give the sense as I understand it.

unbroken line of its bishops, in the ascendant Church of Rome. The value of this ecclesiastical guarantee for Scripture must depend on our belief, how far this traditional feeling of apostolic truth might be open to other considerations in favour of admitting a book, than such as would determine a strictly critical judgment to acknowledge its genuineness. That there was a copious evangelical literature before the time of Irenæus, all the records of that early age seem to indicate. It was, therefore, a question mainly of selection. In how broad and catholic a spirit, with how exquisite a spiritual tact (if I may so describe it), with how fine and discriminating a sense of the essentials of Christian truth, that selection was finally made—we have convincing proof, not only in the precious contents of our actual New Testament, but in the statement of Irenæus himself, that the four gospels, then recognized as canonical, had each been books of authority with different classes of heretics—Matthew with the Ebionites, Luke with Marcion and his school, Mark with some Docetic sect, and John with the Valentinians— while each of these books contained a sufficiency of apostolic truth to confute the sectaries who appealed to them (adv. Hæres. III. xi. 7).

It has been often said, that the strange reasons assigned by Irenæus (III. xi. 8) for there being neither more nor fewer than four gospels, puerile as they are, do not at all invalidate his testimony to the fact, that the gospels received by the Catholic Church as authoritative, were four, and that they bore the names which he gives them. This is perfectly true: and yet the very way in which he introduces the mention of this fact, proves to me that the limitation of number on which he insists as something final and conclusive, was of comparatively recent origin. Hence he sought to establish it by analogies which accorded with the idea of a Catholic Church—viz., that as there were four quarters of the globe, and four chief winds blowing from them,—and as there were four great dispensations of providence, marked by the names of Noah, Abraham, Moses, and Christ, so it might be expected from pervading analogy (εἰκότως ἔχειν) that the Gospel, which is the spirit of life, should be supported by four pillars. Since these things are so, he goes on to argue, (τούτων οὕτως ἐχόντων, and observe, he is not arguing on the ground of established fact, but on that of assumed necessity resulting from the physical and moral order of the world) all those are to be treated as weak, unlearned, and presumptuous, who disregard this analogy, and admit either more or fewer than four gospels.[1] But the most significant illustration adopted by Irenæus—because it is evidently intended to assimilate the Old and New Testaments and put them on the same level—is his symbolizing the Four Evangelists under the form of the creatures that sustained the living throne of God in Ezekiel (x. 14-22). This was, no doubt, one of the considerations that determined him to regard four as a mystic and pre-ordained number. As God sate between the cherubim, and those cherubim were τετραπρόσωπα (exhibited in a fourfold shape) typifying the future four-fold agency of the Son of God (εἰκόνες τῆς πραγματείας τοῦ υἱοῦ τοῦ Θεοῦ), so the Word, the artificer of the universe (ὁ τῶν ἁπάντων τεχνίτης) dwells by his Spirit in the Gospel, which he puts forth under four different forms, symbolized by the Lion, the Calf, the Man, and the Eagle. This symbolism was at once an assertion of the sanctity of the number four, and (in full accordance with the leading design of Irenæus's work) a reply to those who wished to make the New Dispensation entirely independent of the Old.[2]

[1] Irenæus clenches his argument, that there can be neither more nor fewer than four gospels, by the following inference from analogy; "Quum omnia composita et arta Deus fecerit, *oportebat* et speciem Evangelii bene compositam et bene compaginatam esse." I understand this as a protest against the number of unauthorized gospels that were in circulation.

[2] So far as I know, this is the earliest mention of the symbolical representation of the Four Evangelists, which afterwards became so marked a feature in the poetry and art of the Christian Church. According to Irenæus, John is placed at the head of the four, expressed as the Lion ; then comes Luke, as the Calf ; then Matthew, as the Man ; lastly, Mark, as the Eagle. This is different from the order and distribution which finally prevailed—viz., Matthew, Man or Angel ; Mark, Lion ; Luke, Ox ;

TESTIMONIES TO THE FOURTH GOSPEL. 75

There can be no doubt that Irenæus considered the Fourth Gospel to be the work of the apostle John; though he has nowhere expressly designated its author an apostle. He simply describes him in general terms as "a disciple of the Lord" (μαθητὴς τοῦ κυρίου, III. i. 1); but then he speaks in the same way of the writer of the Apocalypse, whom he undoubtedly understood to be the apostle John. To exclude all misapprehension, he further specifies him (III. i. 1) as ὁ ἐπὶ στῆθος τοῦ κυρίου ἀναπεσών ("he who leaned on the bosom of the Lord").[1]

Tertullian, the contemporary of Irenæus, in a most decisive passage of his work against Marcion (iv. 2), speaks of the gospels as the work of the apostles, or if not of apostles, yet of apostolic men, who were associated with apostles and succeeded them; and then signalises John and Matthew as apostles.[2] It is unnecessary to multiply citations from this writer, as I have explained so fully, in speaking of Irenæus, the circumstances which led to the demand for a canonical or authoritative Scripture at the end of the second century. Kirchhofer (Quellensammlung zur Gesch. des Neutestam. Canons, p. 154), from whom I have taken the foregoing quotation, refers also to the following passages of Tertullian: De Præscript. Hæret. c. 36; Adv. Hær. iv. 2, 5; Adv. Prax. 23; and adds in a note: "In all these passages, Tertullian speaks with unhesitating certainty of the authenticity and canonicity of the Fourth Gospel; and as he may be con-

---

John, Eagle. So they are given in a Latin Commentary on the Four Gospels, which bears the name of Theophilus of Antioch, and which probably dates from the latter half of the fifth century; and also in some verses of Sedulius (quoted by Feuardentius on this passage of Irenæus) which belong to the same period, where John, the last of the four, is thus described:

"More volans aquilæ verbo petit astra Joannes."

[1] ὁ ἐπιστήθιος became from this time forth a perpetual epithet of the apostle John.

[2] "Constituimus in primis, evangelicum instrumentum Apostolos autores habere;—si et apostolicos, non tamen solos, sed cum apostolis, et post apostolos.— Ex apostolis Johannes et Matthæus." His object in this passage is evidently to claim authority of the highest kind for the "evangelicum instrumentum."

sidered a representative of the Latin African Church, that part of the Christian world must have shared the same conviction. Moreover, he uses this gospel—not only in the works which he wrote after he became a Montanist (and might, therefore, be supposed to have conceived a prejudice in its favour), but also in those belonging to an earlier period of life —as a work whose claims were uncontested."

Before I quit this part of the subject, I must very briefly notice one or two writings which have a bearing on the character of the Fourth Gospel. In the work "Against Heresies," ascribed to Hippolytus, references constantly occur to every part of that gospel, with the well-known forms of citation— τὸ εἰρημένον, εἴρηται, τὸ γεγραμμένον, τὸ λεγόμενον, etc., which prove that the book from which such quotations were made was already recognized as a part of Scripture; although it is noticeable, that the name of the author, as an apostle, is never adduced to give weight to them. Perhaps this will appear less surprising, when it is recollected that it seems to have been the custom of that age to allege the gospels in the gross as apostolic memorials, without specifying the names of the respective writers.[1] It is curious that in one or two passages Hippolytus has blended with his quotations from John, forms of expression that are peculiar to Matthew and never occur in John. For instance (v. 8), in alluding to Christ's first miracle at Cana in Galilee, for John's words, after ἐφανέρωσε—τὴν δόξαν αὐτοῦ, he substitutes the Matthæan

[1] The only evangelist mentioned in Hippolytus by name is Mark, and that in a single passage (vii. 30) where he is described as κολοβοδάκτυλος, "wanting a finger." According to a tradition preserved in a Latin preface to Mark's gospel, contained in the "Codex Amiatinus," Mark is said, after his conversion, to have cut off his thumb, that he might not be forced into the priesthood. The same story seems to have got into an Arabic narrative. (See Duncker's note in loc.)—In vii. 20, where the first edition reads Matthew (Ματθαῖος), we must probably read with the recent editors, Matthias (Ματθίας). The only other writers of the New Testament mentioned by name are Paul—v. 7, where the epistle to the Romans is cited at some length—vii. 31 and 32, where he is associated with Peter—and viii. 20, where he is called "the blessed," and 1 Timothy iv. 1-5 is quoted;—and, lastly, John—vii. 36, where he is cited as the author of the Apocalypse.

form, βασιλείαν τῶν οὐρανῶν; and in an almost verbal citation of John vi. 44, he replaces the words of the Fourth Gospel, ὁ πατὴρ ὁ πέμψας με, by ὁ πατήρ μου ὁ οὐράνιος, which is found nowhere in the New Testament but in Matthew. At the close of his work, Hippolytus gives an outline of his theological system, as "the true doctrine of the Deity" (ὁ περὶ τὸ θεῖον ἀληθὴς λόγος). It is based on the doctrine of the Logos, and is an expansion and development of the idea which underlies the whole of the Fourth Gospel. In unfolding a theory of providence and human salvation, so strikingly coincident, it is certainly not a little remarkable, that if he received the Fourth Gospel, with which he was evidently acquainted, as a work of the apostle John, he should never once have thought of sanctioning his own views by so very high an authority.[1]

In the Shepherd of Hermas, which I have already noticed as a specimen of the apocalyptic literature of the early church, and which may be regarded as a milder expression of that same spirit of revival which gave birth to the enthusiastic movement of Montanus—we find these words: (Lib. III. Simil. ix. 12) "The gate is the Son of God, who is the only means of access to God. No man, therefore, will enter into the presence of God, otherwise than through his Son" (porta vero Filius Dei est, qui solus est accessus ad Deum. Aliter ergo nemo intrabit ad Deum, nisi per Filium ejus). This is clearly the doctrine of the Fourth Gospel: see x. 9, and xiv.

[1] The exalted language applied in the latter part of this treatise to human nature, when it has been transformed by faith and obedience, should not be passed over without notice: "thou art become a God (γέγονας θεός); and all that accompanies deity, God has promised to bestow" (ὅσα δὲ παρακολουθεῖ θεῷ, ταῦτα παρέχειν ἐπήγγελται θεός) (x. 34). It is when we consider the startling force of such expressions, that we are hardly surprised to find the same writer speak of Christ, who is the perfection of humanity, as ὁ κατὰ πάντων θεός ("God over all"); language, which appeared so extraordinary to the late Baron Bunsen, that he ventured on an emendation of the text, which made it refer not to the Son, but to the Father. The germ, however, of the thought may be found in John's assertion of the spiritual unity of God and Christ and the disciples (xvii. 21), and in the remarkable assurance in 2 Peter i. 4, that through faith and obedience, believers may become "partakers of the divine nature" (θείας κοινωνοὶ φύσεως).

6. The writer too holds distinctly the doctrine of the Logos.[1] But it can hardly be said that we have a quotation in this passage; nor is the source from which it is taken indicated. There is no other passage in the Shepherd which has the same affinity with the Fourth Gospel as this. Throughout the work, the name of John, as the author of an apostolic book, nowhere occurs.

In what are called the Clementine Homilies, a curious religious romance, which belongs most probably to the latter part of the second century, and presents us with a form of Jewish Gnosis, allied to Ebionitish and more remotely to Essenian tendency, exalting Peter and not obscurely repudiating Paul (see Homil. xvii. 19),—it had long been contended, there was no conclusive evidence of the author's being acquainted with the Fourth Gospel. But as the work, when first edited by Cotelerius near two centuries ago,[2] was confessedly imperfect, the argument was only valid *pro tanto*. Since then, in the year 1837, while engaged in examining the literary treasures of the Vatican Library, Dressel lighted on a MS. of the Homilies which contained the wanting portions of the work.[3] In one of the recovered sections, the incident of the man born blind is referred to in language so closely agreeing with what occurs in the Fourth Gospel (ix. 2, 3), that though it is applied in a very different way from the original narrative, no one who compares the two passages, can doubt that the author of the Homilies must have seen and read the Gospel. But no intimation is given whence the story was taken. Christ is quoted at once as "our Teacher," who said so and so, on such an occasion; and his words are used with a freedom approaching to license, to justify a doctrine which, as I understand the passage, is tacitly

---

[1] "Filius quidem Dei antiquior est totius creaturæ Dei, ita ut consilio fuerit patri suo in constituenda tota creatura, quæ est in ipso." Ibid. edit. Dressel.

[2] In 1672, contained in his edition of the "Apostolic Fathers."

[3] The entire work consists of twenty Homilies. The only MS. of which Cotelerius had the use in preparing his edition (contained in the royal library at Paris) broke off at Homil. xix. 14. See Dressel's preface prefixed to his edition.

condemned in the gospel. In the gospel our Lord denies, that the possible sin of the parents can have had anything to do with the son's being born blind; and the miracle was wrought "that the works of God might be made manifest in him." In the homily, on the other hand, the connection of sin, or at least of ignorance, in one generation with infirmity in the next is assumed as a fact, and the cure is performed ἵνα δι' αὐτοῦ φανερωθῇ ἡ δύναμις τοῦ θεοῦ, τῆς ἀγνοίας ἰωμένη τὰ ἁμαρτήματα. ("That through him the power of God should be manifested in healing the sins of ignorance.") What occurs to me in reference to this passage is, that if the author of the Homilies had regarded the book from which he borrowed this incident as an undoubted apostolic production, treating it with only a portion of the reverence with which we of this day should certainly receive any statement which we believed to have come direct from an apostle, I can hardly understand how he should have allowed himself to handle it so unceremoniously, especially in a work the main object of which is to glorify the apostle Peter, with whom the beloved apostle, according to the tradition preserved in Acts, was united in the closest bonds of sympathy and co-operation. On the other side, it must be admitted, that the verbal reverence for Scripture, such as it exists amongst us, and which, in its actual form, was a result of the reaction against sacerdotal authority at the time of the Reformation, was a feeling wholly unknown in the two first centuries of our era. Even an approach to it is hardly discernible till the age of Irenæus and Tertullian. The words of the Master himself were treasured up with the profoundest veneration; but the spirit of the gospel teaching was more regarded than its written form; and scripture still held a subordinate place to tradition. Uhlhorn, in his very able and learned essay on the Clementine Homilies and Recognitions,[1] has shown that the citations in the Homilies from the Old

---

[1] Die Homilien und Recognitionen des Clemens Romanus nach ihrem Ursprunge und Inhalt dargestellt, von Gerhard Uhlhorn. Göttingen, 1854.

Testament, which was already a recognised Scripture, are made in a very loose and irregular way, not seldom modifying the words to suit the sense that was wished to be conveyed. Sometimes they agree verbally with the Septuagint; sometimes they deviate both from it and from the Hebrew, when an object is to be gained; and sometimes they mix up two passages together. In p. 130, Uhlhorn has exhibited in juxta-position a passage in Deuteronomy (xiii. 1-3) and its citation in the Homilies (xvi. 13); and from this it is quite obvious that the original has been purposely altered, to avert from God the possible imputation that he could tempt any one to evil. The words of Christ himself are often quoted, as if they had come from unwritten sources. I may remark that, in quoting the gospels, the Homilies, like Justin Martyr, follow chiefly Matthew, next Luke, last of all Mark and John. Along with these sources, Uhlhorn thinks (p. 137) they must also have used an uncanonical gospel, allied to the "gospel according to the Hebrews."[1]

[1] The Clementines (so called from the name of their supposed author, Clement of Rome) exist in two forms—one in Greek, entitled the Homilies; and another, the Recognitions, which is found only in the Latin version of Rufinus. Both works have interwrought their peculiar theological system with the frame-work of a narrative, which gives to them, especially to the latter, the form of a religious novel. They differ considerably from each other; and it has been a question among critics which should be considered the earlier form. Uhlhorn considers the Recognitions to be a later re-casting of the work, for this, among other reasons,—that the quotations from the New Testament are more conformable to our canonical text, than in the Homilies; and further, that in the Recognitions the narrative is more developed and forms a more important element in the whole composition. Both these circumstances may possibly in some degree be due to the translator; though he says in his preface to Gaudentius, that he has endeavoured to adhere, not only to the sense, but to the very phraseology of his author; and it appears that in his time, there were two editions in Greek of the Recognitions. Anterior to both these forms—the Homilies and the Recognitions—Uhlhorn supposes there was a still older writing, as the nucleus of them, which had its origin among the sect of the Elkesaites in Eastern Syria, where there was a numerous Jewish population, and many Jewish Christian churches. The existence of the work in different forms of greater or less extent, is a parallel case to that of the so-called Ignatian epistles. Uhlhorn assigns the following dates provisionally to these three works: the oldest must have been subsequent to 150 A.D.; the Homilies, to 160 A.D.; and the Recognitions, to 170 A.D. It seems to be certain, that the Recognitions must have been in existence, when Origen wrote his Commentary on Genesis, which was before 231 A.D. (Uhlhorn, p. 434.)

In the letter addressed by the Christians of Vienne and Lyons to their brethren in Asia Minor, giving an account of the persecution which had broken out against them in Gaul, 176, A.D. (preserved by Eusebius, H. E. v. 1), there is a reference, almost verbally coincident, to John xvi. 2, cited as ὑπὸ τοῦ κυρίου ἡμῶν εἰρημένον; and a few sentences before, to the Paraclete, as a spirit of Christian encouragement; but here, as in former instances, without any indication of a written source, or any mention of the name of the apostle John.

In the oldest canon extant (the fragment discovered by Muratori in the middle of the last century), now generally referred by scholars to the end of the second or the opening of the third century, we have the following account of the origin of the Fourth Gospel, which it will be as well to translate at length, according to the corrections of the deeply corrupted text, suggested by Credner:[1] " The fourth of the gospels originated with the disciples of John (quartum evangeliorum Johannis ex discipulis). When his fellow-disciples and bishops had been exhorting him, he said to them: 'Fast with me three days from this time, and then let us relate to one another whatever shall have been revealed to each.' On that same night it was revealed to Andrew, one of the apostles, that John, with the consent or recognition of them all (recognoscentibus cunctis) should write an account of all things in his own name. And therefore, though various principles are inculcated (varia

---

Eastern Syria—where the Clementines had probably their earliest source (the names mentioned Homil. II. 1, it is noticed by Uhlhorn, are mostly Hebrew or Syriac)—has ever been the seat of mystic and ascetic, and later of syncretistic tendencies. Here was the home of Tatian and Bardesanes and Manichæism; and to this day the Druses and the Jezids exhibit in their religious belief a strange intermixture of Jewish, Christian, and Mahometan ideas. In the oldest portion of the Catechism of the Druses, only Matthew, Mark, and John, it is said, are mentioned, the Pauline Luke being excluded—an indication that the religion of the Druses grew up originally on a Jewish Christian basis (Uhlhorn, p. 417, note 96). Matter (Histoire Critique du Gnosticisme, Tom. ii. p. 329) says of the Druses and their probable connexion with the Ebionitism represented in the Clementines —with the characteristic vivacity of a French writer—" On dirait les Druses un reste de ces Ebionites précipités dans le Mahométisme."

[1] Zur Geschichte des Kanons, p. 74.

principia doceantur) in the several books of the gospels, this makes no difference to the faith of believers, inasmuch as in all of them all things are set forth in one predominant spirit (uno ac principali spiritu) concerning the nativity, the passion, the resurrection, his conversation with his disciples, and his twofold advent, first in the lowliness of contempt (which has been fulfilled), and secondly, in regal power and glory, which is to come. What wonder, then, if John should dwell so constantly on particular points even in his epistles, saying, in reference to himself: 'What we have seen with our eyes, and heard with our ears, and our hands have handled, these things have we written.' For so he professes himself to be not only a seer and a hearer, but also a writer in order, of all the wonderful things of the Lord."[1]

This is not very clear ; but two things are sufficiently evident : first, that the writer knew nothing of the actual origin of the Fourth Gospel, otherwise he would not have ventured on so purely legendary an account : and secondly, that believers were already disturbed by the apparently conflicting tendency of the several narratives; and that to quiet them, and induce them to acquiesce in this authoritative collection of sacred writings, he reminds them that on all essential points the four gospels were one in spirit—those points being, it should be observed, not matters of doctrine, but the great facts of the Messianic agency of Christ. The distinction between heresy and catholicism was

[1] I give the Latin (as emended) at length: " Quartum Evangeliorum Johannis ex discipulis. Cohortantibus condiscipulis et episcopis suis dixit : Conjejunate mihi hodie triduo, et quid cuique fuerit revelatum alterutrum nobis enarremus. Eadem nocte revelatum Andreæ ex apostolis, ut recognoscentibus cunctis Johannes suo nomine cuncta describeret.—Et ideo, licet varia singulis evangeliorum libris principia doceantur, nihil tamen differt credentium fidei, cum uno ac principali spiritu declarata sint in omnibus omnia de nativitate, de passione, de resurrectione, de conversatione cum discipulis, et de gemino ejus adventu, primo in humilitate despectus, quod ratum est, secundo potestate regali præclaro, quod futurum est. Quid ergo mirum, si Johannes tam constanter singula etiam in epistolis suis proferat, dicens in semetipso ; ' quæ vidimus oculis nostris, etc., etc., hæc scripsimus.' Sic enim non solum visorem se et auditorem, sed et scriptorem omnium mirabilium domini per ordinem profitetur."

already beginning to be sharply drawn, when the author of this Canon wrote. In another part of the Fragment (8), alluding to the rejection by the Church of a work that had been forged in Paul's name to support the heresy of Marcion, he lays down the broad principle, that we ought not "to mix gall and honey together" (Fel cum melle misceri non congruit).

One feature is significant in all the traditions respecting the Gospel of John—and that is, not only that it was universally regarded as the latest of the four, but that it was also believed to have a supplementary character, developing and completing what was rudimental and defective in the earlier three. Clement of Alexandria, in a passage of his Hypotyposes, preserved by Eusebius (H. E. vi. 14.) says,—" that John lastly, observing that the material or earthly side of the Gospel had been exhibited by the other evangelists, at the request of his acquaintance, and through the inspiration of the Spirit, composed a spiritual Gospel."[1] A curious extract from Theodore of Mopsuestia, which Mill has prefixed to the Gospel of John, in his edition of the Greek Testament, states that "the Fourth Gospel was written to supply the evidence, wanting in the three first, of the divinity of Christ, lest men, familiar only with what they found there, should come at last to regard Jesus as no more than what he seemed (*i.e.* a man)."[2]

I regret to have taxed the reader's patience by this long citation and criticism of passages, and by going over some ground that might seem to have been sufficiently trodden before; but the importance of the subject demanded as thorough an investigation as I could give it, and some passages which have been often quoted, it seemed desirable to examine anew. It must strike every one, I think, who compares the testimonies for the Apocalypse, as the work of

---

[1] τὸν μέντοι Ἰωάννην ἔσχατον συνιδόντα ὅτι τὰ σωματικὰ ἐν τοῖς εὐαγγελίοις δεδήλωται, προτραπέντα ὑπὸ τῶν γνωρίμων, πνεύματι θεοφορηθέντα, πνευματικὸν ποιῆσαι εὐαγγέλιον.

[2] ὥστε μὴ τοῦ χρόνου προβαίνοντος τούτοις ἐνεθισθέντας τοῖς λόγοις τοὺς ἀνθρώπους τοῦτο μόνον αὐτὸν νομίζειν, ὅπερ ἐφαίνετο.

the apostle John, with those that have been produced for
the same object on behalf of the Fourth Gospel,—that while
the former are distinct and express as early as the middle or
even the first half of the second century, none appear for
the gospel that can be adduced with any certainty, till Theophilus of Antioch, 178 A.D.; and that by a curious exchange
of position, the Fourth Gospel should then first obtain the
full and undoubting suffrage of the Catholic Church as the
production of an apostle, when the Apocalypse is beginning
to fall in reputation, and doubts are already insinuated against
its authenticity—that is to say, in the early part of the
third century. Whatever may have been the origin of these
two works, the difference of their character will partly account
for the altered feeling respecting them. It took place when
that change was coming over the educated members of the
Church in respect to their relations to the existing state of
civilization, to which I have adverted in a preceding section,
and which, as I have there shown, was followed by a two-
fold effect. It introduced, on the one hand, a conformity to
the usages of the world, which was regarded by stricter
Christians as a culpable surrender of principle, and did probably in some cases lead to laxity and scepticism; and it
awakened, on the other, as a counteraction, a spirit of earnest
and enthusiastic revival. While this change was in progress,
the doctrine of the Logos was assuming an increased importance, and undergoing a more scientific development in all
the great Christian writers of the period. It furnished a
means of reconciling the Petrine and Pauline tendencies, and
was the grand instrument for reducing the rigidity of the old
Judaic Christianity and moulding it into a more genial and
catholic form. We see in the writings of Tertullian, how
it contributed to develope the earliest phase of the doctrine
of the Trinity, and laid the first stone of that vast edifice of
orthodoxy which ensuing centuries reared up and consum-
mated. But it was equally suited to meet, in another way,

the wants of more enthusiastic spirits. Λόγος and Πνεῦμα, *Word* and *Spirit*, were not yet recognized as distinct spiritual entities, but were still employed, with the old Jewish vagueness, almost indifferently to designate the indwelling power and impulse of the Almighty. Whatever view of Christianity gave additional prominence to the doctrine of the Logos, was embraced with eagerness by all those fervid religionists, who felt that the World was paralysing the Church, and who prayed for a new outpouring of the Spirit on men's souls. Especially in the form of the Paraclete, as a perpetuation of the personal influence of the incarnate Logos in the world, was the doctrine eagerly welcomed by the Montanists, whose movement originated in an enthusiastic effort to bring back in a still purer and intenser form the Christianity of the first age. As far as our imperfect notices furnish us with information, it would seem that, of all the books of the New Testament, the Montanists were most devotedly attached to the Apocalypse and the Fourth Gospel. It was the idea of the Word and the Spirit, so vividly expressed in both, that attracted them, and made them find in both the evidence of a common apostolic source. The Montanists were not originally regarded as heretics. Tertullian, whose doctrinal orthodoxy has never been disputed, became one of them. Even Baronius admitted, that the original views of Montanus were harmless, and that it was only unreasonable persecution, mainly fomented by Praxeas, that drove his followers at length into heretical aberrations.[1] Their principles were at one time widely diffused through Italy and North-west Africa, as well as through Asia Minor. But at length the literal acceptance of Chiliastic views led to extravagances which shocked the judgment of more philosophical believers, who perceived the difference between the Apocalypse and the Fourth Gospel, and employed the spiritual idealism of the one to temper the concrete imagery of the other. There seem at this period, in

[1] Semler, Index Latinit. Tertullian. sub voce *Paracletus*.

the transition from the second to the third century, to have been three distinct tendencies working in the Church. First there were the learned and educated Christians, aiming through the doctrine of the Logos at the development of a Catholic Church. Then there were those who still clung to the primitive Jewish type of faith, and shared its traditional expectations, though they accepted the doctrine of the Logos in its more enthusiastic form. Of this movement Montanism was, perhaps, the most marked and prominent expression. Lastly, there are traces of a class of men who appear to have looked on the doctrine of the Logos, both in its learned and in its popular form, as an innovation on the gospel originally preached by Christ, and on this ground to have strongly protested against it.[1] We know very little of these persons. Their leaders were Theodotus and Artemon. They formed a small secession church for a short time at Rome in the beginning of the third century. They are described as zealous cultivators of human learning, and regarded Christ as in nature a man. They never organized themselves into any permanent sect or school; but their numbers and influence must at one time have been considerable, or Epiphanius would never have thought it worth while to bestow on them the name, which he tells us he himself invented, of Alogi.[2]

In such a state of things, a work like the Fourth Gospel became almost a necessity of the time; and if any apostolic materials existed for producing it, they must have been gathered up and put into shape. We are not yet in a position to offer any opinion as to the probable date, origin and authorship of the Fourth Gospel: but what has struck me through the whole of the

---

[1] They contended, that they held the same views with the apostles themselves, and that these views had continued in the Church till the time of Victor, Bishop of Rome, thirteenth in succession from Peter, when the truth began to be perverted. Eusebius, H. E. v. 28.

[2] It involves an *equivoque* (which he intended), and may be rendered either "without reason" or "without the Logos." See a monograph by Heinichen, "De Alogis, Theodotianis atque Artemonitis" (Lips., 1829); a work of very laborious research, which does not, however, throw much light on the subject.

foregoing inquiry is this; that we have decided traces of the doctrine of the book, some time before we find any clear evidence of the existence of the book itself, and still longer before we meet with any mention of the name and apostolic position of its author. The Logos was the doctrine with which the Apologists of the second century combated Jewish narrowness on one side, and Gnostic wildness on the other, and prepared the way for a Catholic Christianity. It is remarkable, that neither Athenagoras, nor Justin Martyr, nor Hippolytus, filled as their writings are with the spirit of that doctrine, should ever once—if the Fourth Gospel were then generally recognized as a work of the apostle John—have invoked in favour of their views the sanction of so great a name.

SECTION VIII.

On the internal indications of a later age in the Fourth Gospel.

WHEN we proceed from external testimonies to the internal signs of age and authorship, we enter a field where the mind of the inquirer is peculiarly exposed to subjective influences, and where, from the force of preconceived opinion, he is almost unconsciously disposed to assume what under other circumstances he could not have found. Nevertheless, where there is a truth at bottom, outward and inward evidence, when really understood, must be in harmony. Having prepared the way by a tolerably full exhibition of the former, and put the reader previously on his guard against a too hasty admission of the latter, I shall now venture to point out what appear to me very strong indications of a later age in the gospel ascribed to the apostle John.

The doctrine of the Logos, modifying the whole conception of the person and ministry of Christ, which pervades from beginning to end this remarkable book, could not, I think, have blended itself so intimately with the popular preaching of Christianity at a very early age. The facts recorded in the Synoptists, are, it is true, implied in the mingled narrative and argumentation of the Fourth Gospel; but they are kept subordinate to the leading idea of the writer; they are evidently combined and moulded with a view to develop it. As we read, we find it difficult to resist the impression, that the simpler and more natural history contained in Matthew or in Luke must have gone before, and that this was more strictly conformable to primitive tradition than the idealized vision of the incarnate Word held up to us by John. No doubt, the doctrine of the Logos existed anterior to the apostolic age; but it was confined to the higher sphere of philosophical thought, and came into no direct contact with the popular mind. With a few of the more educated Hellenistic Jews, who had imbibed a tincture of Alexandrine culture, it might be already understood and accepted, but to the simple multitudes, to whom Christ's personal teaching was addressed, and to the unlettered fishermen of Galilee, who were the earliest missionaries of the new faith, such a doctrine would probably have been incomprehensible, at war with their traditional beliefs and expectations, too abstract and too intellectual to produce any deep spiritual impression on their souls. As Christianity gradually ascended from the depths of society to its heights, and disengaged itself more entirely from Judaism, especially after the second destruction of Jerusalem, under Hadrian, A.D. 135, when it ceased to be regarded as a mere Jewish controversy, and obtained freer access to that widening border land of syncretistic feeling which then vaguely separated the old regions of Hellenic and Oriental thought,—it could no longer remain a stranger to the philosophical theories that were circulating in the world; and of these theories there was none better adapted for assimilation with it, at once from its partially Jewish origin, and from its facilitating the conception of the mutual relation of the Father and the Son, than the Alexandrine doctrine of the Logos. In the Apologists of the second century, most of whom were converts from heathenism, we already find this doctrine fully accepted. It was an intellectual formula, which enabled them to present, with some approach to scientific precision, and without undue offence to the philosophical fastidiousness of the parties whom they addressed, the apparently discordant representations which the popular tradition conveyed of the person and work of the founder of the new religion. As the world was then constituted, Christianity would hardly have made its way into the better mind of heathenism, without this sort of metaphysical bridge to cross the gulph which separated them. But as the doctrine may be regarded as, in a certain sense, a necessity from this time forth, so it could hardly have been such at a much earlier period. So far as we can judge from the very dim and imperfect records of that remote age, there was neither room nor occasion for a work like the Fourth Gospel, much before the middle at least, of the first half of the second century.

In the epistles of Paul we find ourselves in the very heart of the controversy which broke out on the first attempt to carry a Palestinian movement beyond the limits of Judaism. It was the question of faith and works, as the condition of admission into the Kingdom of God—a question which, as we learn from the story of Izates and Ananias in Josephus,[1] had already, in a somewhat different form, been agitated among the Jews. The Spirit, a more strictly Palestinian idea, performed, in the preaching of Paul, the same office of conciliation which later on was assumed by the Alexandrine Logos. All who hearkened to the divine call, and walked not after the flesh but after the spirit, whatever had been their previous condition, became thereby the children of God and the heirs of the promises. Of the doctrine of the Logos, as it was subsequently developed, I can discover little beyond an incipient trace in the Pauline letters. In Colossians, which was probably written during the apostle's captivity in Cæsarea, when the results of his Asiatic experience had taught him the necessity of some common point of view for bringing the Hellenic and the Jewish mind into harmony, we find an approach to that doctrine—language, at least, applied to Christ which is most easily interpreted in reference to it, and on the assumption of its truth. I allude particularly to Colossians, i. 15, 16, and ii. 3, 9, 10,—where such expressions as εἰκὼν τοῦ θεοῦ τοῦ ἀοράτου, πρωτότοκος πάσης κτίσεως,—πάντα δι' αὐτοῦ καὶ εἰς αὐτὸν ἔκτισται,—ἐν αὐτῷ κατοικεῖ πᾶν τὸ πλήρωμα τῆς θεό-

---

[1] Antiquit. XX. ii. 3, 4.

τητος σωματικῶς, and others associated with them—seem to me significant. But in the larger and most unquestionably authentic epistles, written before this time, Romans, Corinthians, Galatians, and Thessalonians, I cannot call to my remembrance a single instance of language of this kind. Here, as I have already remarked, the Spirit, not the Word, is the dominating idea. And in these larger epistles, especially Romans and Galatians, if I rightly interpret them by the collateral light of the book of Acts, the parties chiefly addressed are not so much either Jews or Gentiles in their sharply contrasted opposition to each other, as that large intermediate class—much larger, I am inclined to believe, than is usually supposed—of devout Gentiles, who had been heathens, but who had embraced the grand and noble doctrines of the Hebrew prophets, and who were, therefore, of all men the best fitted for transition to a new faith, which in its earliest form was exhibited as a simple spiritualizing of Judaism.[1]

When we turn to the Fourth Gospel, we find ourselves at once in another atmosphere. The storm of controversy has passed; the air is clear and still. Throughout there is a serene tone of conscious superiority, as if the first struggle were over, and the victory had been substantially won. "The Jews," a collective expression for the opponents of Christ peculiar to this Gospel, are indeed described as arrayed in habitual hostility against him, yet kept in check from first to last, and subdued in the midst of their fiercest assaults (see John xviii. 6,) by the overpowering presence of the incarnate Word and manifested Son of God. On the other hand, the direct access of Greeks ("Ελληνές τινες) to the very heart of the new religion, and the glorious prospect of its world-wide dominion which is anticipated from the coincidence of this event with the ensuing death of Christ,

---

[1] Our Lord, in one of his most authentic utterances, preserved in the Sermon on the Mount, says: "Think not that I am come to destroy the Law and the Prophets; I am not come to destroy but to fulfil" (οὐκ ἦλθον καταλῦσαι, ἀλλὰ πληρῶσαι). Matth. v. 17.

are set forth in the most striking way, as indicative of a new era in the development of Christianity, in John xii. 19—28. The words ascribed to the Pharisees on this occasion are remarkably significant, (v. 19)—" Perceive ye how ye prevail nothing? *Behold the world is gone after him*," (ἴδε ὁ κόσμος ὀπίσω αὐτοῦ ἀπῆλθεν).[1] Just before the crucifixion the enemies of Christ could never have entertained so improbable an expectation. We seem to me to be transported by the feeling so clearly expressed in this passage, to a time when the Jewish nationality was broken up, and the Gospel, released from its moorings on the narrow strand of Jewish prejudice, had set out with expanded sails on its boundless voyage of cosmopolitan conversion. If, in the absence of positive data, one might venture on a conjecture, when this was,—I should say, after the suppression of the Jewish revolt under Bar-Cochba, by Hadrian. It was then that the Jewish Christian church, which had hitherto subsisted at Jerusalem, was finally dispersed; and those who had previously been its members, were either absorbed into the Gentile church which succeeded it, or went back into Judaism, or else subsisted for a century or two longer as a dwindling heresy, under the name of Ebionites and Nazarenes. During the revolt of Bar-Cochba, the Christians had been cruelly persecuted by the Jews. His defeat and the establishment of Ælia Capitolina on the site of the Holy City, was the day of their deliverance and comparative peace.[2]

---

[1] Notice the use of ὁ κόσμος here. It is not introduced without a special meaning, and signifies a great deal more than ὁ ὄχλος or ὁ λαός, which the context seems to require. Wahl, in his Clavis Nov. Test. gives, among other meanings, under this word, that of *multitudo, omnes*; but the passages, of which this is one, cited in support of his rendering, imply, every one of them, something very different and far more specific. Comp. John vii. 4; xiv. 22; xviii. 20; 2 Cor. i. 12; 2 Peter ii. 5.

[2] Speaking of Hadrian's measures to prevent the Jews, after Bar-Cochba's defeat, having any access to Jerusalem, Sulpicius Severus, Hist. Sacr. II. 31, (quoted by Gieseler, Lehrb. der Kirchengesch I. § 42,) adds: " Quod quidem Christianæ fidei proficiebat, quia tum pene omnes Christum Deum sub legis observatione credebant. Nimirum id Domino dispositum, ut legis servitus a libertate fidei atque ecclesiæ tolleretur. Ita tum primum Marcus ex gentilibus apud Hierosolymam episcopus fuit."

Other indications offer themselves confirmatory of the date which I have conjecturally suggested. If I am right, two destructions of Jerusalem had now taken place, and the last dream of a spiritual dominion, with Jerusalem for its earthly centre, was effectually dispelled. Twice had destruction come; and twice had the Lord failed to reveal himself as an avenging Judge from heaven. In conformity with such an experience, we find the rich concrete imagery associated with the second coming, which is so strongly marked in Matthew and even in Luke, softened down and idealized into the more general expression of a final conflict, a κρίσις, between the powers of good and evil, or more generally still, of "a last day" (ἡ ἐσχάτη ἡμέρα). See John xii. 31; xvi. 8; vi. 39; xii. 48, and *passim*. Of the Chiliasm, which was so prominent an article in the faith of the first Christians, and which is so vividly set forth in the Apocalypse, not one clear trace exists in the Fourth Gospel.

Events are long ante-dated in this Gospel, to bring out from the first the transcendent power of the Son of God. It is unnecessary to dwell on the familiar instance of its putting the expulsion of the traffickers from the Temple at the beginning instead of at the end of the ministry of Christ. A less obvious but equally conclusive example is furnished by the conversion of Samaria. This is represented as having been substantially effected quite early in the course of Christ's public teaching, during one of his journeys from Judea to Galilee. (See ch. iv. and especially vv. 40-42). But such a statement is wholly at variance with Matthew x. 5, where Christ forbids the twelve to enter any city of the Samaritans; with Luke ix. 53, when, on his last journey to Jerusalem, the Samaritans refused to receive him and his followers into one of their villages; and still more with Acts viii. 5, where we learn that Christ was first preached in Samaria by Philip. Compare Acts viii. 14, which leaves no doubt as to the meaning of the former passage. There is something almost apologetic in the way in which the mention of Samaria is introduced (John iv. 4) : "he must *needs* go, etc." (ἔδει δὲ αὐτὸν διέρχεσθαι). The intrusion, as it were, of Samaria into the ordinary succession of events, had to be accounted for. Except in this chapter, Samaria is never once noticed again throughout the Fourth Gospel. In John x. 8, are some words which, if we call to mind the Jesus of the synoptical narratives, and the attitude uniformly assumed by him there towards the law and the prophets, we shall find it difficult to believe could ever, in their present unqualified harshness, have been uttered by him: "All that ever came before are thieves and robbers; but the sheep did not hear them." De Wette with Tholuck confesses himself pained and puzzled by them : and what trouble has been taken in all ages to wrest them from their natural and obvious meaning may be seen in the commentaries of Lücke and Meyer.[1] Christ is asserting, that there is only one sure entrance into the sheepfold of eternal life—the way by which he himself enters, the way of which he himself is the door. He distinctly repudiates the possibility of there being now, and of there having ever been, any other access. The feeling of the whole passage is strongly, not to say narrowly, anti-Jewish. Can any period better suit such an utterance than the one to which I have already alluded—when the final and decisive rupture with Judaism had just taken place, when the Christians were still smarting from the recent persecutions of the Jews, and rejoicing at the emancipation which in the name of Christ opened the whole of the heathen world before them? The figure of Christ's being the 'gate of life' passed, probably from this source, into the current theological phraseology of the ensuing century. In the Clementine Homilies,

---

[1] There seems no sufficient reason to question the authenticity of this passage. The oldest MSS. have it, A. B. D : and it is admitted by Lachmann entire into his text. The Codex Sinaiticus omits πρὸ ἐμοῦ ; and the corresponding words are wanting in the Vulgate. This omission is a proof of the difficulty which they early occasioned.

some thirty or forty years later, we find almost the identical words: "I am the gate of life; he that enters through me, enters into life" (ἐγώ εἰμι ἡ πύλη τῆς ζωῆς· ὁ δι' ἐμοῦ εἰσερχόμενος εἰσέρχεται εἰς τὴν ζώην. Hom. iii. 52). The Shepherd of Hermas at the close of the century, has the same idea in a passage quoted in a preceding section: " that there is no access to God, except through his Son, who is 'Porta Dei'" (III. ix. 12).

It is curious, that although the Fourth Gospel omits all mention of the institution of the eucharistic supper with the forms which subsequently became traditional in the Church, yet the doctrine of that observance, as it was developed in the course of the second century, we find nowhere in the New Testament so fully expounded as in the Gospel which is ascribed to John. There is nothing mystical in the account of the Last Supper given by the three first evangelists, nor in the almost identical statement of Paul (1 Cor. xi. 23-25). If anything beyond a simple memorial is indicated, it is less the idea of spiritual nourishment mysteriously conveyed into the soul through participation in the elements, than a reference to some atoning efficacy attached to the passion of Christ. Now turn to the description of the early Christian eucharist in the first Apology of Justin Martyr (66), already referred to. It is here expressly called τροφή (nutriment), which the bread and wine through some change (κατὰ μεταβολήν) effected by the form of benediction, are rendered capable of furnishing. The words of Justin are difficult to render exactly. One thing, however, is clear, that the elements are something more than common bread or common drink (κοινὸν ἄρτον—κοινὸν πόμα). The idea of the passage, as I interpret it, seems to be this: "That as the divine Logos became flesh and blood for our salvation, so our flesh and blood — our humanity — by partaking of this heavenly nourishment, enters into communion with a higher spiritual nature." There is descent on one side, and ascent on the other, and so mutual approximation. Underneath the whole conception lies the strong belief of that first age, that even in the heavenly world the spirit would be clothed with a glorified body. What is this but the doctrine set forth in the sixth chapter of the Fourth Gospel, which the Jews found it so hard to receive? "Except ye eat the flesh of the Son of man, and drink his blood, ye have no life in you. Whoso eateth my flesh and drinketh my blood, hath eternal life; and I will raise him up at the last day. For my flesh is meat indeed, and my blood is drink indeed. He that eateth my flesh and drinketh my blood, dwelleth in me and I in him" (vi. 53-56). Not less close is the affinity of thought in the so-called Epistle of Ignatius to the Romans (c. vii), which, whoever be its author, or whatever be its precise date, certainly exhibits the ideas of the early Christian Church on this subject: "I desire the bread of God, the heavenly bread, the bread of life, which is the flesh of Jesus Christ, the Son of God, who was born in later days of the seed of David and Abraham: and as drink I desire his blood, which is love incorruptible and ever-flowing life."[1] In another passage, also ascribed to Ignatius (Epist. ad Smyrnæos, vii), we have the same idea in a more generalised form: "They abstain from the eucharist and prayer, because they do not confess that the eucharist is the flesh of our Saviour Jesus Christ, which suffered for our sins." The coincidence of the doctrine in all these passages with that contained in the sixth chapter of John's Gospel, must strike every one. But they exhibit the doctrine in an advanced state of development, as it existed in the middle of the second century. Does not its presence, therefore, in the Fourth Gospel, imply such a date as would leave sufficient time for the growth of the doctrine into that

---

[1] Ἄρτον θεοῦ θέλω, ἄρτον οὐράνιον, ἄρτον ζωῆς, ὅς ἐστι σὰρξ Ἰησοῦ Χριστοῦ, τοῦ υἱοῦ τοῦ θεοῦ, τοῦ γενομένου ἐν ὑστέρῳ ἐκ σπέρματος Δαβὶδ καὶ Ἀβραάμ· καὶ πόμα θεοῦ θέλω, τὸ αἷμα αὐτοῦ, ὅ ἐστιν ἀγάπη ἄφθαρτος καὶ ἀένναος ζωή.

maturer form, out of the simple rudiments described by Paul? (1 Cor. xi.)[1]

In the curious passage (John xix. 34) all the attempts to explain by natural causes the flowing of blood and water from the wounded side of Jesus (see De Wette and Meyer in loc.) appear to me utter failures. Meyer, with his usual candour and fine exegetical sense, admits that a significant miracle, a σημεῖον, is here intended, marking the corpse as that of the Messiah, of whose specific agency blood and water are the characteristic symbols—the former denoting his expiatory death, and the latter, regeneration by baptism. The passage receives light from a similar one in 1 John v. 6: "this is he that came by water and blood, Jesus the Christ" (δι' ὕδατος καὶ αἵματος). In a verse immediately following, the spirit is united to the two former tokens of Messiahship; and of these three, the spirit, the water and the blood, it is added, that "they are joint witnesses, and issue in one" (εἰς τὸ ἕν εἰσιν). Taken by themselves, these passages do not, perhaps, prove much either way; but viewed in connection with the probable indication of the later doctrine of the Eucharist in the sixth chapter of the gospel, they seem to me to furnish some additional evidence of a time when the new religion had already become an established system of ecclesiastical discipline, with the expiatory death of Christ for its fundamental idea,

[1] The ancient Fathers, with scarce an exception, interpret John (vi. 53-56) of the eucharist. See Meyer (in loc.), who admits that the passages from Justin Martyr and Ignatius would be an admirable commentary on the meaning of the evangelist, if his gospel really belonged to the second century. Lücke (in loc.) calls this passage of John, the most obscure and difficult in his gospel. How next to impossible it is to extract any clear, consistent sense out of it, if the reference to an institution of later date be excluded, is evident from the long, elaborate, and very unsatisfactory expositions attempted by Lücke and Meyer. Compare the very similar language of Irenæus (Contr. Hær. V. ii.), where he argues, that the bread and wine in the eucharist are the true body and blood of Christ, who was really not apparently human; that these eucharistic elements are our spiritual nourishment, by partaking of which we imbibe the principle of eternal life, so that after death we rise again with a real body from the grave.

with baptism as its recognized mode of initiation, and the spirit as the witness and warrant of its effect.

Before I close this section, I must observe that the choice and arrangement of miracles is a significant feature of the Fourth Gospel. They are just seven in number, rising in importance on the whole as they proceed, and terminating with the raising of Lazarus from the dead, after he had lain in the grave four days, and corruption had already commenced. Of this greatest of all the miracles ascribed to Jesus, the Synoptists say not one word; though the Fourth Gospel represents it as the chief cause of the triumphal procession that went forth to meet him and welcome him with palm-branches, as he approached Jerusalem (xii. 13, 18). This procession is expressly mentioned by the three Synoptists; and therefore it is difficult to understand, how they should have omitted all allusion to the extraordinary occurrence which, we are told by John, was its immediate occasion. Without raising here the general question of the miraculous, so obscure and so mysterious, it is impossible not to remark, that the miracles recorded in the Three First Gospels, seem to drop into the general narrative more naturally, and, as it were, undesignedly, and to be more easily explicable as a spontaneous product of popular tradition, than the symmetrical disposal of them according to the mystic number seven, in the Fourth.

Other and less obvious traces of late origin will probably occur to those who read through this gospel without a strong and deep-fixed bias against the admission of such a conclusion. I have dwelt only on such as have struck me most forcibly on repeated and careful perusal. But the most formidable argument against the decision of the Church, that the Fourth Gospel is the work of the Apostle John, has yet to be adduced; I mean the precedent that was drawn from the Apostle's own practice,—so contrary, apparently, to his reputed words—in the celebrated Paschal controversy.

SECTION IX.

The bearing of the Paschal controversy on the authorship of the Fourth Gospel.

BY far the most extraordinary divergency between the Three First Gospels and the Fourth, relates to the time and circumstances of the Last Supper. It is necessary to understand distinctly wherein this divergency consists. Each of the Synoptists, in the most explicit terms, describes Jesus as partaking of the Jewish passover with his disciples in the usual manner on the evening of the 14th of the month Nisan; and at the conclusion of the supper, in the breaking of bread and the distribution of wine, instituting a memorial of himself. Let the following passages be noticed : Matthew xxvi. 17-29; Mark xiv. 12-26; Luke xxii. 7-20.—Paul (1 Cor. xi. 23-36), by recording the institution almost in the words of Luke, bears indirectly his testimony to the correctness of the synoptical account. According to this, Jesus was crucified on the 15th of Nisan, the first entire day of the feast of Unleavened Bread. The memorial then instituted has continued with widely-varying significance it is true, as a standing ordinance of the Christian Church, to the present day.

Now let us turn to the Fourth Gospel, and see what account it gives of this matter. In the opening verse of chapter thirteen, we are told, that the Supper was " before the feast of the Passover;" and, to exclude all possibility of mistake, we are further told (xiii. 29), that at the conclusion of the Supper, some words spoken by Jesus to Judas were understood to be an instruction to him, to buy what was necessary for the celebration of the feast. In this narrative not a word is said of the commemorative institution of breaking bread and distributing wine, but in place of it a symbolical act is introduced—the washing of his disciples' feet by Christ—to which the Synoptists do not once refer, and for which, indeed, they leave no room. Had we only the Fourth Gospel, we could never have known, that Christ had instituted any memorial of himself, like that described in the Synoptists; and how it had become an usage in the Church, would have remained inexplicable. Curiously enough, however, as I have shown in the preceding section, there are expressions in the body of this same gospel (vi. 50-56), which seem unintelligible, except on the supposition of a tacit allusion to the later conception of the eucharist.[1] According to the Fourth Gospel, then, this Supper must have taken place not on the 14th but on the 13th of Nisan, and Christ himself have suffered on the 14th, the same day on the eve of which the Passover was celebrated. That this was the meaning of the writer, is evident from two passages in the sequel of the narrative: first (xviii. 28), where we are told that the Jews, when they led Jesus from Caiaphas to Pilate, would not enter the heathen judgment-hall, lest they should disqualify themselves by defilement for eating the Passover; and, secondly, (xix. 14), where it is expressly stated, that at the time of the crucifixion "it was the preparation for the Passover." The two narratives, therefore, are utterly incapable of reconcilement. If the account of the Fourth Gospel be the true one, it is impossible that Christ should have eaten the Passover with his disciples, as he was crucified before it could be legally celebrated: and

---

[1] That the essential form of the eucharist in all existing sections of the Christian Church (in the use, for instance, of the bread and wine) should correspond to the description of its origin in the synoptical gospels, is a proof that it must have taken firm and deep root in ecclesiastical usage, before the Fourth Gospel with the authority of an apostle, and above all of the beloved apostle, could have had time to modify it. And it must have so modified it, at least in some part of the Church, had it been publicly recognized as the work of John within the limits of the apostolic age. This fact alone seems to me to imply a comparatively late date for the Fourth Gospel.

we have thus the three first Evangelists, with the apostle Paul, convicted of gross mistake as to a matter of historical fact, which it is hardly conceivable how they could have made, depositories, as we know they were, of the earliest Palestinian tradition respecting Christ. The mistake, too, has endured through all time as the basis of the most solemn and characteristic rite of the Christian Church; for we all refer, for the authorization of the Lord's Supper, not to the strange silence and substitution of the Fourth Gospel, but to the clear, simple, and self-consistent statements of the three Synoptists and Paul. But the difficulty does not end here. In a dispute which broke out in the second century between the Churches of Asia Minor and that of Rome, respecting the time and mode of keeping Easter, the authority of the apostle John was appealed to by the former on behalf of their own usage, in a way which seems altogether incompatible with his being the author of the Fourth Gospel, though conservative criticism has done its utmost to show that he still might be so. This will require a somewhat fuller exposition.

The word πάσχα (pascha) is a rendering into Greek letters of the Hebrew פֶּסַח, or in the later Aramæan form, from which the Greek is more immediately derived, פִּסְחָא, which denoted the lamb that was sacrificed, and sometimes generally the feast accompanying that sacrifice, at the annual commemoration of the passing over or sparing of the first-born of the Israelites on their exodus from Egypt. It comes from a root which signifies "to move onward," or "pass over." It is well rendered by our English word, "Passover." It was also the festival of the vernal equinox, marking the commencement of the new year.[1] In Leviticus (xxiii. 5-7) combined with

[1] Gesenius, Hebr. Wörterb. sub voc.; also Fürst's Hebrew and Chaldee Lexicon, translated from the German by Dr. Davidson. Fürst observes, that the root פֶּסַח "may perhaps have originally denoted the breaking through of the Spring-sun, or the new sprouting of nature or Spring; which is justified by analogy. A historical allusion may have originated with the exodus from Egypt." sub voc. p. 1142. The word πάσχα for the Jewish Passover was first used in the Septuagint; and thence it came into the New Testament.

Exodus (xii. 3-11), we have a full and particular account of the institution of the rite. The lamb was to be selected on the tenth day of the first month (Nisan) and kept till the fourteenth, on the evening of which day it was to be killed and roasted, and eaten whole with bitter herbs. On the fifteenth was to commence the feast of Unleavened Bread, lasting seven days, the first and last to be kept as specially holy, on which no servile work was to be done. The pascha, then, in its origin and primitive meaning, was essentially a Jewish observance, embodying Jewish ideas, and wrought up with the traditions of Jewish history. But at the commencement of the fourth century, subsequent to the Council of Nice, we find that the word had acquired a permanent meaning of quite another kind; and that it had come now to signify the annual Christian commemoration of the resurrection of Christ—what we call Easter. To effect so complete a transition from a Jewish to a Christian meaning, requiring, as we shall see it did, a surrender of the old lunar for the more modern solar reckoning of the year, and the substitution, in the fixation of fasts and festivals, of the days of the week for the days of the month—a long intervening period of strife and controversy was inevitable, embittered by the concurrent effort of Catholic Christianity to shake itself entirely free from its original Judaic trammels. The successive steps of this transition it is difficult to trace, not only from the imperfect nature of the evidence which we can now command, but also from the party spirit in which that evidence, defective as it is, has been manipulated. Nevertheless, the Quartodeciman controversy, as it is called, will become more intelligible, if we keep constantly in view the transformation which Christianity was quietly undergoing in the course of the second and third centuries. The use that was made of the name of the Apostle John by the partisans on one side of this dispute, combined with the remarkable silence of their adversaries, will be found to have a very decided bearing on the immediate object of the present inquiry.

The earliest notice, so far as I am aware, of a difference of usage in the celebration of the *pascha*, between the Asiatic and the Western Churches, occurs in a letter of Irenæus to Victor, Bishop of Rome (185 or 189-201 A.D.), which has been preserved by Eusebius (H. E. v. 24). The circumstances under which it was written, indicate the effort which the Roman hierarchy was now making to assert its supremacy by the establishment of an uniform ecclesiastical system all over the world. In consequence of the refusal of the churches of Asia (that is pro-consular Asia with the adjoining districts) to conform to the practice of the West, Victor had issued a proclamation,[1] excluding the Asiatic Christians, on account of their dissidence, from communion with the Catholic Church. Against this intolerant proceeding, Irenæus, in the name of the churches on the Rhone, over which he then presided, respectfully but firmly protested,—showing that the practice, which had called forth this excommunication, was of very ancient date, and had never till then occasioned any division in the Church. "The predecessors of Victor," he said, "in the Roman see—Anicetus, Pius, Hyginus, Telesphorus and Xystus, up to the very commencement of the second century—though they had not observed the usage in question themselves, had always been on friendly terms with those who did, and had freely sent them the eucharist." In proof of this he tells a story of Polycarp visiting Rome in the time of Anicetus (156-168 A.D.), when the two bishops had a friendly disputation on this very point. For Anicetus could not persuade Polycarp to abstain from the observance (μὴ τηρεῖν), inasmuch as he believed it authorized by the example of "John, the disciple of our Lord, and the rest of the apostles" ('Ιωάννου, τοῦ μαθητοῦ τοῦ κυρίου ἡμῶν, καὶ τῶν λοιπῶν ἀποστόλων); nor Polycarp induce Anicetus to follow the observance (τηρεῖν), for he said he must keep to the

[1] στηλιτεύει διὰ γραμμάτων, "placarded" (as we should say) "in public places." (Euseb. H. E. v. 24).

usage of the presbyters who had preceded him. Notwithstanding their difference, they partook of the communion together; and to show his respect, Anicetus allowed Polycarp to administer the eucharist in his church.[1] One thing is evident from this fragment of Irenæus: viz., that Anicetus quoted the precedent of the presbyters who had gone before him; while Polycarp appealed to the authority of the apostles, and especially of John. Still it is not clear from the passage itself, wherein the τηρεῖν and the μὴ τηρεῖν consisted; especially as Irenæus says, that the controversy turned "not only on the day to be observed, but also on the very form and mode of the fast."[2] Advantage has been taken of this ambiguity to show, that there is no actual inconsistency between such an appeal to the alleged practice of John, and the statements of the gospel which bears his name. If, however, we turn to a previous chapter of Eusebius (H. E. v. 23) where he first introduces the mention of this controversy, we can have little doubt, what the subject of it really was. "The churches of all Asia," we are there informed, "following an ancient tradition, thought it right to keep (ᾤοντο δεῖν—παραφυλάττειν) for the celebration of the pascha of salvation (τοῦ πάσχα σωτηρίου) the fourteenth day of the month—the day on which the Jews were enjoined to kill the lamb; it being absolutely necessary to close the period of fasting at that celebration, on whatever day of the week it might chance to fall." This practice, it is argued, was contrary to the usage of the churches in all the rest of the world, who pleaded apostolic tradition[3] for their uniform belief down to the present time, that it was unseemly to terminate the fast before the day commemorative of the

---

[1] This seems to me the meaning of the original, though the commentators differ. Τούτων οὕτως ἐχόντων, ἐκοινώνησαν ἑαυτοῖς· καὶ ἐν τῇ ἐκκλησίᾳ παρεχώρησεν ὁ Ἀνίκητος τὴν εὐχαριστίαν τῷ Πολυκάρπῳ κατ' ἐντροπὴν δηλονότι.

[2] οὐ μόνον περὶ τῆς ἡμέρας—ἀλλὰ καὶ περὶ τοῦ εἴδους αὐτοῦ τῆς νηστείας.

[3] ἐξ ἀποστολικῆς παραδόσεως. All churches were then in the habit of claiming an apostolic origin for any ancient usage prevalent in them. The Asiatics, as we have seen, did the same for the opposite practice. Collateral circumstances must determine which had the clearest evidence on their side.

resurrection, which, it should be remembered, was always the first day of the week. We observe here already a collision of Jewish and Catholic tendency. None who were of Jewish extraction, could entirely shake off the old reverence for the time-honoured festival of the Passover: whereas to the Gentile Christian under the ever-deepening influence of Rome, Hebrew usages and traditions were of little moment in comparison with the glorious memory of the resurrection, which marked a new era in the prospects of humanity, and promised the reversion of a spiritual inheritance. This feeling was strengthened into a deep popular conviction, when Constantine, by an imperial edict, consecrated the *dies solis* as a day of rest and religious observance throughout Christendom.[1] Towards the end of the second century, in the reign of Commodus, as we gather from the somewhat vague chronological indications of Eusebius (comp. v. 22, and 23 sub. init.), councils were held on this question in various parts of the world,—at Cæsarea in Palestine, at Jerusalem, at Rome, in Pontus, in Gaul, in Osroene, and at Corinth—which came to the unanimous conclusion, that the festival of the resurrection should be celebrated on no other than the Lord's day, and that only on that day should the foregoing fast be terminated.[2] The question was a vital one, whether in fact a Jewish or a Catholic Christianity should finally prevail. But the Asiatics were not to be silenced all at once. A letter from Polycrates of Ephesus to Victor of Rome, still extant (Euseb. v. 24), of which the substance is as follows, clearly explains their views: "We observe the day with scrupulous exactness, neither adding nor taking away.[3]

---

[1] τὴν σωτήριον ἡμέραν, ἣν καὶ φωτὸς εἶναι καὶ ἡλίου ἐπώνυμον συμβαίνει (Euseb. Vit. Const. iv. 18). Constantine's ordinance was issued in 321 A.D. See Guerike Kirchengesch. § 78.

[2] The resolutions of these councils were still extant in the time of Eusebius. He has preserved a fragment of the synodical circular issued by that of Cæsarea. (H. E. v. 25). It expresses agreement with the church of Alexandria; and its object is to enforce uniformity in the observance of the day. Routh has inserted this fragment in his Reliquiæ Sacræ, II. i.

[3] ἀρραδιούργητον ἄγομεν τὴν ἡμέραν· μήτε προστιθέντες, μήτε ἀφαιρούμενοι.

For there are great luminaries sleeping in Asia (pro-consular Asia, of which Ephesus was the centre) who await the resurrection of the saints—Philip, one of the twelve apostles, with his two daughters—John too, who leaned on the Lord's bosom and was a priest and wore the *petalon*—further, Polycarp of Smyrna—Thraseas of Eumenia (a city of Phrygia on the Cludrus), Sagaris of Laodicea—Papirius and Melito of Sardes —all of whom have kept the pascha on the fourteenth, according to the gospel, without any deviation, following the rule of faith; lastly, myself, Polycrates, least of you all, after the tradition of my family, some of whom I have succeeded, for seven of them were bishops, and I am the eighth. This day my family have uniformly observed, when the people cleared away the leaven.[1] I then, brethren, being now sixty-five years of age, having conferred with brethren from all parts of the world, and gone through the whole of holy Scripture, am not alarmed by threatenings; for greater than I have said, 'we ought to obey God rather than man.' I might mention the names of the bishops who have been associated with me, whom, as you requested, I appealed to. They are many; and though they perceived that I was myself an insignificant person, they nevertheless approved of this letter —seeing that I have not borne my grey hairs in vain, and that I have always had my conversation in the Lord Jesus."

We learn from a fragment of Melito, whose name occurs in

The word ἀρρᾳδιούργητον is found in no lexicon or glossary. I believe I have expressed the sense of it. See Routh, in loc. II., p. 17. There is still an ambiguity about "the day." We ask, "What day?" The question on which the whole controversy turned was: Which should be considered the great day of commemoration— the proper πάσχα—the fourteenth of Nisan, or the Sunday? Which was the day that terminated the fast, and opened the festival?

[1] This passage leaves no doubt, that the day observed by the Asiatics, of which Polycrates is speaking, was a perpetuation of the Jewish Passover (Comp. Exodus xii. 15, 19, 20). ὅταν ὁ λαὸς ἤρνυε τὴν ζύμην. Some MSS. read ἤρτυε, but the best give ἤρνυε, which has the force of ᾖρε, 'took away.' See Valesius and Routh in loc. Hilgenfeld (Paschastreit, p. 294, note 2) understands λαός in this passage as equivalent to Jews, " the people of the Old Covenant." This may be the meaning; but the context does not seem to me to require it.

the preceding list (Euseb. H. E. iv. 26), that there had been at an early period a great discussion (ζήτησις πολλή) about the pascha at Laodicea.[1] Melito himself wrote a work in two books on the pascha, as well as a treatise on the 'Lord's day.' From his association with the other Asiatic bishops by Polycrates, and from the fact that his work on the pascha gave occasion to a treatise on the same subject by Clement of Alexandria, we may reasonably conclude that he took the side of the Quartodecimans: and the inference is confirmed by the probability that he was a Montanist; for between the Quartodecimans and the Montanists there was a very close sympathy.[2] In Apollinaris of Hierapolis, a contemporary of Melito, we discern at length, among the Asiatic bishops, clear traces of a conversion to the Catholic view, though expressed with a gentleness which is in marked contrast with the harshness of Victor, and bears an indirect witness to the strength and wide diffusion of the opinion to which he was opposed. In a fragment of his work on the pascha, preserved in the Paschal Chronicle (edit. Du Cange, p. 6, Niebuhr, p. 13),[3] we have these words: "There are some, then, who through ignorance are disputatious (φιλονεικοῦσι) about these things, experiencing a pardonable weakness; for ignorance does not admit of blame, but demands instruction. And they say, that on the fourteenth the Lord ate the Lamb with his disciples, and suffered himself on the great day of Unleavened Bread: and they explain Matthew as stating the matter in accordance with their own ideas. Hence their notion is irreconcilable with the law, and according to their views the gospels seem at variance."[4] In

---

[1] It was at the time of the martyrdom of Sagaris, when Servilus Paulus was proconsul of Asia.

[2] He is described by Polycrates (Euseb. H. E. v. 24) as τὸν ἐν ἁγίῳ πνεύματι πάντα πολιτευσάμενον; and Tertullian, himself a Montanist, says of him, as quoted by Jerome (de Script. Ecclesiast.) "eum a plerisque nostrorum prophetam putari."

[3] It is also given by Routh, I. p. 160.

[4] ὅθεν ἀσύμφωνός τε νόμῳ ἡ νόησις αὐτῶν· καὶ στασιάζειν δοκεῖ κατ' αὐτοὺς τὰ εὐαγγέλια. Two evils are here said to result from the Quartodeciman theory: first, a contravention of the Law, which enjoined that the paschal lamb, and hence

another fragment of the same work, (Chron. Pasch. ibid.) Christ is called " the true pascha, the great sacrifice, that was offered in place of the lamb, and was buried on the day of the Passover." Among the other works of Apollinaris, he wrote one, we are told, against the Montanist heresy, which had then recently broken out (Euseb. H. E. iv. 27)—a circumstance which further marks the decided contrariety of his theological position to that of Melito.[1] But the tendency had now set in and was gradually spreading, to regard Christ as the one true pascha; and more effectually to prevent any confusion with old Jewish usage, his crucifixion was declared to have taken place on the very day, on the evening of which the Passover was legally celebrated. The Quartodecimans were those who adhered to what I believe to have been the original and true view, represented by the Synoptists—viz., that Christ

à fortiori (according to the view of Apollinaris), Christ, the true Passover, should be sacrificed on the fourteenth day of the month ; and secondly, by the acceptance of Matthew's as the true account, an introduction of discordance between the evangelists. The language of Apollinaris seems to me to imply, that in his time the statement of the Fourth Evangelist respecting the Last Supper was already received by a portion of the Church as the true account, which ought to control the divergent narrative of the earlier three. It is singular to observe, how the most learned men of a former generation shrank from fairly encountering the facts of this critical problem. Dr. Routh (Reliq. Sacr. I. p. 168) fights shy of it, and modestly pleads his own inability to grapple with it. " Celeberrima est atque difficillima quæstio—cui me virum pusilli ingenii interponere noluerim."

[1] It is surprising, that in the face of such facts, Weitzel (quoted by Hilgenfeld Paschastreit, p. 266) should contend, that Melito and Apollinaris, so far from being dogmatically opposed to each other, joined together in resisting an Ebionitish tendency in the Council of Laodicea, where the Quartodeciman controversy was agitated. But the question is, not whether Melito was an Ebionite, but whether he was a Quartodeciman. The fragments published by Grabe from the Bodleian library, and inserted by Routh in his Reliquiæ Sacræ (I. p. 122 seq.), prove that he was much given to a typical interpretation of the Old Testament, and saw in all its histories a constant foreshadowing of Christ. They indicate, perhaps, the commencement of a tendency of mind which might lead, if persisted in, to the conclusion already reached by Apollinaris. In all the passages now extant, however, Christ is typified, not by the Passover, but by Isaac or by the ram which redeemed him; and even had he been expressly called pascha, this would no more have proved that Melito did not believe him to have been crucified on the 15th of Nisan, than Paul's saying (1 Cor. v. 7) " Christ our Passover is sacrificed for us," is any evidence, that he did not accept the synoptical account of the Last Supper, which we know he did.

ate the paschal supper with his disciples in the regular way on the evening of the fourteenth, and suffered on the fifteenth, the first day of Unleavened Bread. As recent critics have denied that this was the real subject of the Quartodeciman controversy, it becomes necessary to specify with some distinctness the testimony of ancient writers respecting it.

Origen, on Matthew xxvi. 17, in a passage quoted by Hilgenfeld (Paschastreit, p. 211, note 1), argues, "that it is a kind of Ebionitism, to infer from the fact, that Jesus celebrated the Passover in the Jewish way (more Judaico), that we, as imitators of Christ, should do the same."[1] From this observation we may conclude, that Origen regarded Christ's eating the real Jewish Passover as an undoubted historical fact, which many Christians of his day were accustomed literally (corporaliter) to copy; whereas he, from his spiritual way of interpreting Scripture, considered such an observance to be in no wise obligatory. Tertullian (adversus Judæos, c. 10) understands the words of Moses (Exod. xii. 11) as a foretelling of the passion of Christ, and then adds: "which prophecy was fulfilled by your putting Christ to death on the *first day of Unleavened Bread :*" (prima die azymorum) which was the day following the Passover, and therefore the fifteenth day of the month.[2] Tertullian, in saying this, must have accepted the synoptical account of the crucifixion. From two passages of Athanasius (quoted by Hilgenfeld, Paschastreit, p. 322) we learn, that down to his time, at the beginning of the fourth century, "the churches of Syria, Cilicia, and Mesopotamia were at variance with the Catholic Christians, and

[1] " Secundum hæc forsitan aliquis imperitorum requiret, cadens in Ebionismum, ex eo quod Jesus celebravit *more Judaico* pascha corporaliter, sicut et primam diem azymorum et pascha, dicens quia convenit et nos *imitatores Christi* similiter facere." On which passage, Hilgenfeld remarks : "What Origen designates as Ebionitism, was, originally, nothing but the natural celebration of the Passover after the example of Jesus."

[2] This is a direct inference from Leviticus xxiii. 6, where the language is express; nor is it contradicted by Matt. xxvi. 17 ; Mark xiv. 12 ; and Luke xxii. 1. For the first day of Unleavened Bread began with the Passover on the evening of the 14th; in other words, the 15th began with the evening of the 14th.

observed the pascha at the same time with the Jews;[1] and that
to procure uniformity in this respect was one reason for con-
voking the council of Nice. From their pertinacious adherence
to ancient usage, the Quartodecimans were considered unreasonable and crotchety; and we notice a certain peevishness in the
language used respecting them, as if they were disturbers of the
peace for a fancy of their own. This is very evident from the
words of Athanasius in the fragment of a letter to Epiphanius,
which has been preserved in the Paschal Chronicle (ed. Niebuhr,
p. 9, Ducange, p. 4): "Cease to find fault, but rather pray that
henceforth the Church may preserve her peace unbroken; then
will cease those cursed heresies, and those disputatious people
(φιλονεικοῦντες) will also cease, who devise difficult questions for
themselves, under the pretext of zeal for the pascha of salvation,
but really to gratify their characteristic love of strife (τῆς ἰδίας
ἔριδος χάριν), because seeming to be of us and boasting of the
name of Christian, they are zealous, nevertheless, for the practices
of the Jews, who betrayed our Lord. For what a plausible answer
might be given to them in those words of the Scripture: ' on
the first day of Unleavened Bread, when they must needs kill
the Passover.'[2] In those days (i.e., the apostolic times) everything went on rightly; but now, as it is written (Ps. xcv. 10),
'they do always err in their heart.'" φιλονεικοῦντες is an
epithet constantly applied to the Quartodecimans by the
Catholic writers of this time. It expresses the feeling with
which an ascendant party always regards contumacious dissi-
dents. To the same effect is the very instructive passage of
Hippolytus (Hær. Refutat. viii. 18): "And there are certain
others, disputatious (φιλόνεικοι) by nature, unlearned in their
views, and of a rather pugnacious turn, who maintain that
they ought to keep the pascha on the fourteenth day of the

---

[1] διεφώνουν πρὸς ἡμᾶς, καὶ τῷ καιρῷ ἐν ᾧ ποιοῦσιν οἱ 'Ιουδαῖοι, ἐποίουν καὶ αὐτοί.
(de Synod. Arim. and Seleuc. c. 5.—ad Afr. episcop. Epist. I. p. 892).

[2] Athanasius has here blended, in the way so common in that age, the words of
Mark xiv. 12 with Luke xxii. 7, and has availed himself of the loose reckoning of
the Jews (see p. 109, note 2) to justify his own view of the day of the Crucifixion.

first month, as required by the Law, on whatever day (of the week) it may fall—out of reverence for the imprecations pronounced in the Law on disobedience—not observing, that this commandment was given to the Jews, who were destined to slay the true Passover, which has passed to the Gentiles, and is apprehended by faith, and is now no longer kept according to the letter. But in other respects these people accept entirely the things which have been delivered to the Church by the apostles." The Church, in fact, was now experiencing all the perplexity and conflict which must accompany the transition of an institution, which had originated in national beliefs and usages, to a condition of world-wide recognition and ascendancy —which had undertaken, in other words, to translate a historical fact into a Catholic idea. The simple-minded, who could not be convinced, and clung to the tradition of their fathers, had to be silenced by authority. To other causes of confusion the difficulty (to which I shall briefly allude to bye-and-bye) of bringing the lunar and solar reckoning of the year into harmony, was now added.

Latterly the controversy took the more practical form of a question, when the fast—which we find had already in the third century begun uniformly to precede Easter— should cease, and how long it should last.[1] The point, as we shall see, was not finally settled till the Council of Nice in 325 A.D. That things were now tending to the issue, which finally prevailed, and in the Catholic Church effectually abolished the old Jewish usage, we learn from a letter addressed to Basilides ("On the Great Sabbath: when the Fast should cease") by Dionysius, bishop of Alexandria, in the middle of the third century, of whose critical ability, and decided opposition to the Judaic form of Christianity, I have cited proofs in a former section, when discussing the

[1] According to Hilgenfeld (Paschastreit, p. 356, note), Quadragesima, our Lent, is first mentioned by Origen (Homil. on Levit. x. 2), in Rufinus's translation, and in the time of Athanasius, extended over six weeks.

authenticity of the Apocalypse.[1] Dionysius had been consulted by his friend about the cessation of the fast (τῇ τοῦ πάσχα περιλύσει); some affirming, that "it should commence from evening, others not till cock-crowing." Dionysius replied, "that it was difficult to fix the precise time; but that it would be universally admitted" (he must mean of course by the Catholic Church, and his strong assertion should be noticed, as marking the point which the triumph of the Catholic principle had already reached) "that the fast should be continued to the hour of Christ's resurrection, and that from that time the festival with its season of rejoicing should begin." The Scriptures, he observes, determine nothing as to the exact time when the resurrection took place. He notices that the four evangelists represent the parties, whom they severally speak of, as coming at different times to the sepulchre, and all finding the Lord already risen; no one stating precisely when he rose (πότε μὲν ἀνέστη), but all agreeing substantially that it must have been some time on the night of the Sabbath, or very early on the first day of the week. In accordance with this indefiniteness in the Scriptural narrative, "Some persons," he continues, "anticipate the conclusion of the fast before midnight; others lengthen it out to the farthest point; and some again pursue a middle course. Each must be allowed to do as he is moved, or feels himself capable. For all cannot stand six days of fasting (the week before Easter, our Passion week). Some, indeed, go through them all. Some fast two, some three, some four days; some not one day." It is quite evident, from this curious passage, that in the time of Dionysius, the word πάσχα, in the view which had then become predominant in the Catholic Church, had passed on from its original association with the fourteenth of Nisan, to a fixed position in the first day of the week, on

---

[1] This epistle occurs among those which are called the "Epistolæ Canonicæ," and will be found in Harduin's "Editio Conciliorum." It is also inserted by Routh in his Reliquiæ Sacræ, III. p. 223.

which Christ was believed to have risen, and had acquired a meaning equivalent to our Easter, as the anniversary of the resurrection; so that the only controversy remaining among Catholic Christians was, over what length of time the preceding fast should extend.

The schism, however, would never have healed of itself: it demanded the intervention of an authority that could not be gainsaid. Even according to the statement of Eusebius (Vit. Constant. iii. 5), the strife between the contending parties was so nicely balanced (a remarkable admission from no prejudiced quarter of the extreme tenacity of Quartodeciman resistance), that only the omnipotent God, and Constantine, his sole minister on earth for good, could put an end to it.[1] In other words, the Church could only be pacified by the State. The letter of Constantine to the churches, a copy of which was transmitted to every ecclesiastical province, explains how this was done, and throws light on the matter really at issue in the Quartodeciman controversy.[2] " The object was "—says the imperial missive—" to fix the celebration of the feast, which assured to men the hopes of immortality ($\pi\alpha\rho'$ $\tilde{\eta}\varsigma$ $\tau\grave{\alpha}\varsigma$ $\tau\tilde{\eta}\varsigma$ $\dot{\alpha}\theta\alpha\nu\alpha\sigma\acute{\iota}\alpha\varsigma$ $\epsilon\grave{\iota}\lambda\acute{\eta}\phi\alpha\mu\epsilon\nu$ $\dot{\epsilon}\lambda\pi\acute{\iota}\delta\alpha\varsigma$) on one and the same day throughout Christendom, and to break off a degrading dependence on an usage of the blood-stained and infatuated Jews, who could so little calculate the time of their own festival, that they sometimes kept it twice in the same year.[3] Nothing could be more unseemly, than that some should be feasting, and others fasting, on the same day. The churches of the west, the south and the north, and some even of the east, had already concurred in one usage; and it was hoped that the rest would follow their example." "In

---

[1] οὐδεὶς οἷός τε ἦν ἀνθρώπων θεραπείαν εὕρασθαι τοῦ κακοῦ ἰσοστασίου τῆς ἔριδος τοῖς διεστῶσιν ὑπαρχούσης· μόνῳ δ' ἄρα τῷ παντοδυνάμῳ θεῷ καὶ ταῦτ' ἰᾶσθαι ῥᾴδιον ἦν· ἀγαθῶν δ' ὑπηρέτης αὐτῷ μόνος τῶν ἐπὶ γῆς κατεφαίνετο Κωνσταντῖνος.

[2] Euseb. Vit. Constant. iii. 17-20. Hilgenfeld has given the greater part of it in the original (Paschastreit, p. 360-63).

[3] The allusion is, probably, to the occurrence of the fourteenth of Nisan, sometimes before, and sometimes after, the vernal equinox. See Valesius in loc.

one word," concludes the emperor, "it has seemed good to the general judgment, that the most holy festival of the pascha should be celebrated everywhere on the same day; for it is not fitting, that in so holy a matter there should be any diversity, but far better to acquiesce in this decision, in which there is no intermixture of foreign error and sin." The observance was henceforth to be purely Christian, without a remnant of Jewish association.

Such was practically the solution of the Quartodeciman question; though the old usage still lingered in some districts, and even yet is not entirely extinct.

If we impartially sum up the collective evidence of the foregoing citations, it seems a legitimate inference from the original and proper meaning of the word πάσχα, from the objections urged by the Catholics against the Quartodeciman usage, and from the part of the world where that usage most widely prevailed, and was longest retained,—that the Jewish, who were also the earliest Christians, kept, as the oldest Christian pascha, the anniversary of the farewell supper on the evening of the fourteenth of Nisan. They were confirmed in this observance by their strong Jewish predilections, as it coincided with the great national festival of the Passover, which Jesus himself had always kept; and it was moreover the traditional belief of the Jews, that Messiah would appear on the night of the Passover.[1] When the old Jewish

---

[1] Jerome, on Matt. xxv. 5, (referred to by Hilgenfeld, p. 306 note 2). Clement of Alexandria, in a fragment of his work on the Pascha (Chron. Pasch. p. 14 Niebuhr, p. 7 Ducange) tells us, that it was only in the years preceding his crucifixion, that our Lord ate the Jewish Passover, but that at the last, in place of this, he washed his disciples' feet after supper on the 13th, and then suffered himself on the 14th (αὐτὸς ὢν τὸ πάσχα, καλλιερηθεὶς ὑπὸ 'Ιουδαίων). He quotes the evangelist John as his authority, and adds, that with his account, rightly understood, the other gospels agree. I do not, however, think that this passage necessitates any qualification of the statement in the text. Passages to the same effect occur in Hippolytus (see Hilgenfeld, p. 278). They only prove, that at the time of the transition from the second to the third century, the doctrine that Christ did not eat, but was himself, the Passover (πάσχα οὐκ ἔφαγεν, ἀλλ' ἔπαθεν) had already become the belief of the Catholic Church, warranted, it was thought, by the Fourth Gospel, with which the others must be made to agree.

Church at Jerusalem was dispersed in the time of Hadrian, the peculiar type of belief which had distinguished it, still subsisted in the churches of Syria, Mesopotamia, and Asia Minor, especially in the region surrounding Ephesus, where apostles had early settled, and where churches founded by them, inheriting their ideas and perpetuating their traditions, long continued to flourish. In many of these churches, the pascha appears to have retained its semi-Jewish character down to the fourth century. It was essentially a commemoration of the death of Christ, and of all that followed it and was involved in it; and it admitted, therefore, of a ready extension to the most important consequence of the death of Christ—his resurrection. Several circumstances contributed to promote a transference of the term from the earlier to the subsequent event. But there was probably an intervening stage, which merely carried it forward from the evening to the next day, which, according to the Jewish mode of reckoning, was a continuation of it. In this stage pascha denoted the death of Christ, the anti-type of the Jewish festival, at once its absolute fulfilment and its abolition—the true Passover that was sacrificed for the redemption of the world. We observe already an approximation to this view in Paul (1 Cor. xi. 23-26), and also in Luke's account of the Last Supper (xxii); where, though in both cases there is an undoubted allusion to the ordinary legal Passover, yet, as Hilgenfeld has remarked, the Jewish accessories of the occasion are designedly kept in the background, and the Christian elements of faith and feeling are brought prominently into view. But an obvious contrariety was soon experienced between the Jewish and the Christian idea associated with the word pascha. To the Jew it expressed rejoicing—the memory of deliverance; to the Christian it suggested, in the first instance, the remembrance of sorrow and loss, the death of his benefactor and best earthly friend. To one it was a festival; to the other it was a fast. The feeling of this contrariety deepened, as the purely Christian sentiment triumphed in the minds of believers, and a sense of the radical difference between the Old and the New Dispensation was more thoroughly developed. In the West the change in the application of the word was accelerated (as I have already remarked) by the difficulty of adjusting the lunar to the solar year, and by the custom of regulating the anniversary of the Lord's death and resurrection, not by the day of the month, but by the day of the week. The steps of this change it is no longer possible to trace with distinctness; but there are still indications of there having been a time, when πάσχα was peculiarly associated with a remembrance of the sufferings of Christ,— an idea which was fostered in the minds of the Greeks by their confounding the Hebrew πάσχα with their own verb πάσχειν. Mosheim and some others, noticing this, have made a distinction, for which there appears to be no adequate foundation,— between a πάσχα σταυρώσιμον, commemorating the passion, and a πάσχα ἀναστάσιμον, commemorating the resurrection, each of which was observed by the Church—the former as a fast, the latter as a festival.

At length this migratory name finished its course, and settled finally in the first day of the week, as the anniversary of the resurrection: and to prevent any further confusion with the old Jewish usage, the account of the last days of Jesus, which acquired currency through the Fourth Gospel, denied that he ever partook of the Passover at all, but suffered on the very day on which alone it could be legally eaten. Two important consequences resulted from this fixation of the pascha: it was severed for ever from its Jewish root; and it resumed once more its original signification of a festival instead of a fast. But we have seen with what difficulty this transition was made; and how it needed the interposition of an imperial decree to render it effectual. The old Jewish churches of Asia Minor and the farther East still observed the fourteenth of Nisan, not as Jews but as Christians. It was the Christian, not the Jewish, pascha which they kept; and that they could only have kept, in commemoration of the farewell supper,—associated as it was with the death of their Lord, and with their sense of all of which that death was to them the symbol and the pledge. Their usage was, therefore, in conformity with the account which the Three First Gospels have transmitted to us of the closing scenes of the life of Jesus; and they pleaded on behalf of this usage, as we have seen from the letter of Polycrates to Victor, against the newer practice of the West, enforced mainly by Alexandria and Rome—not only the general precedent of apostolic tradition, but more especially the example of the greatest celebrity of the Asiatic churches, the apostle John, whose name had conferred a kind of sanctity on Ephesus and the whole ecclesiastical circle of which Ephesus was the centre. This is the more remarkable, as the gospel which we find in general circulation under the name of John before the close of the second century, contains statements respecting the last supper of Jesus with his disciples, so entirely at variance with the belief on which the Quartodecimans, as their very name implies, founded their practice, that, had they recognized it as the work of John, it is impossible that they could have appealed in their defence to his sanction. What is more remarkable still, those who were opposed to Quartodeciman usage and wished to enforce a Catholic uniformity throughout the Church, never once thought of appealing in the earlier stages of the controversy to the statement in the Fourth Gospel, which was decidedly in their favour. A word from one standing in so close a relation to Jesus as the beloved apostle, would have settled the question for ever. Yet not till quite the end of the second century, do we find the name of John adduced to support the Catholic view.

We cannot, it seems to me, form a correct idea of this and some kindred controversies, without distinctly realizing to ourselves the immense fermentation of ideas, the vehement antagonism of principles, which was going on through the whole of the second and third centuries, as a condition of the development of a Catholic Christianity—in other words, of the evolution of a religion for the world and for futurity, out of the simple rudiments of Jewish belief and a national movement of earnest Jewish reform. Chiliasm, Montanism, Quartodecimanism are only different phases of one and the same strong tendency—the effort to preserve or to revive the faith and practice of the primitive Galilæan institution, under the changes that were stealing over it from wider and more unreserved contact with the world, and the transformation of its simple beliefs and expectations into abstract formulas in accordance with the philosophical theories of the day. A constant looking for the second advent of the Lord, self-surrender to the impulses of the spirit as the only adequate preparation of meeting him, and a punctual observance, weekly and annual, of the appointed memorial, which should "show forth his death till he came," and which took the stronger hold of their imagination, from its coincidence with the most venerable rite of the preceding dispensation—all this implied a state of mind so opposed to the ordinary views and feelings of mankind, that only a degree of enthusiasm amounting at times to fanaticism could perpetuate it. Yet in certain temperaments this very contrariety to the world furnished the aliment of a self-supporting activity and zeal. It bound men by the closest bonds to usage that was consecrated by the holiest traditions, and stirred them up to the most strenuous endeavours after spiritual revival. It generated a heroism, a courage, and a conscientiousness which worldly blandishment could not seduce, and which persecution only rendered more intense. Except on their respective points of difference with the Catholics,—Chiliasts, Montanists, and Quartodecimans, were reputed orthodox.[1] Had the authen-

[1] Epiphanius's artificial multiplication of the different forms of heresy has drawn a sharper line of distinction between these sects than really existed. We should have understood their significance in relation to the history of their times more clearly, if our attention had been drawn rather to the broad principle in which they agreed,

ticity of the Fourth Gospel not been involved, the foregoing explanation of the Quartodeciman controversy would probably have been accepted as the most natural deduction from the extant evidence; but the consequence inevitably flowing from it, was not to be admitted without a resolute endeavour to evade it. It has, therefore, been argued,—among others by the late Professor Bleek of Bonn,[1]—that the point at issue was, not whether John was right or the Synoptists, in the day assigned by them respectively for the Last Supper, but whether the Jewish Passover should continue to be observed in the Christian Church. This seems to me a misstatement of the whole question. No one has ever contended,

than to the minuter points on which they differed. In reading of them we are constantly struck with certain features of resemblance to the sectaries of a more recent date—the Lollards and Puritans of our own country, the Gueux and Huguenots of the Continent. This is particularly the case with the Donatists of Africa, who offered the last and most determined resistance in the West to the encroachments of Catholic ascendancy. But the East, from Asia Minor to Mesopotamia and Armenia, ever continued the great *officina hæresium*, from which issued the strange, mysterious sects that penetrated into Europe in the eleventh and twelfth centuries of our era. Unfortunately we know little of these opponents of the dominant church, except through the reports of their enemies. This remark applies to the Montanists and Quartodecimans of the second and third centuries. Of the former, Eusebius has preserved some curious notices, though evidently drawn from a prejudiced source, in the fifth book of his Ecclesiastical History. His authority, Apollonius, (c. 18), charges them with luxurious living, personal vanity, and worldliness. He says that "they dye their hair, and tinge their eyes with stibium, and array themselves in gaudy attire, and play at tables and dice, and put out money at interest." Such a statement may seem at first view irreconcileable with the prevalent idea of their principles and practice. But it is not in itself at all incredible. Heinichen, in a sensible note on the passage, has shown that it is the natural tendency of an exaggerated spirituality to break out at times into the opposite extreme : and I call attention to the circumstance here, for the opportunity it affords me of noticing a parallel instance in our own religious history. The Independents of the Commonwealth were the most advanced and spiritual section of the Puritan body. Yet they scandalized their Presbyterian contemporaries, by their easy conformity to the manners of the world. "They wear strange long hair," says Edwards in his Gangræna (p. 63), "go in fine fashionable apparel beyond their places, feast, ride journeys, and do servile business on fast days." Their ministers were well paid, and lived in great worldly comfort. John Goodwin, one of the most eminent among them, did not scruple, any more than Calvin at Geneva, to go to bowls and other sports on days of public thanksgiving. It must not be supposed, therefore, that in the controversy between the Quartodecimans and the Catholics, all the fanaticism or all the worldliness was on one side.

[1] Beiträge zur Evangelien-Kritik. II. 6, 7, 8.

that the great dispute of the second and third centuries turned on the superior claim of the Three First Gospels or of the Fourth, to chronological accuracy in the date of Christ's passion. Such a discussion was not in accordance with the spirit of those times, at least among those who commenced the controversy. If the only matter to be settled were, whether a strictly Jewish festival should be perpetuated among a Christian people, this would of course leave it possible, that John might be right in putting the Supper on the 13th, and have also kept the Jewish Passover, and been quoted as an authority for doing so by a later generation of Christians. But not to insist on the extreme improbability, that the author of the Fourth Gospel could have remained a Jew in this more rigid sense; —not to press the unquestionable fact, to which I have before adverted, that the usage of the Christian Eucharist in all ages has been founded on statements contained in the Synoptical Gospels, and has no warrant whatever in the Fourth:—if one thing is clearer than another in the language of ancient writers, it is, that the question related not to a Jewish but to a Christian observance, or rather, as the word pascha itself implies, to a commemoration which had been originally associated with Jewish usage, but which had become in process of time exclusively Christian. More recently, Weitzel, whose theory has been fully detailed by Hilgenfeld (Paschastreit, *passim*), has suggested, with much ingenuity, that the Asiatic mode of keeping the 14th of Nisan, was founded on a combination of the Pauline and Johannine conceptions of the death of Christ, as the true Passover, abolishing the shadow in the substance; that instead of repudiating, the Quartodecimans really accepted the chronology of the Fourth Gospel, putting the supper on the 13th, and the crucifixion on the 14th of the month; and that they could, therefore, properly claim the authority of the apostle for their usage;—that, in fact, the only difference between the Asiatics and Catholics amounted to this—that, whereas the former thought the Old Dispensation

THE PASCHAL CONTROVERSY. 121

ended and the New began on the 14th of Nisan, the latter carried forward the separation between them, to the anniversary of the resurrection on the ensuing Sunday; otherwise expressed, that one party fixed the boundary line of the two dispensations on Good Friday, the other on Easter Sunday.

It is possible, that this theory of Weitzel may so far have historical truth on its side, that it represents a stage in the controversy, when pascha denoted pre-eminently the anniversary of the death of Christ, the πάσχα σταυρώσιμον as it has been called by some. The modern critics, who have gone into the history of this controversy, have perhaps drawn too absolute a line of separation between the Quartodecimans and their opponents, without sufficiently recognising the intervening steps of transition through which primitive Christianity gradually passed into Catholicism.[1] But that this theory does not go to the bottom of the question, or suggest its true origin, appears to me quite evident from the following consideration. If the death-day of Christ was observed on the 14th of Nisan, it must have been observed as a fast day, and would therefore have been in harmony with the prolonged course of fasting which preceded the anniversary of the resurrection. But the complaint

---

[1] Epiphanius, speaking of the Quartodecimans (Panar. 1. 2). expresses the idea of Weitzel in the following passage : ἔδει τὸν Χριστὸν ἐν τῇ τεσσαρεσκαιδεκάτῃ ἡμέρᾳ θύεσθαι κατὰ τὸν νόμον, ὅπως λήξῃ παρ' αὐτοῖς τὸ φωτίζον αὐτοὺς φῶς κατὰ τὸν νόμον, τοῦ ἡλίου ἀνατείλαντος καὶ σκεπάσαντος τῆς σελήνης τὸ σέλας. ἀπὸ γὰρ τεσσαρεσκαιδεκάτης καὶ κάτω φθίνει τὸ φαινόμενον τῆς σελήνης. οὕτω καὶ ἐν τῷ νόμῳ ἀπὸ τῆς τοῦ Χριστοῦ παρουσίας καὶ πάθους ἠμαυρώθη ἡ 'Ιουδαϊκὴ συναγωγή, κατηύγασε δὲ τὸ εὐαγγέλιον, μὴ καταλυθέντος τοῦ νόμου, ἀλλὰ πληρωθέντος, μὴ καταργηθέντος τοῦ τύπου, ἀλλὰ παραστήσαντος τὴν ἀλήθειαν. "Christ must needs be sacrificed on the 14th day, that among them should cease the light which lighteneth them according to the law, the sun having arisen and overpowered the brightness of the moon. For, from the 14th and downward the appearance of the moon waneth. So also in the law, from the time of the presence and passion of Christ, the Jewish congregation has become dim, and the gospel has shone forth—the law not having been destroyed but fulfilled, the type not being made void, but exhibiting the truth."

This, with similar passages, represents the intermediate state of feeling, in which the Church endeavoured to combine in one system the observance both of the 14th and of the Sunday, so as to avoid the occurrence of two paschas in one and the same year.

against the Quartodecimans, as we have seen, was this :—that by
keeping the 14th of Nisan, they interrupted with a feast, which
the old pascha or Passover properly was, the continuous fasting
of Passion-week,—so that it did not terminate the fast, but
merely broke it for the occasion. Weitzel himself is so im-
pressed with this difficulty, and some others attaching to his
theory, that he is obliged to assume the existence of two parties
among the Quartodecimans, a more Catholic party, and one
decidedly Ebionitish. But for such an assumption there is no
ground whatever. All extant evidence goes to show, that the
whole party was imbued with Jewish tendency, and represented
the old Jewish Christianity. The idea of cutting them up into
two sections, would never have occurred to any one, had it not
been required by the exigencies of a theory. Down into the
Middle Ages, and even, it is said, to this day, in some remote
parts of Asia, traces may be found of the use of unleavened
bread and of the sacrifice of a lamb in the celebration of the
Lord's Supper, which seem clearly to indicate its derivation
from the Jewish Passover, and serve to show, that the original dispute between the Quartodecimans and the Catholics
related to something more fundamental than a mere reckoning
of days.[1] On the whole, I am compelled to believe, by a fair

[1] See the evidence of this statement in Mosheim (De Rebus Christ. II., § lxxi.*
1) and Routh (Reliq. Sacr. II. p. 19). According to existing records it would seem
(contrary to what might have been expected from the earlier stages of the controversy), that Jewish usage lingered longer in the West than in the East. One of
the disputes between the Greek and Latin Churches, which accelerated the final
schism between them, related to the kind of bread which should be used in the
eucharist, the latter Church insisting on the use of unleavened bread, which was
disapproved by the former. See Riddle's Christian Antiquities (iv. § 7, 1). Still
more remarkable was the charge brought by the Greek, in the ninth century, against
the Roman Church, of "offering a lamb on the altar, after the manner of the Jews,
at the time of the pascha, and of blessing it along with the Lord's body," (agnum
in pascha, more Judæorum, super altare pariter cum dominico corpore benedicere et
offerre.) That the charge was not wholly without foundation, is evident from a
passage in Walafrid Strabo (de rebus eccles. c. 18.) There was even a form of benediction appropriate to the occasion, still preserved in some old rituals of the Roman
Church, from one of which it appears, that the Pope and eleven Cardinals had
solemnly partaken of a lamb at Easter. It was eaten on the Sunday. See Gieseler
(Kirch. Gesch. II. i. § 41, m.), who has given the original authorities at full. The

interpretation of such evidence as has come within my reach, that the real struggle in this dispute was between the retention of Jewish and the substitution of Catholic usage; that the apostle John, if he were, as I have attempted to show, a Jewish Christian, naturally shared in the Jewish predilections of his Asiatic brethren, and was therefore quoted by them as an authority for their own practice; that the Synoptists have given the true account of the Last Supper, and the crucifixion; and that the author of the Fourth Gospel, by assigning the Passion to the 14th of Nisan, and holding up Christ himself as the true Passover, evidently intended to do away with the last pretext for retaining any semblance to a Jewish rite, and to free Christianity from the swathing bands of Hebrew thought and Hebrew usage, which checked its healthy growth and still kept it in spiritual childhood.

remonstrance of the Greek Church probably put an end to this Jewish practice in the West. In the latter half of the fourth century, we find Aerius, a heretic of Arian tendencies, and a contemporary of Epiphanius, protesting against the Jewish usages with which the Pascha, in his time, continued to be celebrated. He seems indeed to have objected to the retention of the Pascha in any sense, and to have disregarded the fasting with which it was accompanied: οὐ χρὴ τὸ Πάσχα ἐπιτελεῖν. (Epiphan. Panar. lxxv. 3.)

The Armenian Christians are charged by the Patriarch Nikon (Patr. Apost. Coteler. I., p. 236), with eating a lamb on Easter Sunday, smearing their door-posts with its blood, and using unleavened bread. To this day, according to Grant (The Nestorians) the Nestorian Christians in the mountains of Kurdistan, who call themselves Nazarenes, still celebrate Easter in accordance with the Old Testament regulations about the Passover, substituting, however, the elements of the Christian eucharist for the paschal lamb. See Hilgenfeld (Paschastreit, p. 399, note 1). All these instances justify the conclusion, that in the Christian pascha there was a gradual transition from Jewish to Christian usage.

SECTION X.

Some points in the Chronology of the Paschal question.

THE purely critical issues of the paschal controversy, in relation to the authorship of the Fourth Gospel, have been complicated by chronological difficulties, resulting from the substitution of the solar for the lunar year, which have had the effect of diverting attention from the real nature and origin of the subject in dispute. The Hebrew Passover was at once a festival of nature and a historical anniversary. It marked the opening of the year, coincident with the vernal equinox; and it was also a memorial of national deliverance. But the old Hebrew year was reckoned by successive lunations, the periods of which were themselves determined by very imperfect observations, and were only kept in a sort of rough and general harmony with the annual revolution of the sun, by means of occasional intercalations.[1] The occurrence of the death of Christ at the time of the Passover introduced a new historical element into the yearly celebration, and was the cause of fresh difficulties in calculating it. The one fixed point for Jews and Christians was the vernal equinox. When Christianity spread out of Palestine through the Roman empire, the different usages prevalent in the ancient populations of Asia and among the more civilized peoples of the West, led to a contrariety of practice which was the means under providence of more completely detaching the new religion from its parent root in Judaism. The Hebrew Passover commenced on the eve of the 14th of Nisan, without any reference to the day of the week; the Christian anniversary of the

[1] Ideler, Lehrbuch der Chronologie, p. 204.

resurrection was associated immutably with the first day of the week, irrespective of the particular day of the month. The points of departure for the subsequent regulation were different in the two cases, and collision was the unavoidable result. The first influence which modified the conception of the Christian pascha and prepared the way for the later system—was the disposition, so natural under the circumstances, and favoured by the typological passion of the day, to regard Christ himself as the true Passover. This occasioned, almost inevitably, in the way of reckoning then customary among the Jews (connecting the evening of one day with the morning of the next as one continuous day), a throwing back of the day of the crucifixion from the 15th to the 14th, and a consequent exclusion of the possibility of Christ and his followers having partaken of a proper paschal supper on the evening of the 14th. In this manner the foundation was laid for what was afterwards called the Holy Week, founded on a parallelism between the Jewish and the Christian pascha. It began with the selection of the victim, symbolized by the anointing of Jesus, six days before the Passover, according to the Fourth Gospel (xii. 1); then came the sacrifice itself, the centre-point of the Great Week (on the 14th, as represented by the Fourth Gospel); followed, on the third day after inclusive (*i.e.* on the Sunday), by the resurrection. So conceived and arranged, the week exhibited, according to the Catholic system, a most entire coincidence of type and anti-type—of prefiguration and fulfilment. But although the Catholic pascha, by the practice of dating back from the Sunday, was freed from a servile dependence on any particular day of a Jewish month, it was still necessary to keep it connected generally with the season of the vernal equinox; and hence arose the necessity of scientific interposition, to adjust the relations of the lunar and the solar year. The old Hebrew names for the months had been superseded by Macedonian, as a result of the conquests of Alexander. Josephus employs the altered nomenclature. When these Macedonian months, which were lunar, were changed under Roman influence into fixed solar months, is uncertain. According to Galen (quoted by Hilgenfeld, p. 236, note) this conversion had taken place among the peoples of Asia, as early as the middle of the second century of our era. Soon after, at the beginning of the third century, we find the first attempt made to construct a cycle for determining the time of Easter, by Hippolytus, (Hilgenfeld, p. 332). An observation of the variations between the lunar and the solar year, had early induced the Greek astronomers to try to find out some period of moderate length, in which the solar years, the lunar months, and the solar days should each be capable of expression by whole numbers; so that it might be possible, in any particular year of the period, to refer the new and full moons to the days of that year. Such periods were called lunar cycles. The earliest of which we read, consisted of nineteen years, and bears the name of Meton, who is said to have lived in the latter part of the fifth century before Christ. The cycle of Meton was reconstructed by Calippus, a contemporary of Aristotle, who substituted in place of it a longer cycle of seventy-six years. This cycle of Calippus, with the addition of the *octaeteris* or space of eight years, making it a cycle of eighty-four,—was for a time in use in the Western church, with a view to bring round the new moons not only to the same day of the month, but also to the same day of the week. The old cycle of the *octaeteris*, older it is said among the Greeks than the Metonic cycle of nineteen years, was the element out of which the earliest paschal cycles of the Christians were evolved. Hippolytus doubled it, and so framed his cycle of sixteen years. But it was a rude approximation, which failed of its proposed object, and was superseded at the beginning of the fourth century among the Latins, by the cycle of eighty-four years. (Hilgenfeld, p. 340.)[1]

[1] The canon paschalis of Hippolytus is inscribed on one side of the chair of the statue, supposed to be that of Hippolytus, which was dug up in the catacombs of San Lorenzo at Rome, in the year 1551.

"The whole ecclesiastical division of the year," was henceforth, according to Ideler,[1] "determined by the festival of Easter, which from the commencement of the Christian era had been always solemnized on the Sunday which followed the vernal full moon; and, when this fell on a Sunday, on the Sunday next following. By the vernal full moon was understood either that which coincided with the 21st of March (universally accepted as the commencement of spring) or that which immediately followed it. This was called the 'Easter limit,' *terminus paschalis*. Two things had therefore to be determined in fixing Easter; first, the day of the month, and secondly the day of the week, of the 'Easter limit.'" "When the new moon has been found," he continues (p. 347), "the next thing is to deduce from it the full moon. In all the discussions respecting the celebration of Easter, we find the expression τεσσαρεσκαιδεκάτη, *Luna decima quarta* (the 14th day of the month) employed by ecclesiastical writers to denote the full moon.[2] The full moon occurs nearly fifteen days, on the average, after the conjunction; but the Greeks reckoned the age of the moon from its first appearance in the evening sky, and with that they began their month.[3]

[1] Handbuch der Chronologie, p. 345. In a note, Ideler observes: "the old German *Ostern* is of disputed origin. The usual notion is, that it is derived from *urstan*, which in the oldest language of Germany, signifies to 'rise again.' According to Bede (de temp. rat. c. 13), it comes from the name of an old Anglo-Saxon goddess, *Eostre*, whose feast from the remotest antiquity was celebrated about the time of the Christian Easter. Bede calls April, in which Easter usually falls, *Eosturmonath*, Charlemagne, *Ostarmanoth*."

[2] We have here a curious indication of Jewish origin, in the retention of a mark of time after it had ceased to have any propriety or even meaning in the Christian usage, except as a rough general expression for the middle of a month. In like manner the phrase, σάββατον μέγα, *sabbatum magnum*, is used in the Roman Church to signify the sabbath that occurs in the paschal week, the day when Christ lay in the grave, between Good Friday and Easter Sunday; though among the Jews, it seems to have originally denoted the day which immediately followed the Passover, the first day of Unleavened Bread, the 15th of Nisan, whether it was an ordinary sabbath or not; in accordance with the Jewish practice of calling all their high festival days sabbaths. See the evidence for this last statement adduced by Hilgenfeld (Paschastreit, p. 149, note).

[3] The crescent moon, as marking the commencement of another lunation, would naturally acquire something of a religious character, and might become an object of

The new moons in the ecclesiastical tables must be understood in the same sense. As from the first phase to the full moon thirteen days usually elapse, those who fixed the time of Easter reckoned 13, or inclusive of the new moon, 14 days onwards,—from the beginning to the middle of the lunation, and so ascertained the 'Easter Limit.'" The days on which this fell, were marked in the cycle of nineteen years by numbers, from one to nineteen, which were called "the golden numbers," probably from their having at one time been written in gold.[1] The earliest 'Easter limit' was the 21st of March, regarded universally as the first day of spring. Hence the Easter new moon must fall somewhere between the 8th of March and the 5th of April inclusive. The new moon on the 8th of March would give the earliest 'Easter limit'—that on the 21st. Should it not occur till the 5th of April, it would yield the latest 'Easter limit,'—on the 18th of that month. If the 21st of March should fall on a Saturday, Easter would be celebrated next day, on the 22nd, and this would be the earliest Easter day possible. If, on the other hand, the 18th of April should happen to be a Sunday, then Easter would have to be postponed a week, and fall on the 25th of April, the latest day to which it could be deferred. These are the extreme limits of the possible period of Easter, separated by an interval of five weeks.[2]

The different cycles devised for finding the new and full moons on which Easter depended, were only approximations to rigid scientific truth. From time to time they had to be corrected; and when they had run out their course, they must either be renewed or superseded by others. The altered constitution of the civil year imposed at length the necessity of making such calculations, not less on the Jews in fixing the time of the Passover, than on the Christians in regulating Easter. As the

worship. Relics have been found in the Lake-dwellings built on piles, lately brought to light in Switzerland and elsewhere, from which it has been conjectured that the people who inhabited them worshipped the crescent moon. (See Dr. Ferdinand Keller's work, Engl. Transl.) The new moons were sacred among the Hebrews.

[1] Ideler, Handbuch, etc., p. 346.   [2] Ideler, p. 348.

learned bishops of Alexandria issued their paschal letters year by year, which were authorised by imperial decree throughout the Roman empire; so the Nasi or Jewish patriarchs at Tiberias annually put forth their decrees determining the time of the Passover, which had the force of law in all the synagogues of the West. On both sides there was now the greatest care to avoid any coincidence in the season of celebration, between the Jewish and the Christian festivals. For a long time the Jews were so entirely without any certain rule on the subject, and their calendar had fallen into such a state of confusion, that they are said to have observed the first and the last days of the feast of Unleavened Bread twice over, to diminish the chance of their having possibly missed the true time. About the middle of the third century, Dionysius of Alexandria, still making use of the *octaeteris*, improved on the imperfect cycle of Hippolytus; and so contrived his calculations, that the celebration of Easter could not occur till after the vernal equinox. This was in defiance of the old lunar usage of the Jews, and was no doubt intended to be so; a fact which deserves notice, as indicating the feeling which at that time so powerfully actuated the Christians in the regulation of their great annual festival. Towards the end of the third century, Anatolius of Alexandria introduced the cycle of nineteen years; and this, in the course of the fourth century, was superseded in the Latin Church by the cycle of eighty-four years, to which I have already referred. In relation to the subject of the present inquiry, it is unnecessary to pursue the history of these ecclesiastical cycles any further than to observe, that in the first half of the sixth century, Dionysius Exiguus constructed a table which brought the Alexandrine and the Roman usage into harmony. This Dionysian cycle gradually superseded all others. In the time of Charlemagne it was accepted universally throughout the West,[1] where it continued to be employed until the general reform of the calendar under Gregory XIII., in the latter half of the 16th century. Uniformity

[1] Ideler, p. 378.

in the mode of keeping Easter was first attempted to be made imperative at the Council of Nice, but if any canons were then framed with this view, they have perished. Practically, as the result of these long discussions, Easter was fixed on the Lord's day next after the full moon happening upon, or immediately following, the vernal equinox; with a provision, that if the full moon should fall on a Sunday, then Easter day should be the Sunday after.[1]

It appears, then, that the final regulation of this festival, which had occasioned such vehement disputes between different sections of the Church in the earlier centuries of our era, was framed, as to the main subject of its celebration—(the anniversary of our Lord's passion and resurrection)—in accordance with the account of the closing scenes of the life of Jesus, contained in the Fourth Gospel. The Church, in its official terminology, significantly designates the "Easter limit," which determines Easter Sunday, τεσσαρεσκαιδεκάτη "the fourteenth." The reader will have to consider whether the influences which I have indicated in previous sections, as operating so powerfully within the Catholic Church, appear to him of such a nature as to account satisfactorily for the substitution of the later account ascribed to John, in place of the earlier traditions,—without compelling us to withdraw our faith from the general historical trustworthiness of the three first Evangelists. There is, however, one argument on behalf of the superior credibility of the day assigned by the Fourth Gospel for the crucifixion of Jesus, which has been urged with so much plausibility, especially by the late Professor Bleek, that it cannot be passed over without a somewhat fuller notice. The argument is this.[2] According to the three first Evangelists,

---

[1] This was, of course, done to avoid coincidence with the Jewish Passover.

The chronological details involved in this long paschal controversy, have been discussed with great thoroughness and exuberant learning, by Hilgenfeld, in the work so often referred to : "Der Paschastreit der alten Kirche, nach seiner Bedentung für die Kirchengeschichte und für die Evangelienforschung urkundlich dargestellt."

[2] Bleek's "Beiträge Zur Evangelien-Kritik," II. 6, 7, 8.

Christ was crucified with the two malefactors on the 15th of Nisan, which was the first day of Unleavened Bread, the great day of the feast. This had a sabbatical character, and was observed with sabbatical strictness. It was a day, therefore, on which no public execution could lawfully take place. From this difficulty the narration in John, it is argued, is wholly free. It represents Jesus to have supped with his disciples, the evening on which he was betrayed, "before the feast of the Passover" (πρὸ τῆς ἑορτῆς τοῦ πάσχα). This must have been on the 13th; the Passover not commencing till the evening of the next day; so that there could have been no legal hindrance to the crucifixion during the earlier hours of the 14th. According to this statement, Christ was crucified on the same day on which the paschal lamb was slaughtered; and this is assumed to be strictly in accordance with the language of Paul (1 Cor. v. 7), "Christ, our Passover, is sacrificed for us." Dr. Bleek contends, that the word παρασκευή (preparation) by which the day of the crucifixion is designated in all the four Evangelists, is not used of every Friday preceding an ordinary Sabbath, but only of a Friday falling on the 14th of Nisan, when the Sabbath following would be a "highday," the first day of "Unleavened Bread." He even thinks that the Synoptists who confounded the Last Supper with the Paschal Supper, and therefore carried it forward from the 13th to the 14th, have unconsciously preserved a trace of the original and true account, by retaining the word παρασκευή, though they have applied it to a day, viz., the 15th, of which, as being itself sabbatical, it could not with propriety be used. Other violations of the sabbatical strictness with which the 15th of Nisan in the paschal week was required by the law to be kept, have been noticed by Bleek in the synoptical narratives: for instance, the coming of Simon of Cyrene "out of the country" (ἐρχόμενον ἀπὸ ἀγροῦ), as if from his labour, on that holy day (Mark xv. 21; Luke xxiii. 26); and further, Matthew's statement (xxvii. 62) that "after the preparation" (μετὰ τὴν παρασκευήν), that is, on the Sabbath itself, the chief priests and Pharisees went to Pilate, and made arrangements with him for setting a watch at the mouth of the sepulchre. From all this Bleek concludes, that the Synoptists have related what could not possibly have taken place on a sabbatical day; and that consequently the account in the Fourth Gospel must be received as the true one.

Notwithstanding the plausibility of this theory, it is open to grave, and, as I think, unanswerable objections. In the first place, what authority has Dr. Bleek for limiting the application of παρασκευή to a Friday coinciding with the 14th of Nisan? The three first Evangelists, by his own showing, cannot have so understood it; and as they were either Jews or used Jewish materials, it is inconceivable how such a misuse of the word could have got into their text. Moreover, usage is clearly against him. Mark (xv. 42) explains παρασκευή for his readers by προσάββατον, which would have been a very inadequate definition, if it referred specially to a sabbath falling on the 15th.[1] Luke's expression (xxiii. 54) is equally general: "It was the day of preparation and the Sabbath was dawning" (ἡμέρα ἦν παρασκευῆς, καὶ σάββατον ἐπέφωσκεν).[2] John, on the other hand, who puts the crucifixion on the 14th, seems purposely to limit the generality of the expression by subjoining —(xix. 14) "of the Passover"—"it was the preparation of the Passover" (παρασκευὴ τοῦ πάσχα). Why should he have added τοῦ πάσχα if παρασκευή meant that of itself? Apparently with the same view, when the word occurs again, further on (v. 31), he adds: "for that Sabbath day was a high day" (ἦν μεγάλη ἡ ἡμέρα ἐκείνου τοῦ σαββάτου).[3] The same inference,

---

[1] According to Lachmann, the Alexandrine and the Vatican here read πρὸς σάββατον, which Meyer treats as a mere clerical error.

[2] The Alexandrine and some other MSS. read παρασκευή. But the sense is the same, rendered in our received version: "that day was the preparation."

[3] In speaking of Jewish observances, John has some expressions peculiar to himself. For instance, he qualifies τὸ πάσχα by adding τῶν Ἰουδαίων. See ii. 13; vi. 4; xi. 55. This never once occurs in the Synoptists. In like manner Jesus, in the Fourth Gospel, when addressing the Jews, says, "Your law," (viii. 17, x. 34) as if he wished to mark his own separation from them.

that *parasceue* simply denoted in the Hellenistic Greek of the Jews, the day before an ordinary Sabbath, seems also fairly deducible from a passage in Irenæus, where he is speaking generally of the sixth day of the week (that is, Friday) as *parasceue* (ἐν τῇ ἕκτῃ τῶν ἡμερῶν ἥτις ἐστὶ παρασκευή (Adv. Hær. I., xiv. 6); and again: "*parasceue*, that is the sixth day, which the Lord made conspicuous by suffering on it" (ibid. v. xxiii. 2). This last circumstance, of course, conferred subsequently, and among Christians, a significance on the term *parasceue*, which it did not previously possess.[1]

The incident of Simon's "coming from the field," and meeting Jesus on his way to Calvary, is unduly dwelt on by Dr. Bleek. Nothing is said, which indicates that he had been engaged in any kind of labour, and his 'coming' might be altogether within the limits of a Sabbath-day's journey. It does not appear from the citations adduced by Dr. Bleek, that the Rabbis were altogether agreed among themselves, what acts were and what were not permissible on a Sabbath day or a sabbatical festival. One authority says,[2] that in case of sacrilege, the offender might be seized and brought to the Temple, and there be put to death in the presence of all the people, at one of the three holy festivals. In the eyes of his enemies the case of Jesus would have come within the scope of this decision. He was regarded as a blasphemer, whose death must be an acceptable offering to offended Deity.[3] His crucifixion was a solemn *auto da fe*, which rather enhanced than profaned the sanctity of a sabbatical day; and the execution along with him of two ordinary malefactors, was only intended to augment by bitterness and contumely the force of this expiatory sacrifice.

---

[1] In the "Gesta Pilati" (A. recently published by Tischendorf), παρασκευή occurs in a context, where it cannot mean anything but the day before a sabbath (xv. 5, p. 253).

[2] Bleek, Beiträge, etc., pp. 145 and 6.

[3] It was a doctrine of the Rabbis, cited by Wetstein and Lücke on John xvi. 2; "Quisquis effundit sanguinem impii, idem facit ac si sacrificium offerat." This sentiment involves the seed of all religious persecution. Christ foresaw its application to his followers.

Independently, however, of these considerations, I cannot believe, that either the original provisions of the Mosaic Law, or the later decisions of the Rabbis, who interpreted their ancient Scriptures with a superstitious servility to the letter, are applicable in all their strictness to the disordered times in which Christ lived, when the old Hebrew theocracy was breaking down under heathen influence, and the factions which disposed of the priesthood and raged in the Synedrium, rendered it difficult to exercise any regular Jewish jurisdiction at all. The fear which Matthew (xxvi. 5) and Mark (xiv. 2) ascribe to the rulers, of rousing the people, if they should apprehend Jesus "on the feast day"—implies, that they would have felt no scruple in doing so on account of the day itself.[1] One consideration to which I have already alluded, seems to me to deprive of all weight the argument on which so much stress has been laid by Professor Bleek. There can be no reasonable doubt, that the Synoptists have transmitted to us the earliest Palestinian tradition respecting the life and death of Jesus; and two of

[1] I took this view, when I first became acquainted with Bleek's argument some years ago. I have since found it confirmed by the judgment of the learned Jewish historian, Jost, in his recent work, "Geschichte des Judenthums und seiner Secten" (III. iii. 12. Vol. I. p. 402, seq.). He says, that all the proceedings against Jesus were irregular, arranged probably by some secret understanding between Caiaphas and Herod; and that there is no trace of a formal judicial investigation, still less of a duly assembled meeting of the Sanhedrim. This is indicated, he thinks, by the unseemly haste and precipitation which marked the whole transaction. Their assembling at so early an hour on the Friday morning betrays the perplexity of the chief priests and rulers of the people. He notices the absence of Gamaliel, one of the Sanhedrim, from all their deliberations, as significant: and adds, in language most remarkable, as coming from a Jew: "here was no trial; it was a private murder. It was not the Jews who crucified Jesus, but a number, not more particularly specified, of determined enemies, who took the responsibility on themselves." (p. 408.)

I ought to observe that, according to Jost, the Rabbis accept it as a fact, that Jesus was crucified on the day before the first day of the Passover, that is on the 14th Nisan. They agree, therefore, in this with the statement of the Fourth Gospel. But Jost shows clearly, in the same place, that not the slightest reliance can be placed on these rabbinical statements, which rested on vague traditions, and discover the greatest ignorance of historical facts. The same motive which induced the Christians to put the crucifixion on the day of the Passover, viz., to prevent any possible confusion of the Jewish and Christian paschas, would have equal weight with the Jews, from the time when the hostility between the two religions became marked and irreconcilable.

them, Matthew and Mark, were themselves Jews. Now, admitting for the sake of argument, that the materials left by them were subsequently worked up into their present form by other hands, still those materials were Jewish, and the Jewish impress remains on them most distinctly to this day. If, then, it had been impossible in the actual state of Judea, for the crucifixion to have taken place on the 15th of Nisan, the writers of those gospels must have known that it was so; and it is to me perfectly incredible how they should have admitted into their narrative a statement which was so flagrantly at variance with the established usage of their country, and which must have carried on its face the plainest evidence of falsehood.

SUPPLEMENTARY NOTE.

A learned friend, S. S., in some "Biblical Notes" communicated to the "Truth-Seeker" (March, 1864), has taken up the defence of the chronology of the Fourth Gospel, relative to the time of the crucifixion, against that of the Synoptists. His conclusion is mainly an inference from the abbreviation of time obtained by his mode of reckoning the years of reigns, supported, as he thinks, by the concurrence of ancient testimony. According to the civil reckoning, he tells us, of Egypt, Syria, Babylon and Asia, the fragment of a year, though it should amount to only a few days, was always reckoned as the first year of a sovereign's reign. By applying this principle to the reign of Tiberius, he saves a year, making the 15th of that reign begin August 29th, A.D. 27. Allowing one year and a part of two others for the public ministry of Christ—including the autumn of 27 A.D., the whole of 28 A.D., and the spring of 29 A.D.—we get 29 A.D. as the year of the crucifixion. According to the calculations of Adams and Airy, it was new moon at Jerusalem that year one hour after sunset on Saturday, April 2nd; consequently the next day was the 1st of Nisan (coincident with the first appearance of the new moon). Thirteen days later was the full moon, on the 14th of Nisan, which, according to this reckoning, must have fallen on Saturday, April 16th (the Sabbath). On the evening of this Saturday (the 14th of Nisan) the Passover was eaten; and the following day (our Sunday), the 15th of Nisan, was the first day of the feast of Unleavened Bread. In this manner, S. S., following the determinations of the astronomers, distributes the events of the Paschal or Passion week; and the arrangement, he contends, is more in accordance with the statements of the Fourth Gospel than with those of the three first.

Upon this I have first to remark in general, that the application of scientific tests to a subject like the present, is often fallacious. It may have the appearance of establishing a precise truth; while, in fact, it is only confirming an error. Given the year, we can, of course, determine by the help of science on what day of that year any particular astronomical phenomenon would occur. But we must first determine from independent evidence the year itself; and that is the very point in dispute. Considering the nature of the documents with which we have to deal, I do not think it possible to get beyond *proximate* chronological results; such, for instance, as that sometime about the middle of the reign of Tiberius, a great religious movement, associated with the names of John the Baptist and Jesus of Nazareth, broke out in Palestine. Within the New Testament itself, I find no certain data for determining the duration of Christ's public ministry. We know that it must have terminated while Pontius Pilate was Procurator of Judæa; and therefore could not have extended beyond 36 A.D., when Pilate was removed from his office. I am strengthened in my persuasion of the great uncertainty accompanying all attempts to fix the precise year of Christ's death, by observing how widely the conclusions of the most learned men have been at variance respecting it,—varying from 29 A.D., through all the intermediate dates, to 35 A.D. (see the Comparative Table, appended to Wieseler's " Chronologische Synopse der vier Evangelien").

S. S. affirms that all foreign testimony confirms his view of the year of Christ's death; alluding, I presume, to the general agreement among early Christian writers, to place that event in the consulship of the two Gemini, C. Rubellius and C. Rufius, which is referred by Zumpt (Annales veter. Regn. et Popul.) and by Clinton (Fasti Romani) to 29 A.D. It becomes necessary, therefore, to examine the grounds on which this agreement appears ultimately to rest. It is quite evident to me, that the point of departure for all these testimonies on which my friend lays so much stress, is the one only definite chronological datum which is to be found in the gospels—viz., Luke iii. 1, 2 (comp. iii. 23); and that they have simply followed one another, with the slightest possible variation, in adopting it. We probably detect the earliest use of this date in the "Acta Pilati," which, from Justin Martyr downwards, were constantly cited by Christian writers as a historical authority.[1] If for the reasons so clearly stated by Thilo (Cod. Apocr. Prolegom. p. cxviii.) and Tischendorf (Evangel. Apocr. Prolegom. p. lxiii. lxv.), we may assume the first part of what is called the "Gospel of Nicodemus" to contain the substance of the original "Acta Pilati"—those Acts introduced the account of our Lord's cross and passion with the following date: "in the 15th year of the reign of Tiberius Cæsar, King of the Romans, and in the 19th year of the reign of Herod, King of Galilee, on the 8th day before the Calends of April, which is the 25th of March, in the consulship of Rufus and Rubellio, in the 4th year of 202nd Olympiad, when Joseph, son of Caiaphas, was high priest of the Jews." This chronological determination, it will be observed, is not associated with the baptism, but with the crucifixion of Jesus, and must correspond, therefore, not to 27 A.D., assigned by

[1] See Tischendorf, "De Orig. et Usu Evangel. Apocryph.," p. 95.

S. S. to the 15th of Tiberius, but to 29 A.D., on his theory the assumed year of Christ's death. It seems to have been found by the very obvious process of looking into the Fasti Romani for the synchronism to the 15th of Tiberius, and can only be reconciled with Luke, on the supposition that the baptism and the crucifixion occurred within the limits of one year. We find Epiphanius at the end of the fourth century, when the paschal controversy had led to great differences among Christians as to the proper time of celebrating Easter, still referring to the "Acta Pilati" as a chronological authority, and remarking that several copies of them which he had seen, varied, in assigning the anniversary of the Passion, between the 8th, the 13th, and the 10th before the Calends of April; though it is significant that, according to Epiphanius, the Quartodecimans, who probably preserved the original tradition, appear to have agreed with the date given above, in observing the 8th (Epiphan. Panar. L. 1.).

What I have said about the probable origin of the date of the passion, traditionally accepted by Christian writers, is rendered additionally clear by the more unexceptionable testimony of Tertullian (adv. Judæos, c. viii.). At the close of an investigation of the numbers in Daniel, he adds: "Tiberii Cæsaris quintodecimo anno imperii passus est Christus, annos habens quasi xxx. cum pateretur."—" Quæ passio—perfecta est sub Tiberio Cæsare, Coss. Rubellio Gemino et Rufio Gemino, mense Martio, temporibus paschæ, die viii. Calend. April. die prima azymorum, quo agnum ut occiderent ad vesperem, a Moyse fuerat præceptum." This date agrees with the one probably assigned by the "Acta Pilati;" and though Tertullian does not here quote the "Acta" as its immediate source, yet it appears from Apologet. c. 21, that he was acquainted with them, and appealed to them as an authority. That he included the baptism in the same year with the passion, is evident from another passage (adv. Marcionem, c. 19) : "Anno xv. Tiberii, Christus Jesus de cælo manare dignatus est, spiritus salutaris." Tertullian, then, does not seem to lend any warrant to S. S.'s distribution of time, which assigns the 15th of Tiberius with the baptism to 27 A.D., and carries on the passion to 29 A.D. If we proceed to the next witness in the series, Clement of Alexandria, we find him, like Tertullian, anxious to make out arithmetical symmetries from the mystic numbers in Daniel; and this does not dispose us *a priori* to look with much confidence to his chronological determinations. Nevertheless, he refers distinctly to Luke iii. 1 (Strom. I. cxxi. § 145) for the 15th of Tiberius as the date of the baptism, when Jesus was about thirty years of age; and he quotes Luke iv. 19, to prove that Christ's ministry could not have lasted more than a year: ὅτι ἐνιαυτὸν μόνον ἔδει αὐτὸν κηρῦξαι καὶ τοῦτο γέγραπται οὕτως, κ. τ. λ. In the following section (146), he mentions some who, aiming at more precision (ἀκριβολογούμενοι), put the passion in the 16th year of Tiberius; but that he himself accepted the 15th, is quite clear from his own reasoning,—that between the birth and the death of Christ, the 15th of Augustus and 15th of Tiberius, the thirty years were completed, which had been announced by the prophet and the gospel: τοῦτο καὶ ὁ προφήτης εἶπεν καὶ τὸ εὐαγγέλιον, πεντεκαιδεκάτῳ οὖν ἔτει Τιβερίου καὶ πεντεκαιδεκάτῳ Αὐγούστου, οὕτω πληροῦται τὰ τριάκοντα ἔτη ἕως οὗ ἔπαθεν. From the passion to the fall of Jerusalem he further reckons forty-two years three months. Origen (Contra Cels. IV. 22), probably following Clement, who had been his teacher, says forty-two years elapsed between the crucifixion and the destruction of Jerusalem; and assuming this last event, as is generally admitted, to have occurred in 70 A.D.—by deducting in round numbers forty-two, we get a proximate date for the passion, 28 A.D. But then, it must be kept in mind that Clement reckons, as we have just seen, from the 15th of Tiberius, which S. S. identifies with 27 A.D., putting the crucifixion in 29 A.D. All this seems to show how impossible it is, with our existing data of time, to get beyond a rough approximation. Scaliger (quoted by Spencer in Orig. c. Cels. 1. c.) and Clinton (Fasti Romani) repudiate the numbers of both Clement and Origen as wrong. Clinton says, "the true interval from the Passover of the 15th of Tiberius, 29 A.D., to the fall of Jerusalem, was forty-one years six months." Julius Africanus (Chron. V. Fragm. apud Routh, Reliquiæ Sacræ, ii. 301, 302) verifies dates from numbers in Daniel, ἐπὶ τὸ Τιβερίου καίσαρος ἑκκαιδέκατον ἔτος, postponing the date of the crucifixion a year: but Jerome, his interpreter, as if in obedience to the received tradition, renders his words, "usque ad annum *quintum decimum* Tiberii Cæsaris, quando passus est Christus." Julius Africanus identifies his date of the 16th of Tiberius with Olympiad 202. 2. The "Acta Pilati," as we have seen, give Olympiad 202. 4. Lastly, Lactantius (Div. Instit. IV. x.) adheres to the date in Luke, with his further traditional specifications, varying only as to the day of the month: "Tiberii Cæsaris anno quintodecimo, id est, duobus Geminis Consulibus, a. d. 10 Calend. April. Judæi Christum cruci affixerunt."

After this enumeration, I cannot admit, that "all foreign testimony" is in favour of S. S.'s distribution of the events of Christ's public ministry. An internal indication of time which S. S. adduces as confirmatory of his view, is furnished by John ii. 20: "forty-and-six years was this temple in building." Herod the Great came to the throne 39 B.C., and commenced the third rebuilding of the temple in the eighteenth year of his reign (Joseph. Antiquit. XV. xi. 1), which coincides, according to the usual calculations (see Meyer, on John ii. 20) with 20 or 19 B.C. Assume the former date as most favourable to S. S.'s theory: then, 46—20=26 A.D., one year before the time assigned by S. S. for the baptism; and this, on the supposition, that the expulsion of the money-changers from the temple, which gave occasion to these words, is left where it occurs in the Fourth Gospel—*i.e.*, at the opening of Christ's ministry. Carried forward, as S. S. contends the event ought to be, to the later period assigned to it by the Synoptists,—we find it two years at least in excess beyond the point of time to which the calculation so obtained conducts us. How little ground there is, and was early felt to be, for chronological exactness in this matter beyond the one date in Luke, which the Fathers for the three first centuries blindly followed and arbitrarily interpreted, is evident from the example of Irenæus (adv. Hæres. II. xxii. 4, 5, 6), not the least intelligent or instructed of their number, who, influenced partly by a feeling of inherent probability, partly by his understanding of a passage in John (viii. 56, 57), and partly, it would seem, by what he accepted as the testimony of the presbyters,— maintained that Jesus only began his ministry when he was about thirty years, but must have prolonged it till he was between forty and fifty.

But the most serious objection to the reckoning which S. S. has founded on the determinations of the astronomers, is, that it is as much at variance, if I understand it rightly, with the chronology of the Fourth Gospel itself as with that of the three first. The difference between them is this: that whereas the Synoptists represent Jesus as eating the Passover with his disciples on the evening of the 14th of Nisan, and suffering on the 15th; the Fourth Gospel, substituting the supper with the feet-washing on the evening of the 13th, puts the passion on the 14th (Friday), and makes the following day (the Sabbath), the first day of the feast of Unleavened Bread. All four agree as to the days of the week; but, in reckoning the days of the month, the Fourth Gospel is one day behind the Synoptists. The chronology of the Fourth Gospel ultimately determined the practice of the Catholic Church, which assumed, on the alleged authority of the apostle John, that the death of Christ, as the true Passover, and the slaughter of the paschal lamb, occurred on one and the same day—viz., the 14th of Nisan. I can find nothing in the Fourth Gospel, to give even plausibility to S. S.'s assertion, that the 14th of Nisan in the year of the crucifixion fell on a Saturday. The Saturday, according to every indication that I can discover in that gospel, was the 15th. If we appeal to astronomical determinations at all, we are at liberty to select for their application the year which, on independent grounds, combines the largest amount of probabilities in its favour. Wieseler, in his very elaborate inquiry into the chronology of the gospels, taking his stand on the narrative of the Synoptists, has given strong reasons for considering this to be the case with 30 A.D. as the year of the crucifixion; and he further states, that Wurm, a German astronomer of high reputation, has ascertained, by calculations made quite irrespective of any theory about the Gospels, that in the year 30, the 15th of Nisan might fall on a Friday—a possibility which I believe S. S. himself would not deny.

In reply to the objection raised by S. S. against the probability of the synoptical account of the Last Supper,—that it represents the company as reclining, after the Roman fashion, on couches, whereas, according to the Law (Exodus xii. 11), they were required to eat the Passover standing, as in haste, like men prepared for a journey—I can adduce the high authority of Otho (Lexicon Rabbinicum), who not only affirms generally (p. 440), "tempore salvatoris nostri Pascha non amplius omnibus illis ritibus celebrabant, quibus celebrabatur ab initio,"—but has shown particularly, in the following passages of his work (pp. 5, 6, 447, 454) that reclining (accubitus) was the mode observed in the celebration of the Passover in the time of our Lord and subsequently.

For the reasons now stated, I am unable to give up the chronological and historical statement of the Synoptists, recommended as it is by its internal probability and self-consistency, for the ingenious theory of my friend, which seems to me as irreconcilable with the Fourth Gospel as with the three first.

SECTION XI.

Recapitulation and Result.

It is time to collect into one view the evidence that has been exhibited in the preceding sections, and to inquire what is the result to which it points. It will be difficult, I think, after an unbiassed comparison of the matter contained in the Apocalypse and the Fourth Gospel, and of the very different form into which it has been cast by each—to believe that both books are the production of the same author. Nothing, probably, but a sort of religious reverence for the traditions of the Church, could ever have allowed a critical mind to acquiesce in such a conclusion. As both works have been ascribed to the apostle John, the first and most obvious method which suggests itself for determining the claim of either to such a parentage, is to compare the tone of thought and sentiment which they respectively exhibit, with the character of its reputed author. No two works can possibly be more strongly contrasted in their form and underlying type of mind, than the Apocalypse and the Fourth Gospel. The former is intensely Jewish in its spirit; abounds in rich, concrete imagery; and is pervaded by a vivid Chiliasm from beginning to end. Its language is so broken and rough, so ungrammatical and solœcistic, as to be absolutely barbarous. The latter, on the contrary, bears traces throughout of a marked antipathy to Judaism; is free from every vestige of Chiliasm; deals rather in the mystic abstractions of the later Alexandrine schools, than in the sensuous pictures of the old prophets; and like the bed of some deep river, is filled to the brim with a continuous flow, if not of pure, at least of such smooth and perspicuous Greek as indicates a long habitude of speaking and thinking in that language. Now, compare with this striking difference between the two works, all that we know from the New Testament and from ecclesiastical tradition, of the personal character of the apostle John. From the former source we learn, that with his mother and elder brother he ardently shared in the Messianic hopes of his age and country; that in him those hopes were profoundly Jewish, tinged with a narrowness and national prejudice which all his love and reverence for the Great Master but imperfectly kept in check. After the death of Christ we find him actively engaged with Peter in establishing the earliest church at Jerusalem, which we know was Jewish,—and, as we not obscurely gather from Acts and the Epistles, identified with the party that opposed itself to the more liberal movement set on foot by Stephen and Paul. Drawing our inferences from the New Testament alone, exclusive of the Fourth Gospel, we should say that John, the son of Zebedee, as there exhibited, was a complete specimen of the primitive Jewish Christian, warm-hearted, honest and devoted, full of zeal for his Master's service, but withal unlettered and uncultivated, and wanting the breadth of mind which only culture can give. The few and vague traditions which have come down from the ancient church of Ephesus, are on the whole—certainly the oldest and most reliable amongst them—in harmony with this description of the apostle John. Upon such evidence, then, as now lies before us, if we had to decide which of the two works under consideration best corresponded with the character of their reputed author, we could hardly hesitate in replying—the Apocalypse.

The direct testimony of antiquity, so far as we can now recover it, is in favour of the same conclusion. Not to insist on the doubtful witness of Papias and Clement of Rome, the earliest distinct citations of the Apocalypse in Justin Martyr and Hippolytus refer it by name to the apostle John as its author; a specification the more remarkable, as it is not attached by these writers to their general citations, numerous as they are, from the other books of the New Testament.[1] In the great writers at the end of the second, and in the first half of the third century, Irenæus, Tertullian, Clement of Alexandria, and Origen, who are our chief authorities for the books constituting our present canon, the Apocalypse is certainly quoted or alluded to in the most express terms, as an undoubted work of the apostle John. Not till the middle of the third and the beginning of the fourth century, in the time of Dionysius of Alexandria, and Eusebius the historian, do we find doubts beginning to be intimated; and we can pretty clearly point to their source in the growing aversion to the old popular Chiliasm, and the conviction that such a doctrine could never have had the sanction of an apostolic name. The superior critical discernment cultivated in the learned school of Alexandria, and displayed to such advantage by Dionysius, had led to the conclusion, that the Apocalypse and the Fourth Gospel could not be by the same hand; while, in adjudicating between them, the strong subjective feeling of what was and must be Christian truth—which in those days mainly decided in the last instance the question of apostolic authorship—gave the preference to the Gospel. So long as learning and intelligence had free play, the question remained an open one; till criticism was suppressed by authority, and the Church decreed, that the Apocalypse and the Gospel were both to be accepted as the work of the apostle John. In the line of testimony on behalf of the Gospel, we are struck with a singular contrast to that alleged for the Apocalypse. It begins to be express and full about the time that the latter becomes faint and wavering, in the period of transition from the second to the third century, when the feeling first clearly manifests itself, which ultimately separated the Catholic Church from the primitive Judaic Christianity. The earliest notice of the Fourth Gospel with the name of the apostle, occurs

---

[1] The only exception that I can call to mind, is a passage in Hippolytus (vii. 32), where Mark's gospel is referred to.

in a work of Theophilus of Antioch, 178 A.D. That gospel expressed distinctly and decidedly the principles which now grew into ascendancy in the Catholic Church, and contained the germ of all the doctrines that were gradually elaborated by successive councils into the scientific formulas of orthodoxy. From the third century downwards its authority in the Catholic Church was undisputed and supreme. Of the ineffectual protests of the Alogi we catch only obscure and uncertain rumours. Already in the third century we perceive a tendency on the part of the Fathers—in the case of variations between the evangelical narratives,—to appeal to the authority of John as decisive—as something normal, to which the statements of the Synoptists must be made to conform. But this, it is obvious, was a dogmatic resource, not a critical judgment. If we compare the contents of the Fourth Gospel with those of the Apocalypse, we cannot fail to be struck with numerous internal indications of the later date of the former. The Apocalypse is deeply impregnated with the Jewish spirit, which entered, we know, so largely into the earliest form of Christian belief, and with the strong colouring of which the original teachings of Jesus himself, as represented by Matthew, were decidedly tinged. Chiliasm was a sure mark of primitive Palestinian Christianity; and the Apocalypse is steeped in the very essence of Chiliasm. That this Chiliastic element should be so entirely wanting in the Fourth Gospel, must be regarded as a sure indication of subsequent origin. Moreover the calm, elevated tone of conscious superiority which pervades it, implies that the first fierce stage of controversy had been triumphantly terminated, and that the Jews, the oldest and bitterest opponents of the Gospel, who stand here in a very different relation to Christ from that which is disclosed by the Synoptists, had been already reduced to a condition of comparative weakness and subjection. We all feel as we read, that it is not the same social atmosphere which we breathe in the epistles of Paul. The unmistakeable influence of philosophical ideas on the language of this gospel, is a phenomenon which can only be explained on the supposition, that a sufficient length of time had now elapsed to allow of the new religion emerging from the sphere of popular sympathies and expectations, where it had its source, into those higher regions of thought which brought it into contact with the speculative theories of the age. Its indications, too, of the relations of Christianity with the outward world, and its significant glances—the more significant that they are but glances— at the mystical belief already associated with the eucharist, furnish another and equal proof of a time when the doctrine and ritual of the church had undergone a development which it could have taken little less than a century from the death of Christ to effect. Any one who keeps in view what apostolic Christianity originally was, and compares it with the features which I have just noticed as marking the Fourth Gospel,—will hardly persuade himself that a work which bears on it such distinct traces of later thought and later usage could have been produced within the limits of the apostolic age, even if we extend that period to the close of the first century.

It is remarkable, that in searching for the evidence of the Fourth Gospel through the second century, we first come upon traces of the doctrine which it contains; then we discover proofs, more or less distinct, of the existence of the book; lastly, but not till quite towards the end of the century, do we find the apostle John mentioned by name as its author. The doctrine of the Logos, which had already been rendered familiar to the more educated Jewish mind through the influence of Philo and other Alexandrine teachers, supplied the grand metaphysical formula, as I have endeavoured to explain in a former section, for reconciling philosophical heathens to the idea of a revelation of God in man. It was the controversial weapon with which the apologists of the second century combated the polytheistic tendencies of the Hellenic world on the one hand, and the monotheistic narrowness of the Jews on the other. We might almost say, that it was evoked out of preexisting elements as an intellectual necessity of the age. As Catholicism predominated over the conflicting tendencies which, in the earlier part of the second century, had shaken the Church to its foundations, the doctrine of the Logos became the binding and consolidating principle of the whole ecclesiastical fabric, which not only recommended itself to the syncretistic spirit that brought the most advanced minds of heathenism and Christianity into vital proximity, but was now urged on the acceptance of the great mass of traditional believers by the authority of the most distinguished of the apostles.

On the subject of the Last Supper the Fourth Gospel and the Synoptists are irreconcilably at variance; and in the Quartodeciman controversy, the Asiatics of Ephesus and its neighbourhood, who must have known from tradition what was the usage of the great apostolic head of their Church, appealed to the example of John in favour of their own practice of keeping the *pascha* on the 14th of Nisan. The most intelligible explanation of this practice, and of the whole controversy that sprang out of it, is to be found in the assumption, that it was at first an annual commemoration on the same day of the month, in obedience to Christ's own command, of the farewell supper, of which he partook with his disciples at the regular celebration of the Jewish Passover; and that this usage became offensive to the Catholics, as perpetuating Jewish ideas, when the Church finally broke with Judaism and transferred the *pascha*, as an essentially Christian observance, from the 14th of Nisan to the Sunday following the full moon on or next after the vernal equinox. The controversy, therefore, though itself occasional, involved the deeper principle on which the whole future of Christianity turned, whether the new religion should henceforth be Judaic or Catholic in tendency. Of the origin of this Quartodeciman practice the Synoptists give a plain and intelligible account; whereas the statement in the Fourth Gospel is not only inconsistent with that account, but makes the usage itself, in the

Christian sense, absolutely impossible. Nothing can appear more strange, than that the author of a book so strongly anti-Judaic as the Fourth Gospel, should be quoted as the authority for a custom which was one of the last relics of Judaism that lingered in the Christian church:—and the legitimate inference is, that the apostle John, whose ways were well known and long remembered at Ephesus, cannot have written the gospel which bears his name. Considered as historical documents, the Synoptical Gospels carry in them much stronger indications of internal probability than the Fourth. They clearly embody the original Palestinian tradition respecting Jesus, which is simple and self-consistent; and in their description of the closing scenes of his life, they furnish the only extant explanation of the origin of the most expressive rite of Christendom, which in its characteristic features still corresponds to that description, and finds in it its Scriptural warrant and justification. That the crucifixion, according to their narrative, should have fallen on a sabbatical day is not, when we consider both the disordered state of the times and the conflict of Rabbinical testimony on the subject, any indication of contrariety to historical fact. At all events, the Synoptists were Jews, who were acquainted with the actual usages of their country at the time, and would never have ventured to introduce into their history what they knew was impossible or absurd. The absence from the Fourth Gospel of the particulars recorded by the Synoptists, and its identifying the time of the crucifixion with that of the Passover on the evening of the 14th, so as to exclude the possibility of Christ himself having legally celebrated it—are remarkable and significant instances of the contrariety between the two accounts, which cannot on either side have been the result of mere chronological oversight, but must on one side or the other have proceeded from design.[1] It is inconceivable, that the synoptical

---

[1] The feet-washing in the Fourth Gospel takes the place of the paschal supper in the Synoptists. In the fifth century the Lord's Supper and the ceremony of feet-

narratives, even that of Matthew, could have been written to subserve the interests of a Jewish Christianity as opposed to Catholicism. What is still Jewish in their tone, is the natural reflexion of a living and genuine tradition. But when we observe how the arrangement of events at the end of the Fourth Gospel coincides with the doctrinal aim of the whole work, how, instead of Christ's eating the Passover, it puts his own death in its place—we can hardly fail to see, in these distinguishing peculiarities of the Johannine narrative, the evidence of a time, when doctrinal considerations had begun to control and modify the simple statements of the primitive tradition; when the Church wished to believe, that it had been purely Christian, in other words, wholly un-Jewish, from the first, and with that view conceived and presented the fundamental fact, on which the gospel proclamation of pardon and eternal life was based, in such a light as to mark it for ever as the final abolition of a covenant which God had decreed should now pass away.

In every critical inquiry of this kind it is more easy to obtain a negative than a positive result. The evidence of which I have just exhibited a summary, will not allow me to regard the Fourth Gospel as of apostolic origin in the strict historical sense. But if I am asked, who was its author, and when it was written, I confess I am unable to give a categorical answer. If Papias, as Eusebius informs us, cited testimonies from the first epistle of John—as I can have little doubt that the author of that epistle and of the gospel were one and the same person—the author must have been living, and both works probably written, before the middle of the second century. The death of Papias is usually assigned to 163 A.D. We find thus a

---

washing, or, as it was then called, the *pedilavium*, were both celebrated on the Thursday immediately preceding Good Friday,—what, in later times, has been known under the name of Maundy Thursday (probably *dies Mandati*). But we have the authority of Augustine (Epist. 118 ad Januarium) for saying, that the Lord's Supper was the more ancient and general custom, and the *pedilavium* of later introduction and more partial observance. (See Riddle's Christian Antiquities, Book V. ch. iii. p. 632.)

probable *terminus ad quem*. Can we suggest a *terminus a quo*? It has occurred to me (as I have already intimated), in studying the internal indications of the Fourth Gospel, and comparing them with the known course of historical events, that they point to a time when the Church had finally emancipated itself from Jewish bondage, and Jerusalem had ceased to be its centre of religious interest and reverence.[1] Such a time I find most clearly indicated in the results of the suppression of the Jewish revolt under Bar Cochba, subsequent to 135 A.D. This is, of course, nothing more than conjecture, supported by no direct evidence. Nevertheless, between these two events—the substitution of Ælia Capitolina for Jerusalem by Hadrian, and the death of Papias—I seem to find a period within which the origin of the Fourth Gospel might, without improbability, be placed. I look upon the final disengagement of Christianity from Judaism, which occurred in the reign of Hadrian, as the first decided impulse given by outward events to that great Catholic movement, which Paul commenced, but in his life-time could not effectually sustain against Judaic opposition, and of which we can distinctly trace the influence in the tone of the Fourth Gospel, betraying the same movement at a more advanced stage and in a more comprehensive form. Most providentially the different books of the New Testament reveal to us the successive steps of the internal self-development which the new life imparted to the world by Christ went through, while the religion was yet a free spontaneous energy of popular conviction and zeal, unfettered by the canons of councils and imperial decrees, till it reached its amplest phase of spiritual expansion in the Fourth Gospel.

---

[1] "The hour cometh, when ye shall neither in this mountain, nor yet at *Jerusalem*, worship the Father" (John iv. 21). To which may be added the significant passage (John xi. 43): "If we let him thus alone, all men will believe on him: and *the Romans shall come and take away both our place and nation*:" which seems to me to have a more apposite reference to the destruction of Jerusalem under Hadrian, than to that under Titus; for it was not till the former event that the Jewish nationality was totally destroyed.

It is of less importance to be able to say precisely, by whom it was written, than to feel sure that we possess in it a genuine record of the progressive, self-consistent working of a new and higher truth, by which God was preparing a way for the spiritual renovation of mankind. If from the more elevated position which we now occupy, we are sometimes tempted to regret that the reign of a living faith should have come to an end so soon, only to be followed by the servile worship of a dead letter,—we should recollect the circumstances under which this change took place. In view of the future that was impending, it was fortunate for the world that the spirit of primitive Christianity, in its most diversified manifestations, should have been encased, as it were, in such a body of writings as our present canonical scriptures. The great truths involved in it, were thus preserved from mutilation and corruption by the reverence of superstition itself, ere the storms came on which swept away the ancient civilization, and deformed or destroyed every doctrine and institution, which had no surer vehicle of transmission to posterity than tradition. The ark was now built, and the Gospel was shut up safe within it. Though the rains descended and the floods came, it rode securely on the bosom of the deep, while the earth lay buried under a deluge of ignorance and barbarism; till it rested at length on the tops of the re-appearing mountains, and its windows were opened again, and a free spirit went forth from its sacred enclosure and brought back to it the tokens of a reviving humanity.

F. C. Baur has given it as his opinion, that the Fourth Gospel must be of Alexandrine origin; and if this only means, that it was evidently conceived under the influence of Alexandrine ideas, he is no doubt right. But the tradition of the Church from the first seems to me too steady and uniform, to admit of our looking for any other place, as the immediate seat of its production, than Ephesus. If anything can be accepted as a fact on mere traditional evidence, it is that the Fourth

Gospel came out of that circle of religious influences of which Ephesus was the centre. The intercourse between the great cities of the Levant and of Egypt was in that age so ready and frequent, and the diffusion of ideas under Roman centralization so rapid and easy, that Alexandrine philosophy may well be conceived to have exerted as much influence at Ephesus as in Alexandria itself. Irenæus, who was a native of that part of Asia, distinctly connects the origin of the Fourth Gospel with Ephesus. It may be thought perhaps, that the testimony of Irenæus proves too much for our present argument; and that if we accept it as sufficient to establish the locality of the origin, we ought also to accept it for the person of the author, which can, in that case, be no other than the apostle John. But the distinction is obvious. A person of ordinary knowledge and intercourse with mankind, might be well assured from what quarter a certain production had come, and yet not possess the critical faculty—especially after years of absence in a remote part of the world (as was the case with Irenæus in Gaul)—for deciding on the more difficult question of personal authenticity. Besides, we of the present day hardly familiarize to ourselves sufficiently the loose way of thinking on such subjects, which prevailed in ancient times, and more particularly among the ancient Christians. With all the great centres of Christian activity, the name of some distinguished apostle was associated, as of James the Less with Jerusalem, of Peter with Rome, and of John with Ephesus. Whatever sprang out of the natural impulse originally imparted by such an apostle, and might be regarded as the natural growth of the faith planted by him in that place, was referred to him by the general sentiment as its immediate source. There is evidence, I think, of two successive religious movements, each associated with the name of the apostle John, in the two works which have been the subject of comparison in the present inquiry;—an early one, closely connected with the Jewish Christianity of Palestine, in the

Apocalypse,—and a later, the fruit of more advanced development, in the Fourth Gospel. We find possibly the hidden link of mental connexion between these two works in the doctrine of an *hypostatized* or impersonated Logos, which appears distinctly in a remarkable passage of the Apocalypse (xix. 11-16), and which runs, as we have seen, through every part of the Fourth Gospel. It might be a doctrine which distinguished the teaching of the Church founded at Ephesus by John, as the doctrine of the Spirit may be said to characterize the theology of Paul. But the doctrine of the Logos was one peculiarly susceptible of development, and open to fresh construction and ever-widening application with the new intellectual demands of the age. This part of Asia was the special seat of the sharpest conflicts of tendency which marked the second century. The retrogressive movement which aimed at a revival of the primitive faith and zeal, and the movement in the opposite direction which sought to bring Christianity into closer harmony with the civilization and philosophy of the age—here found their battle-field. It was the country of Chiliasm and Montanism, as well as of the efforts that were made to suppress them. Polycarp and Polycrates, the most zealous upholders of Quartodeciman usage, and Apollinaris, its decided opponent, were all from this district. The two works which bear the name of John, furnish another example from the same part of the world, of productions of divergent tendency, announcing distinct stages of spiritual growth, which, nevertheless, by their common reference to the great apostolic head of the church at Ephesus, excluded the idea of direct antagonism, and seem to indicate a continuous unfolding of organic self-development from a common root. Whether and how far the immediate author of the gospel may have had personal intercourse with the apostle, and to what extent he may have introduced into his work ideas ultimately derived from him, we have no present means of determining. Whatever the writer may have derived from that source, it clearly underwent a great change of form in passing through the deep subjective working of his own mind. If he has delivered to us (as I believe he has), whether through an apostolic medium or not, the 'consummate flower' of the faith which was planted in the world by Christ, he certainly has not presented it in the words of the great Teacher himself. The language in which the Fourth Gospel conveys to us the discourses of Christ, is cast in the same mould with that of the epistle and of those portions of the gospel where the writer speaks in his own person. We are impressively taught by this fact,—which is equally certain, on every theory of authorship,—not to put our trust in a verbal Christianity, "in the letter which killeth,"—but to surrender our whole souls to "the spirit which giveth life." To me there is something far less objectionable and offensive in the supposition, that we have in this gospel the free and genuine utterances of one who gives us his own deep personal conception of the truth which he had imbibed in the heart of the Johannine Church, than in admitting—which we must do, if the apostle John were the author—that one who had leaned on Jesus' bosom and caught the very accents that fell from his lips, instead of treasuring them up with reverent exactitude, has unscrupulously transformed them into his own language, and invested them with a form and colour which did not originally belong to them.

Eusebius informs us, there were two Johns whose names were associated with the traditions of the church at Ephesus: one, the Apostle; the other, known as the Presbyter. When the latter lived, we are not told; but Eusebius says, that in his day their two graves were shown at Ephesus. With his undisguised aversion to the Chiliastic doctrines of the Apocalypse, it was not unnatural for Eusebius to suggest, whether the Presbyter rather than the Apostle might not have been the author of that book. It may occur to some—and the inference would be favoured by the result of the foregoing examination—that the other alternative may possibly represent the truth. It is certainly remarkable, that the Second and Third Epistles, which in their language and manner closely resemble the First, have both of them in their heading the title 'Presbyter' (ὁ πρεσβύτερος)—a fact, which our version conceals by rendering the word 'Elder.' If this John were the author of the Fourth Gospel, we can account for its being so uniformly referred to Ephesus; and we can also understand how, in process of time, when early traditions were easily confounded, the Apostle should be substituted for the Presbyter as the author of the gospel—especially where there was so much readiness to claim an apostolic origin for every work of high ecclesiastical authority and influence, and where the two Johns appear each of them to have stood in such close connexion with the church of Ephesus.

SECTION XII.

The Bearing of this Question on the general conception of Christianity.

" Si l'on veut rendre justice à l'orthodoxie, et donner une explication satisfaisante de sa force et de sa durée, il faut—constater ce désir de communication réelle avec Dieu, cette peur de perdre de vue le Dieu vivant, le Dieu réel et accessible, le Dieu adorable, digne d'amour secourable. On peut tenir pour certain, que si les cœurs étaint rassurés à cet égard, les esprits secoueraint bien vite ces misérables sophismes historiques et speculatifs auxquels ils ont tant de peine à donner créance, mais qu'ils n'osent abandonner de peur de sacrifier un plus grand bien."
—Félix Pécaut,—De l'Avenir du Protestantisme, p. 19.

It will be considered by many an insuperable objection to the views which I have here ventured to maintain, that they exhibit the evangelists as irreconcilably at variance on some fundamental particulars of the gospel history, and that they deprive of direct apostolic authority, what has been usually regarded as the most complete and authentic display of the person and teaching of Christ, and the truest expression of the eternal relation of the human and the divine. There is also something exceedingly repulsive to our modern feeling of reverence for a holy book, that it should seem to lie under the imputation of professing to be what it is not, and should assume an apostolic name, where the hand of an apostle, it is affirmed, has never been. These, as they strike the mind on a first view, are doubtless grave objections, and are entitled to a grave and thoughtful reply. Nevertheless, what the historical critic has alone to consider, when he embarks in an inquiry of this description, is the evidence of facts. To evade the conclusion to which that evidence legitimately leads, from the apprehension of assumed consequences, is really to distrust God, and to interfere with the possible order of his Providence. His truth may have a way and method of its own, which we have no right with our limited field of vision to prejudge. The proper answer to any theory to which we may feel ourselves strongly averse, is to show that the facts on which it is based are incorrectly stated, and the inferences from them illogically drawn.

(1.) I may here remark, that some of the most plausible objections to the natural and obvious issue of the present investigation, have acquired an exaggerated importance from the artificial ground assumed by Protestantism, to set up an adequate counterpoise in the popular belief to the authoritative claims of the Church of Rome. It was felt, in the first great struggle of the Reformation, that the pure Word of God must be produced to encounter the arbitrary decrees of man. Hence the main effort of Protestant learning was twofold: first, to prove that the contents of our New Testament Canon—especially the four gospels—came directly or mediately from an apostolic source, and carried with them an absolute apostolic sanction; secondly, to deduce from their contents a complete and definite system of doctrinal belief, which could be made imperative on the conscience of every individual, as the true Gospel of Christ. It is not my present object to show that neither of these objects has ever been successfully accomplished, as the incurable disagreement among Protestant sects, so forcibly urged by Bossuet and Möhler, unanswerably demonstrates; nor, further, that this intellectual conception of faith, commenced by the Fathers, elaborated by the Schoolmen, and inherited from them by the great divines of the Reformation, who fixed the type of Protestantism,—is wholly at variance with the essential genius of Christianity. I simply mean to assert, that the fundamental assumption of this system lays a burden of responsibility on the several books of the New Testament which there is no internal indication of their having ever assumed, and the gratuitous exaction of which throws unnecessary difficulties in the way of establishing the divine origin and influence of the great spiritual renovation introduced into our planet by the prophet of Nazareth. Books, in our sense of the word, had nothing to do with the earliest propagation of Christianity. A change was wrought in the individual soul, by awakening it to a deeper sense of the Living God, and the need of reconciliation with Him, in expectation of the solemn judgment which He was about to execute on a guilty world. All this was effected by the words of the preacher, thrilling with faith and love, and carrying with them the spirit of God into the hearts of his hearers. A parallel phenomenon in modern times, throwing much light on the earliest history of Christianity, may be found in the extraordinary effects which resulted from the missionary labours of the two Wesleys. The grand three-fold impression produced by such preaching was this: personal devotedness to the crucified and risen Christ, who had brought a new life into the world; earnest craving for redemption from the sinfulness of men's actual condition; enthusiastic belief in a future approaching state of righteous retribution, which took so strong a hold on many minds, that it became to them a greater and nearer reality than the present world. Such was primitive Christianity. It floated from land to land and sank into the lowest depths of society, with the tide of a living tradition, kept pure in its essential elements by the sincerity and holiness of those who sustained and diffused it. When at length it began to deposit itself in a written form, it was at first probably nothing more than a private record or memorandum, made without any reference to posterity—for the world was believed to be on the eve of dissolution. As such record was communicated through the ordinary occasions of intercourse, from hand to hand, and church to church, it became by degrees a sort of common property for the whole body of believers, which every one felt himself at liberty to enlarge or modify, according as he believed he was in possession of additional or more accurate knowledge. The letters of the apostle Paul are, it is true, an exception to this general description of the earliest writings that circulated in the Church. They were not, like the evangelical narratives, composed of divers materials, gradually collected and accumulated—the fruit of a spreading and diversified tradition. They were called forth by particular occasions, and addressed to particular communities. They were definite, therefore, and complete in their form from the first; and were naturally preserved with great care and reverence by the churches to which they had been originally directed. On this account we must regard the Pauline letters as the most authentic documents now extant on primitive Christianity. With this exception, I believe the earliest Christian literature to have originated in the manner which I have described; and to any one who will distinctly realize to himself the circumstances of the case, it must be obvious, how wholly inapplicable to such a state of things, are all our modern notions of literary property and the claims of authorship. Such notions never entered the heads of the good and simple people among whom the message of glad tidings found its earliest welcome. When, indeed, in the course of the second and third centuries, the teaching and defence of Christianity passed into the hands of a literary class, the case was somewhat altered. Room and motive were now given for the production of writings of a properly fictitious character, conceived in the interests of a party, or designed to meet the demands of an impatient curiosity, which the original tradition did not adequately satisfy. Of this kind were most of what are called the Apocryphal Gospels; although such of them as bear this character most strongly, belong, I am inclined to believe, to a later period.[1] It was to counteract incipient tendencies of this kind, especially in the speculative schools of Gnosticism, and to furnish an authoritative rule of

---

[1] Tischendorf, de Evangeliorum Apocryphorum Origine et Usu, P. I. § 3.

faith and practice for the mass of believers, that a movement commenced throughout the Church towards the close of the second century, for collecting a body of trustworthy writings which might be appealed to as a criterion to discriminate heretical error from Catholic trnth. The principle of selection was in no sense critical. Books were admitted or rejected or considered doubtful, according as they were warranted or not by general tradition, or as they were felt in their spirit and contents to correspond or be at variance with the standard of faith and practice which had been upheld from the beginning in the most ancient churches. The reason of the difference which every one feels on comparing the canonical with the apocryphal gospels, between the sober, practical wisdom, and sweet natural pathos of the one, and the coarseness and wild extravagance of the other—is to be found in the fact, that the framers of the Canon kept close to the primitive tradition, which had been handed down in the churches from the earliest times by devout and simple-minded men, and which concentrated the thoughts of believers on the one essential point of preparing themselves by repentance and faith for the great retribution to come; while they excluded from their collection, as it were unconsciously and by a sort of spiritual tact, all such writings as were felt by them to be extraneous to the purely religious tradition, and were mainly of an intellectual or imaginative character. The distinction is a vital one; for it proves that, from the first, Christianity was regarded by those who were mainly instrumental in founding it, not as a philosophical speculation, but as a moral and spiritual work.

To return to the Fourth Gospel, the origin of which, whoever was its author, belongs to the primitive age of the Church, and cannot be brought lower than the first half of the second century;—it is clear, that we must apply to the problem of its authorship, not the principles of our modern literary code, but the looser notions,—not consciously involving any question of moral right or wrong,—which were notoriously current among the Christians of the earliest period, and long retained their influence on the minds of their more cultivated successors.[1] If we keep this in view,—and consider further, that theologians, in their apologetic zeal, have laid an undue stress on the supposed implications of apostolic origin in the book itself—we are in a position to weigh dispassionately evidence for and against a simple historical fact, without finding ourselves reduced to the painful alternative of authenticity or imposture. For in this offensive light some have not scrupled to set the present question. Even a man so large-minded as the late Baron Bunsen, and usually so free and fearless in his criticism, has been driven by his predilection for a foregone conclusion, to the incredible hardihood of asserting, that if John's gospel is not authentic, there can be no historical Christ, and no Christian Church.[2] So long as such strong

[1] Of the freedom with which a common material was used, and the loose, uncertain grounds on which authorship was assigned, we have a signal evidence in the different forms of the Clementines, the so-called Ignatian Epistles, and the Apostolical Canons and Constitutions. Kindred phenomena, with perhaps a distincter consciousness and purpose of fraud, occur at a still earlier period among the Alexandrine Jews and the Greeks; as, for instance, in the Sibylline verses and the poems circulated under the title of "Orphica." See generally on this subject: Valckenaer, "De Aristobulo Judæo;" Wesseling, "De Fragmento Orphei, de Aristobulo, etc.;" and Lobeck, "Aglaophamus," Lib. II.; "Orphica," I. iv. In the earliest movements of religious enthusiasm, the fervour of men's feelings overpowers the clearness of their ideas. The elements of truth and falsehood are often strangely commingled in a sort of spiritual chaos; so that it takes centuries to separate them, and make men sensible of their distinction. Welcker, who has devoted an entire life to the study of this side of human nature, makes the following suggestive remark: "Es gehört zu den Mysterien der Geschichte, wie Gottes Geist, heilige und ehrwürdige Satzungen, Ueberzeugungen und Vorurtheile, und andrerseits Schwäche, Menschenwerk, künstliche durch die Menge getragene Systeme und Duplicität, nach den Zeiten und Umständen, gegen einander stehen, herrschen oder vorherrschen." (Griechische Götterlehre, ii. p. 27.)

[2] "Hippolytus and his Age," I. p. 115. Dr. Bleek, on the whole, perhaps, the ablest defender of the authenticity of the Fourth Gospel, with more judgment admits that, should the question be finally decided against him, this would not affect "the genuine historical truth of Christianity." With regard to the alleged immorality implied in the circulation of a book under an assumed name, he observes that such a fact (supposing it to be established) must not be tried by the standard

prejudices prevail, which stake the existence of Christianity itself on the issue of a critical inquiry, it is impossible that this question should be impartially discussed. Let us see, then, what the Fourth Gospel actually says of itself. Must an honest admission of the result of preponderant evidence, necessitate the conclusion, that the most spiritual and sublime of all the books of the New Testament had an immoral origin? I do not believe, that so startling a contrariety could occur in the order of Providence rightly understood. The semblance of it is occasioned by the gratuitous assumptions and unreasonable demands of an artificial theology.

In the gospel itself we meet with no allusion to the apostle John, till we come to the closing scenes of the history (xiii. 23), where he is introduced (though without being named) as a disciple "whom Jesus loved," and as "leaning on his bosom." That John was meant in this passage, there can be no doubt from the uniform tradition of the Church, which constantly distinguished the apostle by the epithet ἐπιστήθιος. A further reference equally indirect, yet still not to be doubted, occurs in ch. xviii. v. 15, where he is coupled with Simon Peter as 'another disciple,' and represented as entering with Jesus into the palace of the high-priest. His being allowed to remain there unquestioned, while Peter was roughly interrogated, is ascribed to his previous acquaintance with the high-priest. The same disciple is evidently meant, still without being named, in the beautiful passage where the dying Jesus commends his mother to the care of his bosom friend (xix. 25-27). Not till we come to ch. xix. 35, where mention is made of blood and water issuing from the pierced side of Christ, does a single expression occur, which can by any possible construction be made to imply, that the apostle spoken of was the author of the gospel; and even here the inference is by no means unambiguous. The words are these: "He that saw

of our times, and that Ecclesiastes, Daniel, and the Psalms, as usually cited, are open to the same imputation, without having forfeited their title to be received into the Canon of the Old Testament. (See Beiträge zur Evangelien-Kritik, p. 263.)

it bare record, and his record is true: and he knoweth that he saith true, that ye might believe."[1] They do not seem to me to mean more than this: that the writer, whoever he was, firmly believed in the recorded occurrence on the authority of an eye-witness; but he does not say, that he was himself that eye-witness. On the contrary, had he intended that, he would have used another tense, and said μαρτυρεῖ, not μεμαρτύρηκεν. The adoption of the present tense in the latter part of the sentence—ἐκεῖνος, οἶδεν, etc.—is no objection to this interpretation. Having cited his witness, the writer by a form of speech which constantly occurs in historical narrative, throws himself back into the time of his authority, in order to give greater weight to the assertion of his trustworthiness. The same disciple, still unnamed, is next described as going with Simon Peter to visit the abandoned sepulchre, and as believing in consequence of what he saw. These are all the indications that we have of John in the first twenty chapters of the Fourth Gospel; and here I believe the gospel to have originally ended; for no words can more clearly mark the termination of an entire work than ch. xx. 30, 31: "Many other signs also wrought Jesus in the presence of his disciples, which are not written in this book: but these are written, that ye may believe that Jesus is the Christ, the Son of God, and that by believing ye may have life through his name."

Chapter xxi. has all the signs of being a subsequent addition. The appearances of Christ after the resurrection, which in the twentieth chapter, as in Luke's account (xxiv. 49; Acts i. 4), are confined to Jerusalem, are here transferred, as in Matthew (xxviii. 10, 16), to Galilee. Peter is here brought prominently forward, as if to counterbalance the claims of the beloved disciple, so distinctly asserted in the previous chapters; and there is an evident attempt to meet the diffi-

---

[1] καὶ ὁ ἑωρακὼς μεμαρτύρηκεν, καὶ ἀληθινὴ αὐτοῦ ἐστὶν ἡ μαρτυρία, καὶ ἐκεῖνος οἶδεν ὅτι ἀληθῆ λέγει, ἵνα καὶ ὑμεῖς πιστεύσητε.

culty occasioned by the non-fulfilment of the traditional expectation, that that disciple would survive till the second coming of Christ.[1] In this supplementary chapter, we meet for the first time with the assertion, that the beloved disciple was the author of the gospel (xxi. 24): "this is the disciple which testifieth of these things, and wrote these things; and we know that his witness is true."[2] We may, therefore, conclude that this addition could not have been made to the original work, before the belief had become confirmed and general among the heads of the Church (the ἐκκλησιαστικοί, as they are called by Eusebius, who were the reliable transmitters of the primitive tradition, and the earliest framers of a canon), that the gospel was the production of the apostle John; and of this we have no clear evidence till the latter part of the second century. If I am right in this inference, the original gospel and the appendix may possibly have been separated from each other by the interval of about half a century.[3]

[1] The expectation had probably its origin in the words of our Lord, preserved by Matthew (xvi. 28): "There be some standing here, which shall not taste of death, till they see the Son of Man coming in his kingdom." As John outlived all the other apostles, these words, it was naturally supposed, would have their fulfilment in him. When he died, and expectation was again disappointed, a new meaning had to be found for them; and to this there is distinct allusion in this twenty-first chapter, v. 23. The same circumstance gave rise to the fable widely current in the Middle Ages, which has associated a superstitious awe with the eve of St. John—that the apostle is not actually dead, but lies slumbering in his grave till the last day. We have other evidence of the feelings produced by this frustration of the popular hope in 2 Peter iii. 4.

[2] οὗτός ἐστιν ὁ μαθητὴς ὁ μαρτυρῶν περὶ τούτων καὶ ὁ γράψας ταῦτα, καὶ οἴδαμεν ὅτι ἀληθής ἐστιν ἡ μαρτυρία αὐτοῦ. This is a repetition in another form of what has already been stated (ch. xx. 35), with the substitution (which should be noticed) of the present μαρτυρῶν for the past μεμαρτύρηκε, and the further assertion of authorship. Verse 25 is an amplification of ch. xx. 30.

[3] Our oldest MSS. do not go back to the time, when this appendix (if it be one) must have been added to the original termination of the gospel: so it is found in all of them. But it is remarkable, that of the passages which are supposed to refer to the Fourth Gospel in the Apostolic Fathers, in Justin Martyr, in Tatian, in Athenagoras, in Theophilus of Antioch, in Hippolytus, and in Irenæus, not one corresponds to anything contained in ch. xxi.; though most of them allude apparently to ch. xx. The earliest trace of any such allusion I find in Tertullian, De Anima, c. 1. (Semler's Index Loc. S. S. ex Joanne), where, however,

Undoubtedly, in the first twenty chapters, which I suppose to have constituted the original work, it is the design of the writer to place the relation of the beloved disciple to Christ in a very solemn and mysterious light, as an eye-witness and close observer of the trial before the high-priest and of the death on the cross, and as the receiver of the last commands of his Lord. The studious avoidance of his name heightens the effect; and the exclusion of all mention of the sons of Zebedee, so prominent in the synoptical narrative, is very significant. They are alluded to once in the supplementary chapter (v. 2), but without any distinction, lumped up, as it were, in a general enumeration of the disciples assembled in Galilee after the resurrection. It may be suspected, that their traditional reputation was too closely associated with a Jewish Christianity to admit of either of them being put conspicuously forward in their original characters as the authority for a new and higher phase of gospel truth. At the same time, John was reverenced as the founder of the Asiatic Church, where his name had eclipsed that of Paul who preceded him. It was further well known, that he was honoured with strong marks of personal confidence and affection by Jesus during his life-time; and there was also a vivid tradition current among the early Christians, that at the last supper he had been assigned the place of honour, and lay with his head on the bosom of his Master. On the whole, therefore, I do not doubt, that this gospel was accepted from the first as an expression of the faith that had triumphed in the church of which John was regarded as the head, and that, in this way, it claimed for itself indirectly the sanction of his name. This, we know, was in full accordance with the usage of those early Christian times; just as any doctrine or usage emanating from Rome, would have been conceived to

---

the gospel is not mentioned at all, but only the fact stated, that John died, though he had expected to live to the second coming (ch. xxi. 23). Tertullian may have received the story through tradition as well as from a written source.

carry with it the authority of Peter. The tradition perpetuated in these ancient churches, notwithstanding the modifications which it constantly underwent, was still supposed to maintain an unbroken connexion with the apostolic source from which it flowed. I venture, however, to think, that within the limits of the original work, there is not one passage which clearly affirms the beloved disciple to have been its author; and that such an interpretation would never have occurred to any one, had it not been suggested by an external tradition which grew up by the side of the gospel, and gathered strength with its diffusion and acceptance. The historical value of that tradition I have attempted to estimate in a previous section of this essay. Although a careful sifting of such evidence as lies within our present reach, has made me feel all but morally certain, that the apostle John could not have written the Fourth Gospel, yet an examination of its contents, exclusive of what I believe to be a later addition, fully relieves me from the painful alternative, so strongly urged by the advocates of the old theory, of a single choice between authenticity and imposture.

(2.) Another objection to the conclusion at which I have arrived, will to many minds seem still more formidable—viz., that it unsettles the habitual reliance on a directly divine authority, and substitutes for words which we have been accustomed to cherish as those of Christ himself, the language and, to some extent, even the ideas of one unknown. I deeply sympathize with this objection; for it is one that will be felt by the most religious natures. It is a cold and heartless reply to say,—"such is the evidence of facts; they dispel a groundless dream,"—and then leave the disenchanted to find their consolation where best they may. For myself I am convinced, that we are not reduced to this hard necessity; for there is a higher view of Scripture than the popular theory admits, which instead of annihilating faith, only gives it new impulse and wider range.

Words at best, even from the most gifted lips or pen, are a very inadequate exponent of the power of a life and the working of a spiritual principle. Their full meaning can only be pressed into them by the responsive consciousness of the mind to which they come. Even were they inspired by absolute truth, their apprehension and effect must be measured by the capacity of the recipient soul. The same truth, expressed with the same fulness and precision, cannot be grasped and retained in the same way by all the different minds in which it finds a home. In regard to spiritual truth, which is incapable of subjection to the definite test of the outward sense, it is of its very nature, that it should multiply itself into an endless variety of intellectual and imaginative forms. The greater and richer the truth, the deeper it penetrates into the heart of humanity,—the more diversified and apparently irreconcilable will the modes of its utterance and representation become. If it be a living truth which has struck root in the heart and conscience of man, it will grow with the humanity which it inspires. I believe this view to be fully borne out by the general experience of human nature. Let us see how it applies to the case of Christianity.

The new life infused into our race by the gospel, consisted mainly in a quickened sense of the reality of "things unseen and eternal," and of man's personal relation to them and interest in them. As a necessary consequence, it brought with it a stronger conviction of the degrading bondage of selfishness and carnality, and an earnest longing for deliverance into a higher state of freedom, purity and love. This in its essence was primitive Christianity: and the wonderful change which it wrought in multitudes, was not the effect of any formal system of positive doctrine—of lectures and disputations, after the manner of the old philosophical schools—but of the simple working among men of a profoundly spiritual nature, filled to its inmost depths with the consciousness of a divine presence, and obeying with single-minded faithfulness the call which it had received from above, to go forth and bring back mankind to a forgotten Father in heaven, and prepare them for their everlasting inheritance in Him. The grand trusts which this spiritual influence awakened, and which are ever latent in the interior of our humanity, Jesus set forth in language and with illustrations the most homely and popular, suggested by the present wants and level to the actual capacity of those whom he addressed, and therefore clothed in the prevailing beliefs and expectations of his age and country. He spoke with authority, because he spoke with intense conviction. He saw his ultimate object with a clearness, and grasped it with a tenacity, which nothing could dim or shake, though he did not always discern how God would bring it to pass; and of the future he knew nothing but what lay immediately before him. Still he held on his way with deep trust in the final issue of the divine purposes, in spite of disappointment, treachery, and abandonment. With the dauntless courage which only religious faith can inspire, he waged unsparing war on the hypocrisy and hardheartedness and spiritual deadness of the professed teachers and guides of the people, till the malignity of his enemies cut short his brief career by a hurried and violent death. Thus the seed was sown. Gradually it absorbed into its inner life all the kindred elements that had for centuries been silently fermenting in the heart of the old civilization. The simplicity of the means employed stands out in marvellous contrast with the greatness of the effects which ensued. But so God works. This very contrast is, to me, an indication of his presence in the movement. God, who is a Spirit, can only reveal himself through the kindred spirit of man; and the fulness of the revelation must always, therefore, be in proportion to the purity, the elevation, and the spiritual discernment of the human media through which it makes its way. There is this peculiarity in the manifestation of spiritual truth through a human personality,—that its influence is contagious. It spreads to other minds, and stirs up a kindred consciousness in them. For a deep, mysterious sympathy binds together all spiritual natures. Those to whom that higher message comes, turn instinctively to its source. They concentrate their trust and reverence on one who seems to belong to a loftier order of being;—who brings down the divine into the midst of the human,—and holds up before them, in vivid concrete embodiment, that of which they had possessed already in their better moments a dim and vague presentiment, but had never before beheld the actual realization. A great truth now flashes on them for the first time in all its clearness, and brings with it its own warrant of a divine source;—the sense of their personal relation to a living God, and of their need of moral regeneration to become the objects of his complacency, and the sharers of his richest blessing. They pass into the consciousness of another and a purer world than that in which they have hitherto lived, haunted wherever they turn by an awful sense of the divine presence—

"With glimpses of the mighty God delighted and afraid."[1]

A true revelation, therefore, in its first stage is a spiritual influence emanating from some eminently devout and holy personality—in other words, it is the Spirit of God working through a human soul. One in essence, the new life so diffused takes a different outward mould in every mind which it thoroughly penetrates; though in all it is referred to the common personal source, which first brought it into view and exhibited it as a human possibility. The characteristic of primitive Christianity was devotion to the person of Christ. It had this in common with all earnest religious movements that have sprung up either outside it or within it;—that the bond of union was attachment to the person of a founder. But it had two features peculiar to itself: first, that instead of kindling zeal about some insulated point of doctrine or abstract speculation, it took its stand on the fundamental moral

[1] Charles Wesley.

consciousness of humanity, and laid the whole stress of its teaching and example on purity of heart and uprightness of life, on the hope of a better future after death, and an unquestioning self-surrender to the will of God; secondly, that the death of its founder, though seeming at first to blight for ever the fondest hopes of his followers, only rendered more intense and elevating his personal influence, gathered up, as it were, his personality into a diviner form of life, and brought it through faith and prayer into closer spiritual intercourse than ever with the souls of believers on earth, as a mediator and intercessor between them and God.

I have long felt unable to accept, as literally true, the conflicting accounts contained in our four gospels, of the bodily manifestation of Christ to his disciples after the crucifixion. The real fact, whatever it may have been, seems to me dissolved and lost beyond the possibility of distinct recovery, in a confluence of different streams of popular tradition. Nevertheless, I fully hold with the late F. C. Baur—one of the freest and most fearless of modern Scriptural critics—that the belief in a risen Christ is the corner-stone of the Christian dispensation; that apart from that belief, its origin and history are an inexplicable enigma.[1] A belief so firm, constant, and strong, as that of the first generation of Christians in the perpetuated spiritual existence of their lost Teacher and Guide, with the deep and lasting impression which it left on the subsequent history of our race, could not possibly, it seems to me, have been a simple delusion, but must have been based on some evidence which brought it home to their minds as a reality, though it is hidden from us in a mystery which I do not expect the utmost resources of science and criticism will ever be able to dispel. Whatever the reality was, it was grasped by faith ; and the sense of it weakened and lost by the decline and failure of faith.[2] I only notice the circumstance here, to bring out more

---

[1] Das Christenthum und die Christliche Kirche der drei ersten Jahrhunderte, I. p. 39.
[2] Faith, be it remembered, is an essential constituent of human nature. As

distinctly the fact, that as well after as before the death of Jesus, the animating principle of his religion was attachment to his person and sympathy with his spirit. His person, indeed, acquired a new beauty and grandeur, and became encircled with a diviner halo, by its transference to an unseen world. All the broken memories and floating traditions of a love and goodness more than human, which had passed in brief transit across this earthly scene, and left behind them the warm lustre of their spirit on a world of sin and woe, migrated with death into a higher and invisible world. Disjoined for ever there from the disturbing associations of mortal weakness, sorrow, and pain, they combined harmoniously into the most perfect form of human excellence which the believer was able to conceive, and after which he felt himself drawn upward to aspire, as the condition of a final union hereafter with Christ and God.[1] The feeling easily lapsed, especially with the coexisting associations of polytheism, into a secondary worship; but in its origin it was essentially a reverence for the highest conceivable form of human goodness, suggested and inspired by

Novalis has finely said : "Wissenschaft ist nur eine Hälfte, Glauben ist die andere ;" and again, with equal truth : " Wir sind mit dem Unsichtbaren näher als mit dem Sichtbaren verbunden."

[1] The same enhanced and spiritualized conception of departed goodness we still feel disposed to associate, though in an inferior degree, with the memory of all the virtuous whom we think of having passed through death into a more glorious state of existence. And this may be no groundless fancy raised by the weak breath of human regret, but the dawning perception of a more perfect reality to come. A sort of saintly halo invests their cherished remembrance, which elevates while it consoles survivors. Such a feeling was particularly strong among the first Christians; and it was due to the directness and simplicity of their faith. The two worlds had an equal reality in their eyes ; and at times, when faith was stimulated into uncommon fervour by persecution, the unseen overpowered the seen,—literally they 'walked by faith not by sight.' The rude inscriptions on their graves, their commemorative rejoicings on the death-day of deceased friends, and their earliest poetry—attest the extreme vividness of their faith in immortality. Where the gone and the left were thus felt to be so completely one great spiritual family in God, prayers for the dead, and even the wish for their prayers in return—though a usage liable to abuse when artificially upheld as part of a sacerdotal system—do not seem to me, as they were offered and desired in the simplicity of the primitive faith, to spring from an unnatural, still less, as often represented by a narrow Protestantism, from a perverted state of mind.

the life of Christ. Had it been left pure, uncorrupted by the philosophical dogmatism of a declining civilization, it might have proved—as it may yet prove with the return to a simple, genuine Christianity—of inestimable service to the maintenance of a high moral standard and of a devotional spirit at once fervent and sober, by interposing the interpretation of our highest human conceptions between the infinite and unsearchable God and the religious wants of our own souls. It is the feeling of having access to God through Christ,—through the purest human to the highest divine. The New Testament expresses it by the significant word, ἐπικαλεῖσθαι; and it finds constant utterance in the early Christian hymns.[1]

To sum up and apply what I have now said. Christianity, in its origin and essence, was a kindling in men's souls of the dormant consciousness of their personal relation to a living God, a deepening of their moral sense, a quickening of their spiritual insight: and this change was wrought through the influence of one profoundly religious nature on its contemporaries.[2] It was an outpouring of the Spirit of God, through the soul of Jesus, on humanity. It was diffused by the living voice, and circulated through the world in streams of living tradition. The work was progressive. The whole truth did not evolve itself out of the primitive germ all at once, nor in all men's minds in the same way. Time and reflection were required to bring out its full significance, and to unfold it into

[1] "Te, Christe, solum novimus,
  Te mente pura et simplici,
  Te voce, te cantu pio
  Rogare curvato genu
  Flendo et canendo discimus."
      Prudentius, Hymn. Matutin. Cathemer II.

[2] When I speak of deepening the moral sense, I do not, of course, mean that any revelation could bestow a new power of discriminating right and wrong. That belongs to the reflective reason on a comparison of the relative value of actions. I refer to the instinctive feeling of approval or disapproval on the perception of an action as right or wrong, without regard to personal consequences,—which nothing so directly contributes to deepen as the consciousness of responsibility to an absolute Moral Excellence.

all its applications. So long as faith was fresh and strong, and not overpowered by the artificial subtlety of dogmatizing theologians, the great seminal principles infused by Christ into the souls of men, underwent a natural and healthy development, the successive stages of which have been providentially recorded for us in the different books of the New Testament. The synoptical gospels have preserved the oldest Palestinian traditions of the person and public ministry of Jesus. In the epistles of Paul we get an insight into the heart of the earliest controversy to which the new religion gave rise. The Fourth Gospel contains the reflections of a profoundly devout and meditative spirit (probably of the church of Ephesus), on a survey of the ministry of Christ, interpreting it from his own lofty point of view, and giving it the comprehensive application which to that wider ken it seemed at once to yield. Briefly we may say, the Synoptists record the original facts; Paul and John exhibit the results of a later reflection on those facts. Now, this vivid and varied exhibition of the growth and expansion of a great seminal principle is far more instructive and refreshing, far more stimulative of the kindred action of our own spiritual faculties, than the presentment of any positive doctrinal system, however precise and complete. This might have satisfied the understanding, and rested there. Here we are continually roused and interested, and allowed momentary glimpses into the deepest mysteries of our being, as we follow the course of the Divine Spirit in its diversified dealing with the souls of men. It is, therefore, of less importance to be able to pronounce with certainty, of such and such a book, that it came from such and such a particular hand, than to feel sure that it issued from the original circle of apostolic faith and zeal, and that, whoever be its author, it brings with it a true expression of the Spirit of the Living God. Christianity carries us back through the souls of holy men, even of the holiest, that of Christ himself—to God, who is the sole ultimate fountain of all holiness and all truth. This consideration, pursued to its consequences, involves a deeper and broader view of the essence of Christianity. It makes its acceptance, as a truth for the soul, independent of all those obscure and difficult critical questions on which the learning of Protestantism has so precariously based it. It enables us, through faith and sympathy with the person and work of Christ, to renounce the perplexing conception of it as an abnormal phenomenon of the past, breaking the continuity of the divine plans, and virtually denying the constancy of God's parental presence with his human family, and to grasp it now and ever as a present and eternal reality—a κτῆμα ἐς ἀεί— for the soul of man. This is not to take it out of God's hands and make it a work of man. On the contrary, it exalts instead of lowering its true divinity. For it recognizes the great Father Spirit as dwelling constantly in the midst of his children, using all pure souls, that are prepared for their reception, as the media of his revelations; Christ, the purest of all, as the medium of the greatest—that which has become, from the absolute depth and fulness of its communications, the rule and measure of all others. It is through the upward tendency and aspiration of what is highest in our own humanity, that we rise to the least inadequate conception of the Infinite God, and, through the sympathy of a kindred spiritual nature, enter into that filial communion with Him which is the final end of Christianity, and the condition of our immortal happiness. Faith in Christ is trust in, reverence for, aspiration after, a glorified humanity in its ultimate union with God. This is the idea—the final result of the organic operation and natural growth of the spirit brought into the world by Christ— which is developed with such wonderful power and beauty in the Fourth Gospel. In relation to time it lies, it is true, at a greater distance from the living root in Christ, than the simple, fragmentary traditions of the Synoptists. Nevertheless, it is a more complete and perfect expression of the new spiritual life breathed into humanity by Christ, than mere historical details could possibly convey : just as the expanded flower and ripened fruit of a plant reveal to us more of the hidden vitality of the root, than the rigid stalk which grows out of the one and sustains the other. The early Quakers had got hold of a great truth, when they maintained that the Spirit was above the Scripture; that the Scripture had, indeed, a high secondary value, but only in proportion as it was a true vehicle of the Spirit.[1] The Spirit, which had its richest opening and fullest manifestation in Christ, is still flowing from its Infinite Source into the hearts and lives of those who truly believe in him. It is this alone which makes them really his, and unites them through him with God. Through the Spirit alone, the Church proves its identity from age to age, and the Scriptures ripen into meaning and yield their fruit.

(3.) It will be urged, doubtless, by many, that the term "Spirit of God" is very vague, and that all our notions of its action on the human soul are extremely obscure. On this subject the final appeal must, of course, be made to the consciousness of the individual soul. But if any sure inference can be drawn from its distinctest utterances—in literature, in the words and actions of men, and in our own deep personal experience—we certainly do possess convictions and trusts, which are given, not acquired,—which are not the product of reasoning, but the basis of it,—apart from which it would have nothing to rest upon, and could find no test of ultimate truth. Such intuitive states of mind I seem to discover, in our sense of the uneffaceable distinction of right and wrong, of liberty to choose either

---

[1] "From the revelations of the Spirit of God to the Saints have proceeded the Scriptures of Truth ;" but " because they are only a declaration of the Fountain, and not the Fountain itself, therefore they are not to be esteemed the principal ground of all Truth and Knowledge, nor yet the adequate, primary rule of Faith and Manners. They are a secondary rule, subordinate to the Spirit, from which they have all their excellency and certainty." (Barclay's Apology : Proposition III. p. 67.)
—In another place (pp. 69, 70), Barclay shows, that Calvin, the French churches, and the Dutch represented at the Synod of Dort, and even the Westminster Divines, appeal in the last resort to the witness and persuasion of the Holy Spirit, in proof of the truth and divinity of the Scriptures.

one or the other, of dependence on something higher than ourselves, of responsibility and subjection—in all the workings of conscience, and in that dimmer feeling of a perpetuity of existence in God, which involves the germ of a belief in immortality. These trusts and convictions lie close to the soul and are ever dormant in it. At times they come forth with unwonted freshness and force, and carry with them an implicit obligation to accomplish some work, or enforce some truth in relation to them, which is recognized as a commission from on high. Whether viewed in their latent permanence, or in their occasional revival, we refer them to the inspiration of God, because we are conscious we did not create them by any act of reasoning, and because we feel that they exist and work in us independent of our volition. Above and beyond them is the wide field, left open to observation and inference, where knowledge and opinion may properly be regarded as products of our own, limited by the extent of our opportunities, and by our diligence and acuteness in using them. But underneath all these subsequent acquisitions, lie undisturbed and indestructible those deeper convictions and holier trusts by which we morally live and through which we hold communion with God.[1] Within these primary convictions and trusts lies the region of faith; while the operations of the free intellect occupy the field of science. The two regions are conterminous; but as they belong to different sides of our nature, though both are embraced by

---

[1] The general action of the Divine Spirit we all feel to be regulated by the moral condition of the percipient mind. But at times it breaks into the current of thought with a directness and a force, which leave no doubt of its source, where the impulse is in harmony with and strengthens the clearest perceptions of reason and the moral sense. To most men of a meditative turn, seasons probably come and go, few and far between, which flash, as if from on high, a momentary light on the soul. Could such moments be arrested and detained, and made permanently to influence our thoughts and aims, they would invest our words and actions with a prophetic significance. But they pass; and we cannot recall them.

"Sponte sua, dum forte etiam nil tale putamus,
In mentem quædam veniunt, quæ forsitan ultro,
Si semel exciderint, nunquam revocata redibunt,
Atque eadem studio frustra expectabis inani."

Vida. Poet. Lib. I.

the highest reason, they must be kept distinct, and one must not invade or encroach on the other. The men who possess these fundamental intuitions in the greatest force, and cultivate them by faith and a holy life, we call prophets. They are messengers from God, the bearers of his revelations to men—more truly such, as they awaken in other souls a sense of their relation to a Divine Power, and deepen the awe and enforce the obligation of the moral law emanating from it. The spirit which such men introduce into the world, is progressive in its working, and becomes richer of results as the capacity of humanity expands with its growth to receive them. We are not to suppose that there is anything arbitrary or capricious in these operations of the Divine Spirit. They are doubtless governed by laws of the highest wisdom; though, as belonging to an invisible scene of things, they are often beyond our present grasp. Their sudden illapses seem to us at times strange and unaccountable. "The wind bloweth where it listeth, and thou hearest the sound thereof, but canst not tell whence it cometh and whither it goeth: so is every one that is born of the Spirit." But this is the impression of our ignorance, not the effect of any arbitrary change in God. Generally, we may observe, that it is the pure, simple, and earnest mind which is most susceptible of these divine influences; and that these for the most part remain constant, so long as their suggestions are listened to and obeyed. We ourselves are most conscious of their power in our holiest moods; when the world and the senses have least dominion over us; when faith and prayer keep them in check, and lift us into a higher region of thought and feeling. Nevertheless, perfect sinlessness is not the condition even of their most vivid experience. Otherwise our humanity would be shut out from all communion with the heavenly world. Sometimes an unguarded lapse into sin will be the means of bringing them back in all their strength, and of intensifying the consciousness of our personal relation to God. Preservation of the sensitiveness of the moral and spiritual sense, is the chief condition of the perpetuity of their power. This is more completely destroyed by the silent corrosion of worldly selfishness and hardheartedness, than by the passing storm of strong passions and appetites, which are acknowledged and deplored even while imperfectly resisted. The soul feels its degradation, and yearns to be delivered from it: and this protects it against absolute moral perdition. In full accordance with this view, Christ declares, that the publicans and harlots, sinners as they are, will enter the kingdom of heaven before the selfish and hypocritical Scribes and Pharisees.

Nor, again, does it follow, that a true revelation may not, even as regards its moral and spiritual contents, be associated with many false ideas on its first outward announcement to the world. Some correspondence, indeed, to existing beliefs and the actual condition of human intelligence, is indispensable as a medium of communication between the truth offered and the mind accepting it. But such things are the mere historical surroundings of the central truth which they serve to introduce. They drop off when they have done their work, and leave room for another and more suitable investment, like the husk which may be shattered without affecting the kernel. No doubt it does not become the men of a particular period to declare absolutely of any statement in a revealed message, that it cannot be true, because they cannot at present comprehend it, provided always it does not offend their moral sense and contradict the first principles of reason. Some mystery is the inevitable adjunct of whatever comes to us from a higher sphere. There is a healthy reverence for the utterances of a holy mind that stands nearer to God than ourselves, and may have glimpses of truth as yet withheld from us, because incapable or unworthy of them—which should hold us back from saying, in purely spiritual matters, "This cannot be, because I do not understand it." Our religious trust, in Christ for instance, would not on this ground be the less, although we should plainly see, that in matters not spiritual, he thought and spoke like the men of his own age and nation. The final test and consummating evidence of a divine revelation is the tendency of its special influence to unfold and develope into higher perfection the moral and spiritual elements of our nature, and the subsistence, with unimpaired authority over the human heart and conscience, of its great fundamental principles, amid the ceaseless growth and decay from generation to generation of the various speculative theories which have successively gathered round them. The well-known words of Cicero have a deep truth which finds its eminent application here: " Opinionum commenta delet dies, naturæ judicia confirmat."[1]

If these views are correct, we cannot take Christianity out of the general circle of divine providence. It is the utterance of God's spirit in the heart of our humanity: but it is a typical, not an exceptional, utterance. This conception of it rescues it from the hands of archæologists and critics, where it was exposed to all their doubts and harassed by their controversies, and gives it back in perpetuity to the religious consciousness of our race. It is the highest function of a true learning, to set it once more free, and restore it to its original freshness and simplicity, that it may abide with us for ever.

(4.) The views which I have now stated simplify the question of the historical origin of our religion, and spare us several difficulties which attach to the ordinary Protestant theory. The new life given to the world by Christ was, as I have already said, a fresh outburst of the Divine Spirit; and the books comprised within our New Testament are a record of its diversified effects and successive developments, as they were conceived and transmitted by popular tradition, or reflected by minds of higher culture and more philosophic comprehension. We must look for the apostolic root of the whole movement in the synoptical gospels, and more especially in those of Matthew and Mark,— for Luke already betrays an approach to the catholic tendencies of Paul. Here we get the truest idea of Christ and his work as

[1] De Natura Deorum, II. 2.

historical realities. The decision of the question respecting his person, whether it was properly human, or something outside and beyond the circle of humanity, hangs on the decision of a previous question—whether we are to appeal to the Three First Gospels or the Fourth, as our highest historical authority. It is the collocation of both these sources, as partaking of the same character, within the limits of the same authoritative book, that has created the difficulty. Had we only the Synoptists, though undoubtedly they invest the person of Christ with very extraordinary powers, and place him in a most intimate relation to God, we should hardly have claimed for him a nature higher than the human, however wonderfully endowed. On the other hand, did we know him through the Fourth Gospel alone, we could not doubt, that the author of that work regarded him as something more than human—an incarnation of the Eternal Word. This idea is so clearly expressed throughout, that nothing but a foregone conclusion and doctrinal prepossession could have blinded anyone to the perception of it. That gospel is regarded—and rightly, by those who admit its authenticity—as a completion, from an apostolic source, of the inadequate conceptions of the person of Christ conveyed by the synoptical narratives. On a point so vital as this, no authority could equal that of the beloved disciple, who leaned on the bosom of the Lord, and was admitted to his inmost privacy of thought. The interweaving into a narrative so simple and natural, in its main features, as the original Palestinian tradition respecting Christ, —of the idea of the incarnation of a divine person, co-existing with God from the beginning, has something so novel and startling, that nothing short of an authority like that of John could make it credible as a fact. But the question assumes another character, when we find the evidence for the authorship of John decidedly defective;—coupled as it is with another consideration, that the doctrine of the Logos was an attempted solution of the old problem of the mutual relation of matter and spirit, already widely current among abstract thinkers, which soon blended itself with the profound intuitions of Christianity as they rose into the region of philosophical thought. It was a typical example of the hypostatizing tendency which distinguished the later Platonic schools, and a not unnatural exaggeration of their hereditary doctrine of Ideas.

Originally, λόγος and πνεῦμα, *word* and *spirit*, were only different modes of expressing one and the same conception,— that of God's action on created things. The former was the Alexandrine mode; the latter (*Ruach*), the Palestinian. It was Philo who developed the doctrine of the λόγος into a system. Where a type of thought more strictly Hebraic prevailed, the idea of πνεῦμα maintained the ascendancy. For instance, it holds a prominent place in the teachings of Paul. But the distinction which the Church subsequently made between the two ideas, we do not find, as yet, clearly recognized in the New Testament. Even in the Fourth Gospel it is only just beginning to show itself. For the two formulas—'the word made flesh,' and 'the spirit given without measure'— are nearly equivalent in meaning. The decided transference, in that gospel, of the doctrine of the Logos to the conception of Christ, accelerated the hypostatizing process by which an idea was gradually converted into a person, and led finally to a complete separation of the meanings attached to Word and Spirit—the former denoting a divine person, the latter a divine influence. At length, the idea of the Spirit also yielded to the hypostatizing tendencies of the age; and before the end of the fourth century, at the time of the Council of Constantinople, the Spirit had ceased to be regarded as a mere influence, and had become a person. Of this second hypostasis I can find no clear trace in the New Testament. Perhaps the promise of the Paraclete, and the use of the pronoun ἐκεῖνος in reference to it (John xvi. 7 and seq.), mark the commencement of the tendency. But of the personality of the Word and of its incarnation in the man Jesus, there is, I think, no indistinct assertion in the Fourth

Gospel. The doctrine, as I apprehend it, was a metaphysical formula of the time, into which the highest thought of Christianity passed and embodied itself, and which doubtless facilitated the access of the new religion to the minds of philosophical heathens. The difference between this and the orthodox view is an important and an obvious one. The latter regards the doctrine of the incarnation of the Eternal Logos in Jesus, as an essential part of the Christian revelation—a great fact in the spiritual economy of the universe; the disclosure of which completes and, as it were, exhausts the spiritual discoveries of the gospel. The other view looks on the doctrine simply as the interpretation by a reflective mind, through the aid of a conception which the philosophy of the age supplied—of the great ultimate design of Christianity; the intellectual vehicle, so to speak, through which the mind penetrated to, appropriated, and conveyed to others, its sense of the highest of all truths—the possibility of the union of the soul of man with God. While, therefore, I am unable to admit, either on critical or on philosophical grounds, the authoritative character of the doctrine of an incarnate Logos as a part of divine revelation, since it wants, in my belief, direct apostolic warrant, and is capable, moreover, of being traced to its source in an old and now defunct school of philosophy;—I still acknowledge with reverence the relative value of this doctrine, as an important link, assigned its place by providence, in the grand chain of mental development—if not a truth itself, a provisional means of approach to the greatest; an attempt, corresponding to the intellectual resources of the age, to render that truth distinct and intelligible by a concrete presentment of it to the mind. It covered the place, if I may so express myself, where a truth lay hid, and would ultimately be found: the truth, that humanity in its highest form supplies the most perfect interpretation that we can apprehend, of the person and will of God;—and that this ideal, as it is conceived by every pure and earnest mind, must be constantly aspired after, as the medium of present communion with the Father of our spirits, and the condition of future, endless approximation to his unattainable perfection. In this great thought lies the meaning of those wonderful expressions of Paul : "the unsearchable riches of Christ;" "your life is hid with Christ in God;" and of the whole of that glorious chapter, the eighth of Romans.

We must not be repelled from this view by the objection, that an imperfect and exploded intellectual formula—in plain words an intellectual error—is thus assumed to have been employed by Providence as a means of introducing and familiarizing to the human mind a great spiritual truth. For this is one of those fixed conditions of progressive mental development, which the history of religion discloses to us at every step. We constantly observe a central truth bursting the intellectual shell, in which it had been temporarily encased, to adapt it to the period of its earliest communication to the world; and then putting on one after another, broader and more comprehensive forms of expression, as the intellectual advance of mankind requires them; but attesting at the same time its own intrinsic divinity, by surviving, in undiminished force and clearness, all the doctrinal forms through which it has successively passed. The great fundamental truths of Christianity—those which constitute its eternal and unchangeable essence—may be reduced to three : first, a life to come of just retribution and endless progress; secondly, the mercy and forgiveness of God freely offered to the believing and repentant; thirdly, the communion of man with God, as of a child with its parent—of the finite in its earnest striving upward, with the all-righteous will and the all-loving heart of the Infinite Spirit of the universe. Now, it is to be noticed, that each of these great truths was introduced at first as a living element into the popular consciousness, by the help of some belief or conception which belongs to the time of its birth—some form of thought which was itself temporary, though the truth which it conveyed, was destined to endure for ever. Take, for instance, that grand and consolatory doctrine of a future life. It was brought home to the Jewish mind, and passed thence to the heathen, under the Hebrew imagery of a kingdom of heaven, which was to come with the dissolution of the present state of things, before the existing generation had passed away. It was conceived at first, in the concrete, sensuous form of a theocracy on earth, with Christ, as God's vice-gerent, at its head. It took, in other words, the form of Chiliasm, which adhered so closely to the primitive Jewish Christianity. That form did not last, for it was condemned and confuted by the unanswerable evidence of facts. Already in the Fourth Gospel there is a perceptible approach to a more spiritual conception of the future life. Other forms succeeded, not wholly purged in the first instance from the original conception, and therefore not perfectly self-consistent, but shaped to the needs of the time by the speculations of philosophical minds, and the progressive doctrinal development of the Church; till at last, in the refined and elevated anticipations of a Cappe, a Channing, and a Parker, the hope took a shape which the Christianity of the first ages, as I have pointed out in a previous section, would have repudiated as unbelief. The history of this doctrine is singularly instructive and significant. Through all the changes of form under which, from age to age, it had been apprehended and realized to the mind, the fundamental trust endured essentially the same. Once clearly and distinctly announced, it found a welcome and response in the popular heart, which ensured its continuance for ever. Once definitely lodged amidst the deepest moral convictions of the soul, it was not to be displaced by merely intellectual doubts, but rested as a quiet trust within, safe and unassailable—borne witness to by the light of conscience and holy love, which it helped itself to keep alive.

So with the promise of divine forgiveness to the penitent. The great thing was to produce the assurance of being pardoned, and so take away that despairing sense of moral helplessness, which the consciousness of unforgiven sin leaves on the soul. Forgiveness was made contingent on change of mind (μετανοία) springing out of faith,—that is, of sympathy with the spirit of Christ himself; and God's absolute forgiveness of the believing and repentant sinner, was brought home to the mind by the contemplation of Christ's great act of self-surrender to God on the cross. Now this effect was deepened, and perhaps could alone have been rendered operative in the popular consciousness of that time, by the inevitable association of the act with those notions of expiation and atonement which were then universally current, alike among the Gentiles and the Jews. The controversial portions of Paul's epistles are deeply tinged with such notions, which had evidently a sincere and earnest, though perhaps an indistinct hold on the belief of the apostle himself. The expository vehicle belonged to that age; though the truth which it sheltered, has remained a permanent treasure to mankind; and it is this: that the only possible atonement for sin, is with Christ to surrender the whole soul to the will of God and to the service and sacrifice which it demands. I have already shown how the same principle applies to the introduction of the doctrine of human communion with God, as it is presented in the Fourth Gospel. So that the three parts of the New Testament, which respectively mark three stages in the development of Christian truth—the Synoptical Gospels, the Epistles of Paul, and the Fourth Gospel—have each contributed their share to that development, by the help of some belief or dogma which belonged to the popular or philosophical opinion of the time, and can, therefore, possess no doctrinal authority for us: the Synoptists clothing the expectation of a future life in the garb of Jewish Chiliasm; Paul rendering clear and impressive the doctrine of reconciliation with God, through the popular notions of atonement; the Fourth Gospel familiarizing to the mind the possibility of a spiritual union between God and man, by the doctrine of the Logos.

Form and essence are, indeed, closely mixed up with each other in the representation given by the New Testament of these great truths; for they were blended together in the minds of the writers, as they must have been, to justify our reverence for them as honest and genuine men. Any supposition is less offensive to the moral sense, than the old rationalistic theory of conscious and deliberate accommodation on the part of our Lord and his apostles to errors and prejudices which they knew to be such. A vain effort was thus made to spare their intellectual infallibility at the cost of their moral integrity. We, who in the order of providence have outlived their limited and mistaken ideas, must separate the two elements which, in their honest belief, were combined in one: and the test that we apply, must be a moral and spiritual one. The Spirit of Christ must itself help us to disengage it from the historical forms, through which it has been brought to us. We must extricate the human from the divine, the temporal from the eternal, by putting our minds spiritually into the same frame towards God and man as we discern in the authors of our religion,—by cultivating that deep inward principle of faith and holiness and love, which underlies, as an eternal substratum, these ancient forms of thought, and which they were used by Providence as media for infusing into the heart of humanity. The failure to recognize this distinction between the form and the substance of spiritual truth, which I have attempted to exemplify in three of its most important manifestations—has been the ceaseless occasion of heresies and sects, of interminable controversy and unfruitful speculation. If we review the history of doctrine, we shall find that, with few exceptions, the questions which have most fiercely divided mankind, have turned on matters that were either beyond the reach of human determination or did not touch at a single point the heart of a saving faith. A verbal theology has been the death of spiritual religion. Till divines have settled among themselves what the Scriptures really are, and how they are to be interpreted—in other words, till they have determined the premisses of their argument—controversy can only breed controversy, and lead to no pacific issue. On the grounds usually assumed by Protestants, controversy stands pretty much where it did three hundred years ago.

I have alluded to the pain and apprehension with which many good and religious minds regard the present tendencies of biblical criticism, as if they were simply destructive. They look upon them as a thinly disguised form of deism, or even of absolute unbelief. In the foregoing Essay I have endeavoured to show, in relation to a particular point, very imperfectly, I am aware, but honestly and with strong conviction, that this is not, at least is not necessarily, the case. On the contrary, my firm persuasion is, that criticism is performing, unconsciously it may be in some cases, a great reparatory and conservative work. It is sweeping away an accumulation of antiquated beliefs and gratuitous assumptions, which obstruct the access to the pure teachings of Jesus Christ, and crush with their needless weight the free working of the Spirit of God. When criticism shall have accomplished its needful, but for the time painful and invidious task, I feel as sure as I can be of anything not capable of scientific demonstration, that it will be followed by a fresh outburst of spiritual religion, counteracting, as nothing else can, the mercenary and materialistic tendencies which now absorb so large a portion of the thought and energy of mankind, and form the chief ground of apprehension for the future of the wonderful times in which we live. There are indications that a new and more searching reformation is preparing for the Church of Christ; and it will then, perhaps, be seen, that the critics, wherever they have been honest and serious, much as they may now be distrusted and dreaded by those who do not perceive the ultimate aim of their labours, have been among not the least safe and effective agents in accelerating its advent. We complain of the decay of religious zeal; of the alienation of the masses from any form of Christian faith; and of the little interest which some of the most cultivated intellects exhibit in the highest questions of humanity. Is not our cold, hard, pugnacious theology, which fights about defunct abstractions, and keeps us away from the living soul of the Gospel,—chiefly to blame for all this? When men truly believe in a Living God, ever-present to the individual soul; when the Unseen Future becomes a reality to them; when love and purity and inward peace, conjoined with free thought and ever-increasing knowledge, come to be regarded as the true wealth and nobleness of human life,—there will be some chance of the world's returning to simpler manners, more rational tastes, and a more refined enjoyment of our present existence. Higher objects will engage the general interest and activity, than the ceaseless accumulation of riches, the restless struggle for social position, or the enervating pursuit of indolent and voluptuous excitement. It may be hoped, that then, at length, Christianity will begin to exercise some influence on politics, and that Church and State will acknowledge a reciprocal relation fraught with some benefit to mankind. But this cannot be, till politics, under a higher influence, mean something nobler than the interested strife of factions, or the audacious schemes of unscrupulous dynastic ambition, without any reference to the well-being and contentment of millions; not till the Church, ceasing to be an arena for the contentions of "envy, hatred, malice, and all uncharitableness," shall strive through all its sections, though still marked by honest and invincible differences of opinion, to realize the beautiful idea of Catholic unity in one wide brotherhood of mutual service and reciprocal goodwill,—and the old exclamation of an admiring heathenism shall no longer sound as a mockery and a sarcasm,—" See how these Christians love one another!"

By the same author,

A RETROSPECT
OF
THE RELIGIOUS LIFE OF ENGLAND;
OR
THE CHURCH, PURITANISM, AND FREE INQUIRY.
Second Edition, revised.
TRÜBNER AND CO., 60, PATERNOSTER ROW.

CHRISTIAN ASPECTS OF FAITH AND DUTY.
Second (English) Edition.
LONGMAN, GREEN, LONGMAN, AND CO., LONDON.

Also, edited by the same, with Preface and Notes,
THE PENTATEUCH:
AND
ITS RELATION TO THE JEWISH AND CHRISTIAN DISPENSATIONS.
By ANDREWS NORTON, late Professor of Sacred History, Harvard University, Mass. U.S.

CHRISTIANITY:
WHAT IS IT? AND WHAT HAS IT DONE?
12mo. 1s.

A CATHOLIC CHRISTIAN CHURCH,
THE WANT OF OUR TIME.
12mo. 1s.
WILLIAMS & NORGATE, LONDON AND EDINBURGH.

www.ingramcontent.com/pod-product-compliance
Lightning Source LLC
Chambersburg PA
CBHW072127160426
43197CB00012B/2019